THE LETTER AND THE COSMOS

How the Alphabet Has Shaped the Western View of the World

From our first ABCs to the Book of Revelation's statement that Jesus is "the Alpha and Omega," we see the world through our letters. More than just a way of writing, the alphabet is a powerful concept that has shaped Western civilization and our daily lives. In *The Letter and the Cosmos*, Laurence de Looze probes that influence, showing how the alphabet has served as a lens through which we conceptualize the world and how the world, and sometimes the whole cosmos, has been perceived as a kind of alphabet itself. Beginning with the ancient Greeks, he traces the use of alphabetic letters and their significance from Plato to postmodernism, offering a fascinating tour through Western history.

A sharp and entertaining examination of how languages, letterforms, orthography, and writing tools have reflected our hidden obsession with the alphabet, *The Letter and the Cosmos* is illustrated with copious examples of the visual and linguistic phenomena which de Looze describes. Read it, and you'll never look at the alphabet the same way again.

LAURENCE DE LOOZE is a professor in the Department of Modern Languages and Literatures at the University of Western Ontario.

LAURENCE DE LOOZE

The Letter and the Cosmos

How the Alphabet Has Shaped the Western View of the World

UNIVERSITY OF TORONTO PRESS
Toronto Buffalo London

ISBN 978-1-4426-5060-2 (cloth)
ISBN 978-1-4426-2853-3 (paper)

Printed on acid-free, 100% post-consumer recycled paper
with vegetable-based inks.

Library and Archives Canada Cataloguing in Publication

De Looze, Laurence, author
The letter and the cosmos : how the alphabet has shaped
the Western view of the world / Laurence de Looze.

Includes bibliographical references and index.
ISBN 978-1-4426-5060-2 (cloth).–ISBN 978-1-4426-2853-3 (paper)

1. Alphabet – History. 2. Civilization, Western. I. Title.

P211.D44 2016   411   C2015-908590-X

University of Toronto Press acknowledges the financial assistance to its
publishing program of the Canada Council for the Arts and the
Ontario Arts Council, an agency of the Government of Ontario.

Canada Council   **Conseil des Arts**
for the Arts   **du Canada**

ONTARIO ARTS COUNCIL
CONSEIL DES ARTS DE L'ONTARIO
an Ontario government agency
un organisme du gouvernement de l'Ontario

Funded by the   Financé par le
Government   gouvernement
of Canada   du Canada

Canadä

For Aara

Contents

Preface

Writing exists only in a civilization and a civilization cannot exist without writing.

I.J. Gelb, *A Study of Writing*

Il parlait de A qui est comme une grande mouche avec ses ailes repliées en arrière; de B qui est drôle, avec ses deux ventres, de C et D qui sont comme la lune, en croissant et en moitié pleine, et O qui est la lune entière dans le ciel noir. Le H est haut, c'est une échelle pour monter aux arbres et sur le toit des maisons; E et F, qui ressemblaient à un râteau et à une pelle, et G, un gros homme assis dans un fauteuil; I danse sur la pointe de ses pieds, avec sa petite tête qui se détache à chaque bond, pendant que J se balance; mais K est cassé comme un vieillard, R marche à grandes enjambées comme un soldat, et Y est debout, les bras en l'air et crie: au secours! L est un arbre au bord de la rivière, M est une montagne; N est pour les noms, et les gens saluent de la main, P dort sur une patte et Q est assis sur sa queue; S, c'est toujours un serpent, Z toujours un éclair; T est beau, c'est comme le mât d'un bateau, U est comme un vase. V, W ce sont des oiseaux, des vols d'oiseaux; X est une croix pour se souvenir.

J.M.G. Le Clézio, *Mondo et autres histoires*

When I began work on this book, freshly armed with a generous SSHRC grant from the Canadian government, I envisioned a book on Renaissance attitudes regarding the alphabet and how they influenced the reception of the New World. The topic fascinated me, especially because I found in Europe's difficulty to reconcile the magnificence of Meso-American culture with its lack of alphabetic writing, a watershed moment in the Early Modern period (the Spanish, beginning with Hernán Cortés, referred to pictogrammic pre-Columbian texts as "painted books"). In fact, I saw the challenge and incomprehensibility of the New World as a catalyst for major changes in European culture.

As will be evident in chapter 5 of this book, I still hold this view. But this book, like many book projects, came to take on a life of its own, and bit by bit the much larger question of how something as simple and elemental as the alphabet shaped the way Western culture conceived of the world, and had done so for thousands of years, took over. The project began to expand. In order to understand the events of the Renaissance, it was necessary to look at how the alphabet was viewed in earlier centuries: the Middle Ages, for example. But then, the Middle Ages grew out of earlier Latin culture, which meant I needed to go back further to the Romans in antiquity. And of course the Romans built on Greek culture. Before I knew it, I was devouring histories of writing and perusing old Greek and Roman discussions of the origins and meaning of the alphabet. The books around my desk were piling high, and my readings kept branching out in different directions. Every new avenue seemed crucial to understanding how the alphabet had conditioned the way people in the West viewed the world.

Moreover, I realized that the story did not, of course, end with the Renaissance. Nevertheless, the Renaissance with its many significant characteristics – the renewed interest in the culture of pagan antiquity, the encounter with the Americas, the invention of the printing press – was a turning point in Western culture, and European society was irrevocably altered. The succeeding centuries rethought alphabetic letters as they rethought their world, and the changes in letters and in the worldview inevitably went hand in hand. Recent centuries were thus as necessary as earlier centuries for an understanding of how the alphabet had reflected the worldview of Westerners. What was more, as our age became a digital one and "globalization" took over, it was crucial, I felt, to examine the role that alphabetic letters continued to play in how we currently construct our world.

The result has been a writing project vaster and more varied than I initially conceived it. While I was still convinced for a while that in the end I would write on the Renaissance and only the Renaissance, I soon found myself giving a series of lectures in various countries about alphabetic letters – Canada, the United States, Portugal, even Iceland – in which I ranged over a much larger historical period. What initially seemed to me to be background gradually became foreground.

The Renaissance was merely one piece of a much larger puzzle, which meant I was going to write a different sort of book.

I have indeed become convinced that from their inception alphabetic letters have provided an optic for the West's view of the world. That view has varied with the ages, and the metamorphoses are fascinating. But underlying it all is the fact that, beginning with the Greeks, the alphabet has been instrumental in defining a conceptual order for people brought up under the dominion, as it were, of the alphabet. Many scholars have speculated about how the invention of writing changed human consciousness, and I did not doubt that this was the case. But what I was curious to learn was how some twenty-odd characters had provided a unique window on the world. The changes wrought by the invention of writing and those brought about by the adoption of the alphabet were not the same.

There was a moment that brought this home to me most powerfully, and it was the moment when I knew I would write this book. I was giving a seminar on the alphabetic letter at the University of Iceland in Reykjavík. I had projected before a room full of doctoral students the photograph reproduced in this book as fig. 1. This was by way of introduction to the topic of the letter that we were going to explore for the next several hours. I remarked that we all knew that this was a photo of a few children scampering up some sort of waterwheel. But, I said, we all saw it instantly in a second way. In fact, I claimed, we could not help but also see the image as one of children climbing up a large capital "D," despite the fact that we knew that the intention of those who built the waterwheel had surely not been to construct a letter of the alphabet.

I looked around for confirmation from the students of what I had said, and they were all nodding in agreement. The "D" sprang out for them, just as it probably does for most readers of this book.

But at that point a hand went up in the room.

The sole Asian student in the group – a Japanese woman – wished to make a comment. When I called on her, she informed us that until I actually stated that the waterwheel was in the shape of a capital "D," she had not seen this at all. In fact, she had initially wondered what the image had to do with the topic we were going to discuss. Even when I first mentioned that there was a second way of seeing the image, it did not occur to her that I meant that it formed a letter of the alphabet.

I decided at that moment that I would write this book. The Japanese student's vision of the image, and of the world, was, I realized, profoundly different from that of the students who had grown up with alphabetic letters all around them since birth. I saw in her response the truth of what has become the thesis of this book – that how Westerners see their world is, and has for millennia been, conditioned by the experience of the alphabet. As soon as the "D" was pointed out to her, she could "see" it. But it did not leap out at her the way it did for students raised all their lives in the West.

But then the world divides largely into two writing systems: ones based on Chinese characters and ones that are alphabetic. The written languages we use in our world today have adopted *grosso modo* one of these two systems; there is no third system in use. The Japanese student came from a culture in which writing was done with characters; she therefore came from the "other side" of writing.[1]

This book intends, then, to shed some light on the fundamental role played by alphabetic letters in how Western culture has perceived the world. Quite obviously, any one book cannot provide the definitive word on a topic so vast. The goals of this volume therefore are simply to provide an introduction and to begin a dialogue that others may take up. For each chapter of this book, specialists with far more erudition will be able to offer more penetrating analyses. The following pages will both benefit and suffer from the fact that they have been written by a generalist for an audience that may include both specialists and non-specialists. My hope is that what I set forth in these pages will be corrected and improved by friends, colleagues, and strangers.

I am indebted to many individuals and institutions for their help and support as I have made my way through the material for this project. In particular, I have benefitted from the helpful staffs at the Bibliothèque Nationale (Paris), the Österreichische Nationalbibliothek (Vienna), the Pierpont Morgan Library (New York), the Newberry Library (Chicago), the British Library (London), the Herzog August Bibliothek Wolfenbüttel (Germany), the Kunst Historisches Museum (Vienna), the Beinecke Library (Yale University), and the Landesarchiv Nordrhein-Westfalen (Germany). I also wish to thank the Social Science and Humanities Research Council for their generous grant as well as the University of Western Ontario for an ADF grant and for a Rosslyn Kelly Swanson Humanities Fund aid-to-publication grant. I have benefitted as well from the hard work of the editors at the University of Toronto Press, and in particular of my copy editor Miriam Skey. I have been privileged to teach some of this material to bright and engaged students in the Comparative Literature and Theory and Criticism centres at my university, which has provided me with many provocative discussions and ideas. I am also indebted to the Landon Library (London, Ont.), the Medieval Association of the Pacific, the Retired Academics Group (London, Ont.), and the University of Iceland (Reykjavík) for inviting me to give lectures on the alphabetic letter. I owe an especial debt to my graduate student and teaching assistant, Hynek Zykmund, who generously read and debated with me most of the chapters of this book in draft form and whose observations have ended up in the final versions more times than I know. I have also been helped enormously by my bright young research assistant Lina El-Shamy as well as by the comments from the anonymous readers for the University of Toronto Press. Finally, I am most grateful to my colleague and partner, Professor Aara Suksi, for many conversations that have enriched this book.

Abbreviations

BN: Biblioteca Nacional (Madrid, Spain)
BnF: Bibliothèque National de France
OED: *Oxford English Dictionary*
PL: *Patrologia Latina*
fol.:   folio
r: recto
v: verso
fig.:   figure

Illustrations

Fig. 1 Children climbing up a waterwheel (from *Devinez l'Alphabet*).

Fig. 2 Beginning of the Gospel of Matthew. Arnstein Bible (ca. 1172).
British Library Harley 2799, fol. 155r.

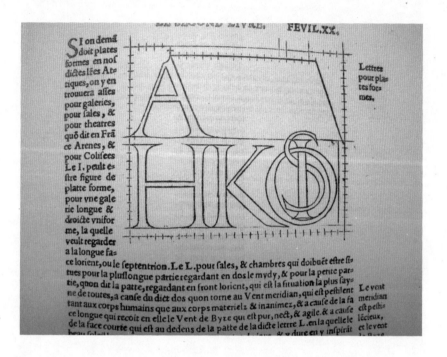

SI on demã doit plates formes en nos dictes lrēs Atiques, on y en trouuera assés pour galeries, pour sales, & pour theatres quõ dit en Frãce Arenes, & pour Colisees Le I. peult estre figure de platte forme, pour vne galerie longue & droicte vniforme, la quelle veult regarder a la longue face

Lettres pour plates formes,

ce lorient, ou le septentrion. Le L.pour sales, & chambres qui doibuét estre situes pour la pluslongue partie regardant en dos le mydy, & pour la pente partie, quon dit la patte, regardant en front lorient, qui est la situation la plus sayne de toutes, a cause du dict dos quon torne au Vent meridian, qui est pestilent tant aux corps humains que aux corps materielz & inanimez, & a cause de la face longue qui recoit en elle le Vent de Byze qui est pur, nect, & agile. & a cause de la face courte qui est au dedens de la patte de la dicte letrre L.en la quelle le beau soleil ... & y dure en y inspirãt

Le vent meridian est pestilécieux, et le vent la Byze

Fig. 3 Geoffroy Tory, *Champ Fleury* (1529), fol. 20r.

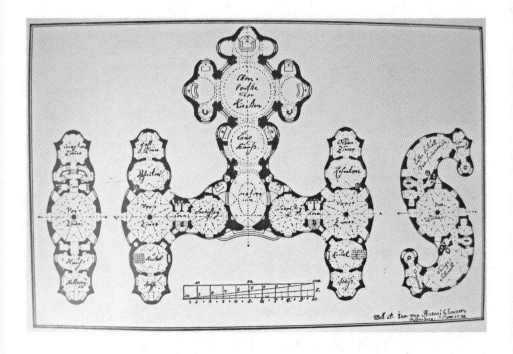

Fig. 4 Jesuit college designed by Anton Glonner.

Fig. 5 Thomas Gobert, *Traité d'architecture* (1690). Letter "L" for Louis XIV
with mirror image, p. 41.

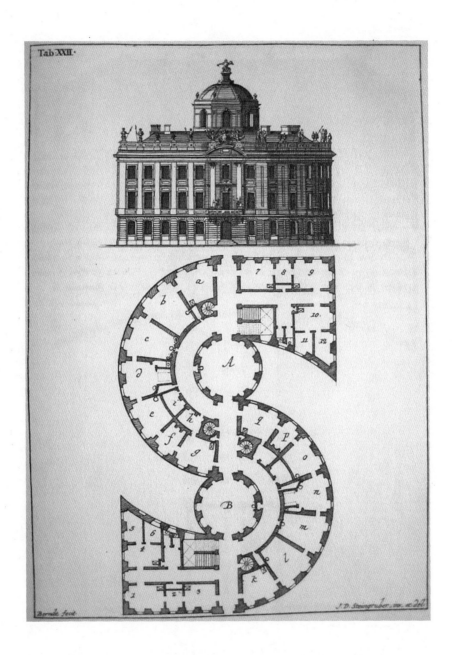

Fig. 6 Johann David Steingruber, *Architectural Alphabet* (1773). Plate 22.

Fig. 7 Daniel Libeskind, sketch for Danish Jewish Museum, Copenhagen,
showing Hebrew word "Mitzvah" becoming floor plan.

Fig. 8 Alfabetgebouw (Alphabet building), Amsterdam.

Fig. 9 Monumental capitals on Trajan's Column, Rome (113 CE).

Fig. 10 The United States Supreme Court, front façade.

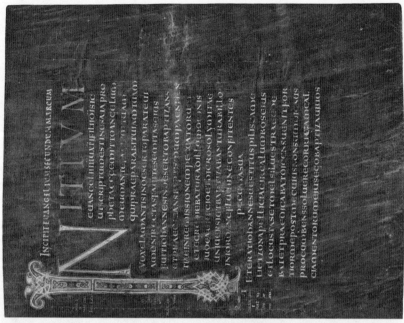

Fig. 11 A and B. Gospel of St Mark. Coronation Gospels (court of Charlemagne, 8th cent.). Vienna, Kunsthistorisches Museum: Schatzkammer, Inv. XIII 18, fols 76v and 77r.

Fig. 12 Commentary on the Apocalypse (1047). Beatus of Fernando and
Sancha: Madrid, BN Vitrina 14–2, fol. 6.

Fig. 13 Beatus manuscript. (Spain ca. 1180). New York, Cloisters. Single leaf.

Fig. 14 Pericope manuscript for Easter Sunday. Herzog August Bibliothek,
Wolfenbüttel (Germany). Cod. Guelf. 84.5 Aug. 2°, fol. 41r.

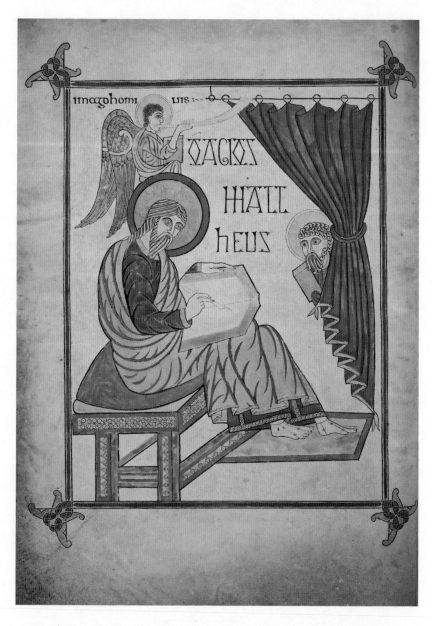

Fig. 15 Lindisfarne Gospels, beginning of the Book of Mathew (ca. 700).
British Library, MS Cotton Nero D IV, fol. 25 v.

Fig. 16 Charter of Emperor Henry IV (1067). Landesarchiv Nordrhein-Westfalen Stift Kaiserswerth, Urk.

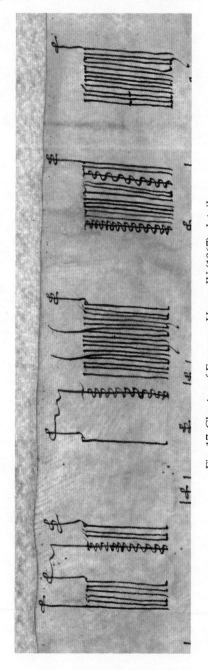

Fig. 17 Charter of Emperor Henry IV (1067), detail.

Fig. 18 Animated alphabet from Charles d'Angouleme Book of Hours
(1475–1500); Paris, BnF MS Lat. 1173, fol. 52r.

Fig. 19 The Drogo Sacramentary (850–5), opening of Mass for Easter Sunday ("D[eu]s"). Paris, BnF MS Lat. 9428, fol. 58.

Fig. 20 "Beatus vir" of St Louis (France, 13th century). Paris,
BnF MS Lat. 10525, fol. 85v.

Fig. 21 Hrabanus Maurus (Raban Maure): *carmen figuratum* with depiction of Louis the Pious (ca. 840). Vienna, Österreichische Nationalbibliothek, Cod. 652, fol. 3v.

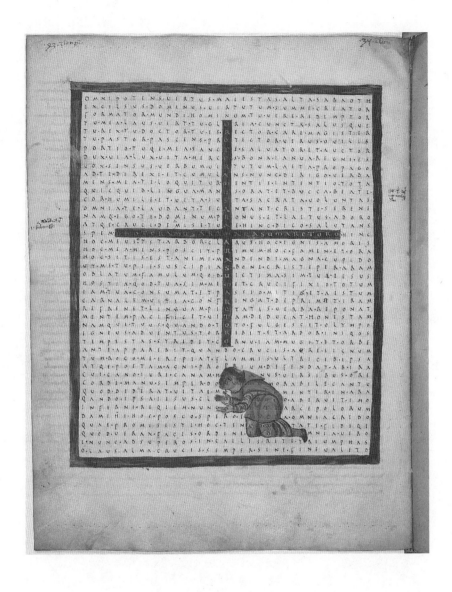

Fig. 22 Final poem of *carmina figurata* of Hrabanus Maurus (De laudibus sanctae crucis). Vienna, Österreichische Nationalbibliothek, Cod. 652, fol. 33v.

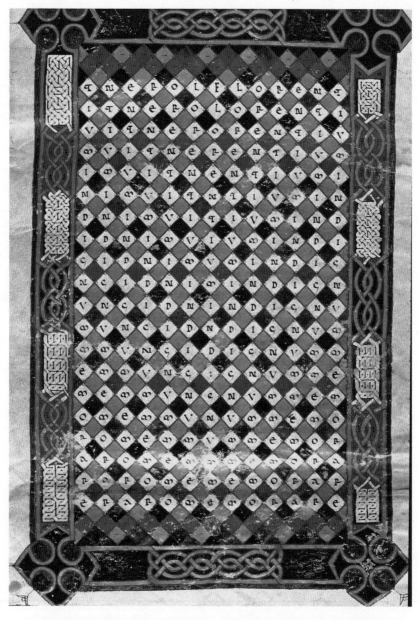

Fig. 23 Moralia in Job, "Florentium indignum memorare" (945 CE).
Madrid, BN Cod. 80, fol. 3r.

Fig. 24 A and B. Book of Hours (end 15th century) belonging to Henry IV. Paris, BnF MS Lat. 1171, fols 11v and 12r.

Fig. 25 Marguerite d'Orleans, Book of Hours (1426). Paris, BnF MS Latin 1156 B, fol. 135r.

Fig. 26 Ein Heysamelere und Predig (A Healthy Teaching and Sermon),
1489–90 BnF, Imprimés, C46159.

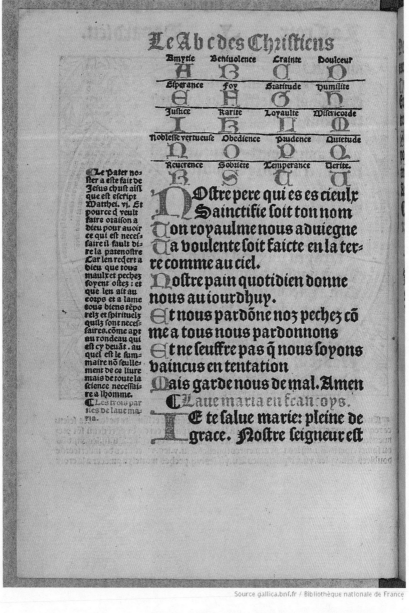

Fig. 27 Moralising Alphabet (ca. 1500); Paris, BnF Mss Rothschild IV. 4., fol. 145.

LE SECOND LIVRE.

IL reste maintenant designer le corps humain en le O .pour bailler cleremēt a entendre ce quauons cy dessus dit en son racourcicement.& pour monstrer que le centre dicelluy O .se trouuera tout droit au nombryl de Lhôme y figure, La quelle chose est en la forme qui sensuyt.

Ordōnā ce de le. O .a lhō me equi= distāmēt pieds & mains estandu. Raison de la figu re Rōde, & de la Quarree,

L Homme, piedz & mains equidi= stāmant estandu, & le O . en ceste figure, accordét en quadrature, en ron deur, & en centre, qui nous signifie la perfection dudit corps humain, & du= dit O . entēdu que la figure ronde est! . plus parfaicte de toutes les figures, & la plus capable. La figure quarree equi angulaire en quadrature est la plus sta= ble & solide, mesmemēt quāt ellest Cu be, cest a dire, Iustemēt quarree en six faces comme est vng det.

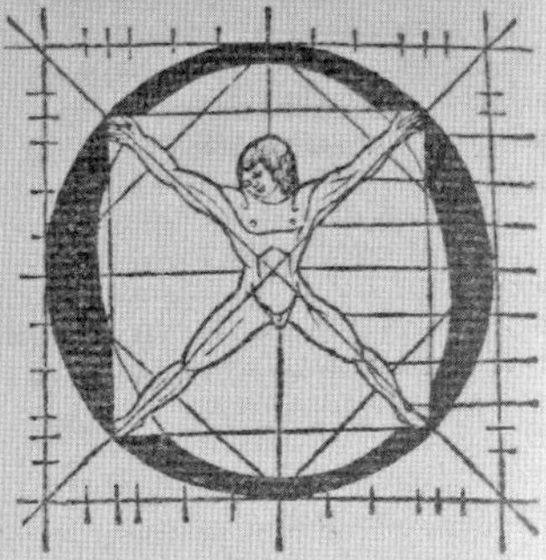

I E ne veulx laisser a mōstrer par figu re accordant a nosdites lettres Atti ques commāt Lhomme estandu sus ses pieds ioincts, & ayant son centré non pas au nombryl, comme le dernier na= gueres cy pres figure en le O, mais au penyl, nous est demonstration tres eui= dente a cognoistre le iuste lieu requis a faire le traict de trauers & la briseure es lettres qui en veulent & requerent auoir en elles.celles sont. A,B,E,F,H, K, P, R, X. Y. Ie nen baille pas figure ne exēple de toutes lune apres lautre pour cause de breuete , mais seullement de trois qui serunt A,H, & K. que nous fi= gurerons cy apres,

Du traict tranerce= ant en le A.accor de au mē bre geni= tal de Lhôme.

Notable singulier.

L A ligne basse du trauerceant tra ict de la lettre A. cy pres desi= gnee & figuree , est iustement assize dessoubz la ligne diametralle de son quarre, & dessoubz le penyl de Lhō me aussi y figure Toutes les susdi= tes autres lettres qui ont trauerceant traict ou briseure, lont dessus la di= cte ligne diametralle.Mais ceste let= tre cy A, pource quelle est close par dessus, & faicte en Pyramide, re= quiert son dit trauercant traict plus= bas que la ditte ligne diametralle . Celluy trauercant traict couure pre cisement le membre genital de lhom me, pour denoter q Pudicite & Chastete auāt toutes choses, sont requises en ceulx qui demandent acces & entree aux bonnes lettres, desquelles le A est lentree & la premiere de toutes les abecedaires,

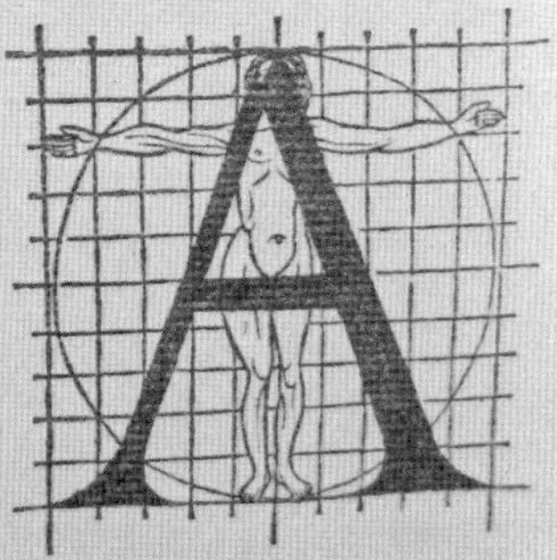

Fig. 28 Geoffroy Tory, *Champ Fleury* (1529): O, A. Fol. 18v.

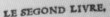

Ordonã=
ce des
neuf Mu=
ſes, &
Apollo.

Moralité
des lignes
Perpédi=
culaire.&
Trauer=
ſante.
Martia=
nus Ca=
pella,
Fulgen=
rius Pla=
ciades.

Liure du
ieu des
Eſchecqs

Confiderez en ceſte prochaine fi=
gure cômant lordonnance eſt ob
ſeruee par nombre & meſure, tant en
ligne trauerſant quen ligne perpendi=
culaire: pour monſtrer ꝗ luſage de tou
tes Scièces eſt & vient principallemét
par lettres, ſoit par inſpiration diuine,
qui eſt ſignifiee par la ligne perpendi
culaire, ou par obſtinee diligence, & la
borieuſe eſtude, qui eſt entendue par
la ligne trauerſante & equilibree. I ay
en la ſuſdicte figure loge leſdictes neuf
Muſes ſelon lordre que tient Martia=
nus Capella ne ignorant que Fulgen=
tius Placiades au. XIII. Capiſtre de
ſon Premier liure des Enarrations alle
goricques les côſtitue & ordonne autrement, comme porra veoir celuy qui ſen
vouldra aller eſbaſtre pour le veoir ſus le dict lieu allegue. Les neuf Muſes e=
ſtoient conſtituees des Anciens pour ſecretement ſignifier autan e de manieres
qui ſont requiſes en ceulx qui veulent acquerir Science. Côme il eſt treſelega=
ment & cleremét eſcript au. XXXIX. Chapitre du liure du ieu des Eſchecqs,
du quel les motz ſont côme il ſenſuit. Il y a donc tel ordre en acquerir Science,
Premieremét il fault bonne volunte de acquerir la dicte Science. Secôdement
ſoy delecter en ce. Tiercemét ſe y arreſter & perſeuerer conſtâment ſans nota=
ble interualle. Quartement bien aprêdre les choſes ou on ſe eſt arreſte. Quinte=
ment retenir & auoir en memoire les choſes entendues. Sextemét ad ouxter de
ſa Science, & trouuer de nouuel aulcunes choſes. Septiememét diſcerner & iu
ger des ſentêces trouuees & comprinſes, & puis eſlire les meilleures, & laiſſer le
ſurplus. Et apres ce finablement vſer de ſa Science, & enſeigner les aultres par
beau langage & par bonne maniere.

A,   trem,

Ordon=
nâce des
ſept Ars
liberaulx
& Apol=
lo.

I E nay encores oublye, Dieu mer=
cy, que iay dict cy deuant que noſ
dictes lettres Attiques ſôt toutes par
ticipantes de le I. & de le O. qui auſſi
eſt faict dudict I. Iay ordône les neuf
Muſes & Apollo êtour le I. Ie veulx
auſſi ordôner les ſept Ars liberaulx,
non pas entour le O . mais dedens,
comme pouuez veoir en la figure cy
pres deſignee. Ie fais ces deux ordon
nâces pour myeulx ſolider mes dictz
cy deſſus eſcriptz, & pour môſtrer cô
mant les bons Anciens ont eſte fi ver
tueux, quilz ont volu loger en la pro
portion de leurs lettres toute perfe=
ction & armonyeux accord tant de=
hors leſdictes lꝛes ꝗ dedans. Ceſt a di
re. tant eſtant eſcriptes a part elles, ꝗ eſtant en la memoire des bôs eſperits hu
mains. La rôdeur ꝗ voyes en le O . & la couche quil a en ſon Quarre, ſignifie ꝗ

pen,   ce.

Fig. 29 Geoffroy Tory, *Champ Fleury* (1529): I, O. Fol. 14v.

ALPHABET,

nouuellement corrigé, augmenté, &
enrichi de lettres. Moyennant lequel
chacun pourra nayuement representer
les paroles : ce que iamais homme n'a
faiɛt, à cause qu'auions si peu de lettres,
qu'estions contraints abuser d'icelles,
& par consequent mal escrire, & met-
tre en peine ceux qui enseignent, &
ceux qui veulent apprendre.

*Qu'il faut bien vser des graces qu'il a pleu
à Dieu nous donner, & qu'il nous en
demandera compte.* CHAP. I.

Le mõde est
vne vigne, en
laquelle faut
trauailler, &
non pas de-
meurer oisif.

P A R la parabole de l'é-
uangile pouuons en-
tendre, que ce monde
est vne vigne, en la-
quelle Dieu nous a
mis

ꝟ ꞁ. φ ꝟ. � ꞁ,
ꝗꝫꝑꞁꞓꞏ7ꝟꞏꝡ7 ꞁꝫ.ꝡ2 ꝡꞓ, ꝟ.ꝫꝑ7ꝫꝡꞏꝛꞓ, ꞓ
ꝟꝡ.ꝡ2ꝼ2 ꝟ ꞁꞁꝫꞏ ꞁ ꞁ ꝫꝫ.ꝗꝟꝡ7 ꞁꞓꞁꞓꞁ
ꝼꝟ.ꞁꝫꝡ ꝑꝫ.ꝡꝟ ꝗꝟ2ꝗꞓꝼꝟꝡ7 .ꝫꝝꝫꝟꝡ7ꞓꝛ
ꞁꞓꞏ ꝑꝟꝛꝏꞁꝝꝫꝛ: ꝼꞓ ꞁ .ꝝꝫꝼꞓꞏ ꝟꝏꝼꝫ ꝗꝟ
φꞓꞁ, ꝟ ꞁꝟꝫꝛꝫ ꞁꝟꝫꝫꝡꞏꝝꝡꞏ ꝼ2 ꝑꝫ ꝟ ꞁꞁꝫꞏꞏ,
ꞁꞁ2ꝫꝡꞏꝫ ꞁꝫ.ꝡꞏꞓꝫꝝꝡꞏ7ꝫ ꝟꝗꝫꝟꞓꝫꞓ ꝟ2ꝼꞓꞁꝫꞏꞏ,
ꞓ ꝑꝟꝫ ꞁꝫꝡ.ꞁꝟꝡ7 ꝼꝟꞁ ꞓꞁ2ꝫꝡꝫ, ꞓ ꝼ-
ꝫꝛꝫ ꝟꝡ ꝑꞓ2ꝗꝫ ꝼꝫꝛ ꞁ2 ꝟ2ꝼꞏꝫꞓꝡ7 , ꞓ
ꝼꝫꝛ ꞁ2 ꝡꝫꞏꞓꝡ7 ꝟꝡꝟꝡꝫꝫꞏ
ꞁ2ꞁ φꝫꝛꞏ .ꝗ2ꞓꝡ ꝫꝟ2ꞓꝫ ꝟꞓꝼ ꝗꝟ.ꞁ2ꝫ ꞁ2ꞁ ꝟ
ꝑꝫ ꝟ ꝟ2ꝫ ꝗꝫꝼ ꝗꝫꝗꞓꝼ, ꞓ ꞁ2ꞁ ꝗꝫꝼ ꝟꝡ
ꝟ.ꝡꝟꝡꝗꞓꝼꝟ.ꞁꝏꝡ.7ꝫ ꞁ ꝼꝟ.ꝑ2ꞁꝫ ꞁ.

ꝟꝡ ꞁꝟ ꝑꝟ.ꝡꝟ.ꝗꝏꞁ2ꝫ ꝟ ꞁꞓ-
ꝼ.ꝟꝟ.ꝡ2ꝼ7ꝫ ꝑꝫꝗꝫꝡꝡ ꝟꝡ-
ꝛ.ꝟꝡꝡꝫ,ꞁ ꝼꞓ .ꝼꝫꝡꝫ
ꞓꞁ ꝫꝗꝫ ꝡ2ꝗꝫ, ꝟꝡ ꞁꝟ-
.ꞁꞓ7ꝫ ꝟ2ꝝ ꝗꝫꝼ ꝟ

528

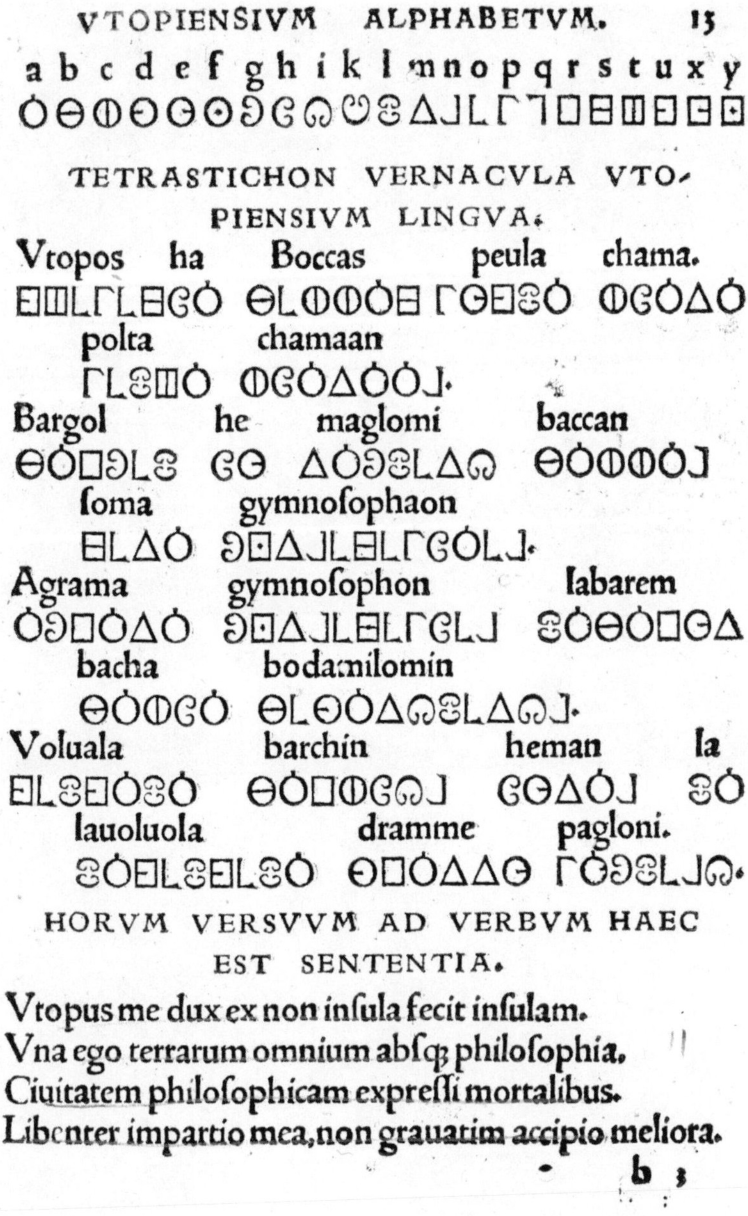

a b c d e f g h i k l m n o p q r s t u x y

Ο Θ Ⓤ Θ Θ Θ Ꝺ Ꞡ ⚀ ꙮ Ꝍ Δ ⅃ Ⴑ Ꝩ Ꞁ Ⴗ 🖿 🖽 ꞑ 🖾 🖵

TETRASTICHON VERNACVLA VTO-
PIENSIVM LINGVA.

Vtopos   ha   Boccas   peula   chama.

🖽ꙮ⅃Ꞁ🖾ꞡΟ   ΘⅬꝌꝌΟ🖽   ꞀΟ🖾ꞑΟ   ꝌꞡΟΔΟ

polta   chamaan

ꞀⅬꞑ🖽Ο   ꝌꞡΟΔΟΟ⅃.

Bargol   he   maglomi   baccan

ΘΟ🖿ꝺⅬꞑ   ꞡΟ   ΔΟꝺꞑⅬΔꙮ   ΘΟꝌꝌΟ⅃

ſoma   gymnoſophaon

🖽ⅬΔΟ   ꝺꞑΔ⅃⅃🖽ⅬꞀꞡΟⅬ⅃.

Agrama   gymnoſophon   labarem

ΟꝺꞑΟΔΟ   ꝺꞑΔ⅃⅃🖽ⅬꞀꞡⅬ⅃   ꞑΟΘΟ🖿ꞡΔ

bacha   bodamilomin

ΘΟꝌꞡΟ   ΘⅬꝌΟΔꙮꞑⅬΔꙮ⅃.

Voluala   barchin   heman   la

🖽Ⅼꞑ🖿ΟꞑΟ   ΘΟ🖿ꝌꞡΟ⅃   ꞡΟΔΟ⅃   ꞑΟ

lauoluola   dramme   pagloni.

ꞑΟ🖽Ⅼꞑ🖽ⅬꞑΟ   ΘꞀΟΔΔΘ   ꞀΟꝺꞑⅬ⅃ꙮ.

HORVM VERSVVM AD VERBVM HAEC
EST SENTENTIA.

Vtopus me dux ex non inſula fecit inſulam.

Vna ego terrarum omnium abſꝗ philoſophia.

Ciuitatem philoſophicam expreſſi mortalibus.

Libenter impartio mea, non grauatim accipio meliora.

b 3

Fig. 31 Thomas More, *Utopia* (Louvain, Thierry Martens, 1516), 13.

Fig. 32 John Dee, *The Alphabet of Enoch* (1659).

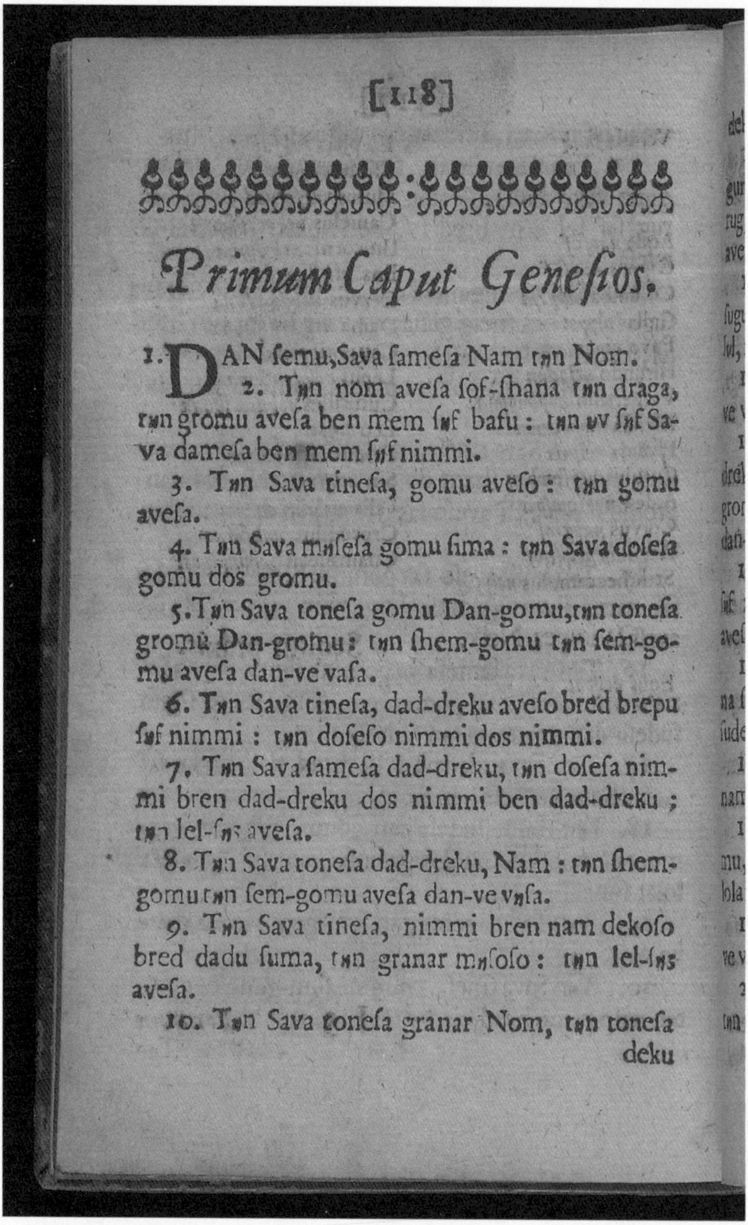

ᵜᵜᵜᵜᵜᵜᵜᵜᵜᵜ·ᵜᵜᵜᵜᵜᵜᵜᵜᵜᵜ

Primum Caput Genesios.

1. DAN femu, Sava famefa Nam tʉn Nom.
2. Tʉn nom avefa fof-fhana tʉn draga, tʉn gromu avefa ben mem fʉf bafu : tʉn ʉv fʉf Sava damefa ben mem fʉf nimmi.

3. Tʉn Sava tinefa, gomu avefo : tʉn gomu avefa.

4. Tʉn Sava mʉfefa gomu fima : tʉn Sava dofefa gomu dos gromu.

5. Tʉn Sava tonefa gomu Dan-gomu, tʉn tonefa gromu Dan-gromu : tʉn fhem-gomu tʉn fem-gomu avefa dan-ve vafa.

6. Tʉn Sava tinefa, dad-dreku avefo bred brepu fʉf nimmi : tʉn dofefo nimmi dos nimmi.

7. Tʉn Sava famefa dad-dreku, tʉn dofefa nimmi bren dad-dreku dos nimmi ben dad-dreku ; tʉn lel-fʉs avefa.

8. Tʉn Sava tonefa dad-dreku, Nam : tʉn fhem-gomu tʉn fem-gomu avefa dan-ve vʉfa.

9. Tʉn Sava tinefa, nimmi bren nam dekofo bred dadu fuma, tʉn granar mʉfofo : tʉn lel-fʉs avefa.

10. Tʉn Sava tonefa granar Nom, tʉn tonefa deku

Fig. 33 John Dalgarno, beginning of Book of Genesis (1661), 118.

All kinds of things and notions, to which names are to be assigned, may be distributed into such as are either more

General; namely those Universal notions, whether belonging more properly to

Things; called TRANSCENDENTAL { GENERAL. I
                                   RELATION MIXED. II
                                   RELATION OF ACTION. III

Words; DISCOURSE. IV

Special; denoting either

CREATOR. V

Creature; namely such things as were either *created* or *concreated* by God, not
excluding several of those notions, which are framed by the minds of men,
considered either

Collectively; WORLD. VI

Distributively; according to the several kinds of Beings, whether such as do
                                                                      (belong to
Substance;

Inanimate; ELEMENT. VII

Animate; considered according to their several

Species; whether

Vegetative

Imperfect; as *Minerals*, { STONE. VIII
                             METAL. IX

Perfect; as *Plant*, { HERB confid. accord. to the { LEAF. X
                         SHRUB. XIII   FLOWER. XI
                         TREE. XIV   SEED-VESSEL. XII

Sensitive; { EXANGUIOUS. XV
              Sanguineous; { FISH. XVI
                              BIRD. XVII
                              BEAST. XVIII

Parts; { PECULIAR. XIX
          GENERAL. XX

Accident;

Quantity; { MAGNITUDE. XXI
             SPACE. XXII
             MEASURE. XXIII

Quality; whether { NATURAL POWER. XXIV
                    HABIT. XXV
                    MANNERS. XXVI
                    SENSIBLE QUALITY. XXVII
                    SICKNESS. XXVIII

Action; { SPIRITUAL. XXIX
           CORPOREAL. XXX
           MOTION. XXXI
           OPERATION. XXXII

Relation; whether more { *Private.* { OECONOMICAL. XXXIII
                                       POSSESSIONS. XXXIV
                                       PROVISIONS. XXXV
                         Publick. { CIVIL. XXXVI.
                                     JUDICIAL. XXXVII
                                     MILITARY. XXXVIII
                                     NAVAL. XXXIX
                                     ECCLESIASTICAL. XL.

Fig. 34 John Wilkins, *Essay towards a Real Character and a Philosophical
Language* (1688), 23.

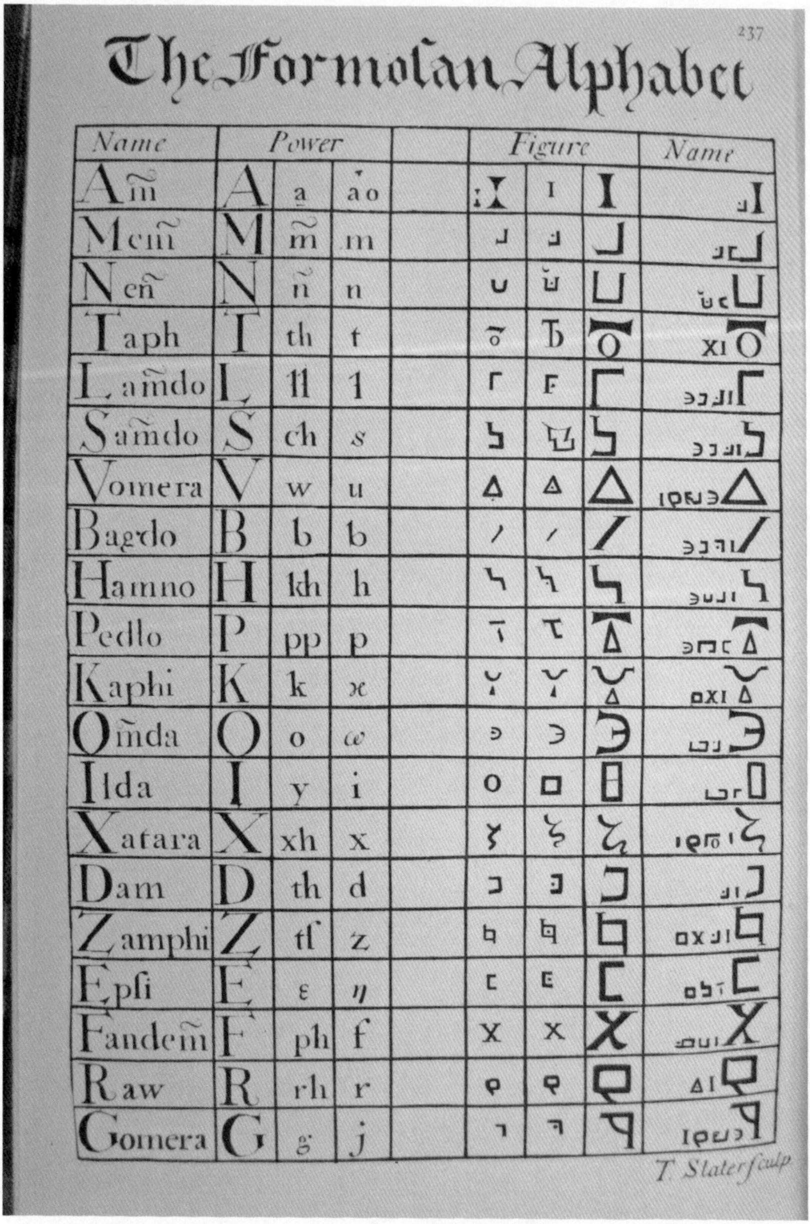

The Formosan Alphabet

Name	Power			Figure			Name
Am	A	a	a o		ːI	I	I	ɟI
Mem	M	m	m		ꓶ	ꓸ	J	ɔCꓶ
Nen	N	ñ	n		u	ŭ	U	ŭcU
Taph	T	th	t		ō	Ƀ	O	xɪO
Lamdo	L	ll	l		ſ	F	Γ	ɔɟɪCE
Samdo	S	ch	s		ʅ	ꓹ	ʅ	ɔɔɪʅ
Vomera	V	w	u		Δ	Δ	Δ	ɪꝺ Δ
Bagdo	B	b	b		⁄	⁄	/	ɔɔꓶ/
Hamno	H	kh	h		ꓵ	ꓵ	ꓵ	ꓴꓴɪ ꓵ
Pedlo	P	pp	p		ꓔ	τ	Δ	ꓱꓴcΔ
Kaphi	K	k	x		ꓯ	ꓯ	ꓯ	ꓷxꓷ ꓯ
Omda	O	o	ω		ꓱ	ꓱ	Ꜫ	ꓶꓲꓴꜪ
Ilda	I	y	i		o	□	Ꮎ	ꓶꓸ⌐Ꮎ
Xafara	X	xh	x		ꓑ	ꓹ	ꓗ	ɪꝺ꜠ꓗ
Dam	D	th	d		ꓶ	ꓷ	ꓶ	ꓺɪꓶ
Zamphi	Z	tſ	z		ꓧ	ꓧ	ꓧ	ꓷxꓶɪꓧ
Epſi	E	ε	ŋ		ꓛ	E	ꓚ	ꓷꓸꓸꓚ
Fandem	F	ph	f		X	X	X	ꓺꓴꓲ X
Raw	R	rh	r		ꝓ	ꝓ	Ꝙ	ΔɪꝘ
Gomera	G	g̈	j		ꓶ	ꓶ	ꟼ	ꓲꝺꓴꟼ

T. Slater ſculp

Fig. 35 George Psalmanaazaar, *An Historical and Geographical Description of Formosa* (1704), 237.

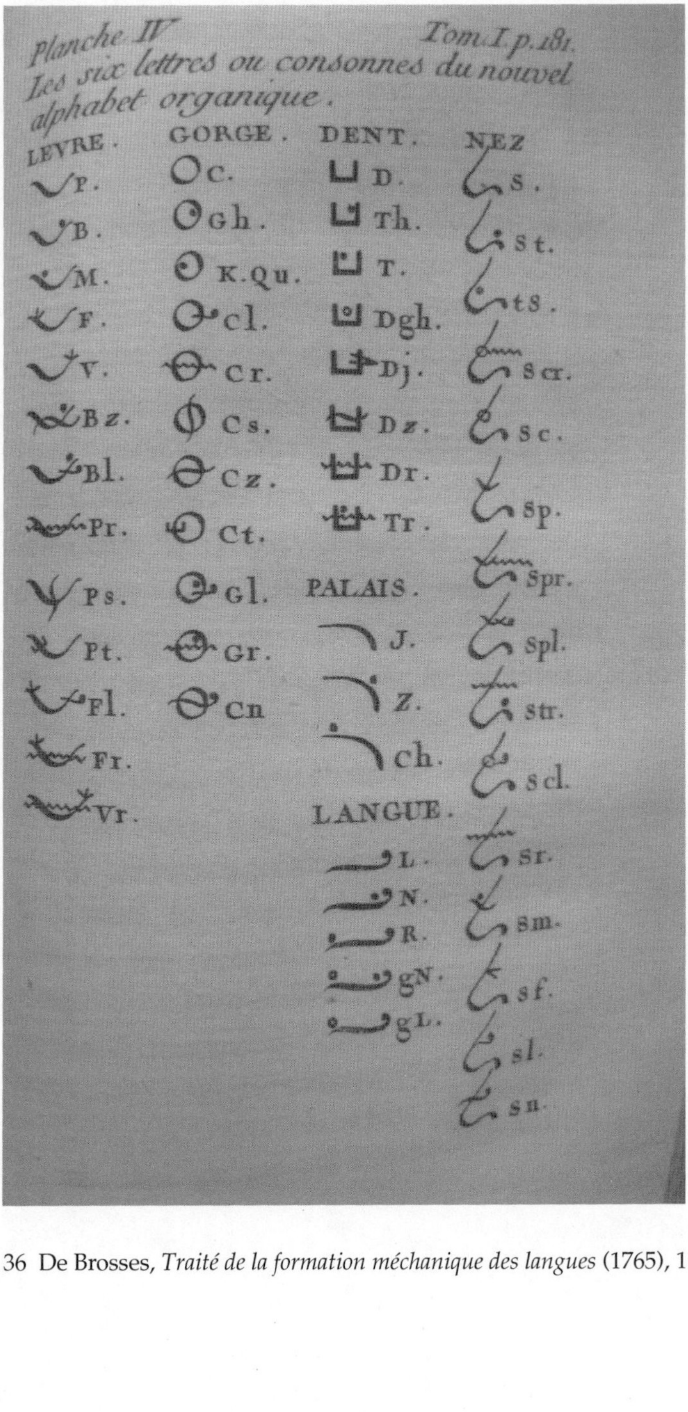

Les six lettres ou consonnes du nouvel alphabet organique.

LEVRE.	GORGE.	DENT.	NEZ
P.	c.	D.	s.
B.	Gh.	Th.	st.
M.	K. Qu.	T.	ts.
F.	cl.	Dgh.	scr.
r.	cr.	Dj.	
Bz.	Cs.	Dz.	sc.
Bl.	Cz.	Dr.	
Pr.	Ct.	Tr.	sp.
Ps.	Gl.	PALAIS.	spr.
Pt.	Gr.	J.	spl.
Fl.	cn	Z.	str.
Fr.		ch.	scl.
Vr.		LANGUE.	
		L.	sr.
		N.	sm.
		R.	sf.
		gN.	sl.
		gL.	sn.

Fig. 36 De Brosses, *Traité de la formation méchanique des langues* (1765), 1:181.

Fig. 37 A and B Diderot and d'Alembert, *L'Encyclopédie*. Vol. 2, "Art d'écrire," Planche 2 and Planche 3. Position of the Body for Writing.

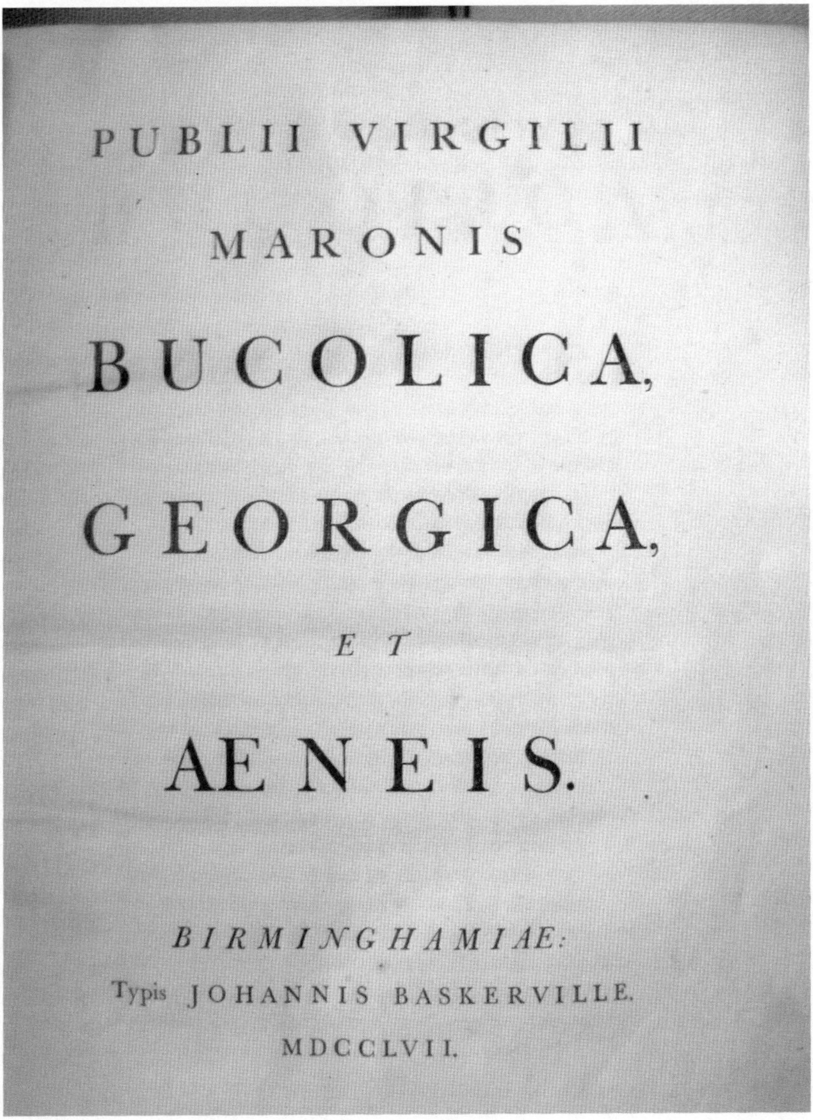

PUBLII VIRGILII

MARONIS

BUCOLICA,

GEORGICA,

ET

AENEIS.

BIRMINGHAMIAE:

Typis JOHANNIS BASKERVILLE.

MDCCLVII.

Fig. 38 Title page, Baskerville edition of Virgil (1757).

3rd.　ɑi turd cwesçun hwiç wi had tuı cunsidur woz ¶ Iz it posibul ər eospidiunt tuı briŋ suç an alfubet az ɑis intuı comun ys ?" Alfubeticul ritiŋ woz surtinli intended orijinuli tuı bi ɛ gid tuı ɑi ssnd ov wurdz, and ɑat onli ; hweɑur at furst sufiʃunt utenʃun woz ped tuı ɑis pònt, hweɑur ɑi furst alfubet woz purfect, duz not ns admit ov satisfacturi investigeʃun ; but it wud sim at eni rɛt ɑat ɑi vɔil dipartmunt woz muç disrigarded, and purhaps not ivun el ɑi consonunts wær propurli discriminɛted.　ɑi furst

Fig. 39　Passage written in Alexander Ellis's "alphabet of nature." *The Alphabet of Nature* (1845), 183.

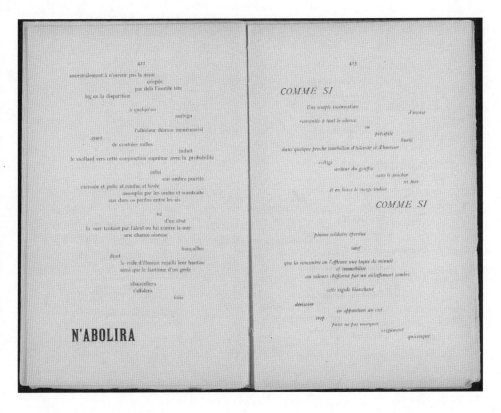

Fig. 40 Stephen Mallarmé, *Un Coup de dés* (1897).

LA CRAVATE ET LA MONTRE

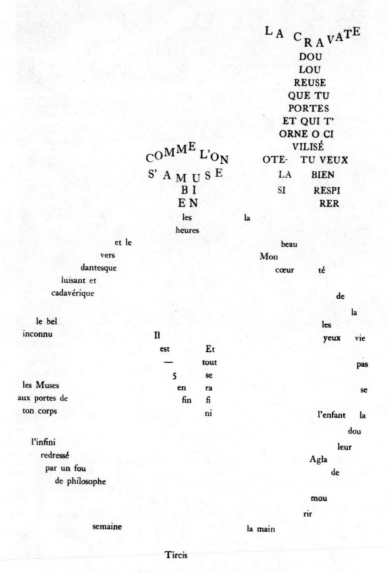

Fig. 41 Guillaume Apollinaire, "La Cravate et la montre" (1914).

Fig. 42 Filippo Tommaso Marinetti, *Parole in libertà* (1914).

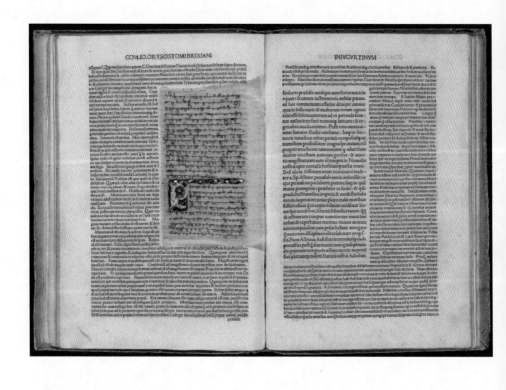

Fig. 43 Sylvia Ptak, *Intervention: Sallust. Works, 1495* (2004).

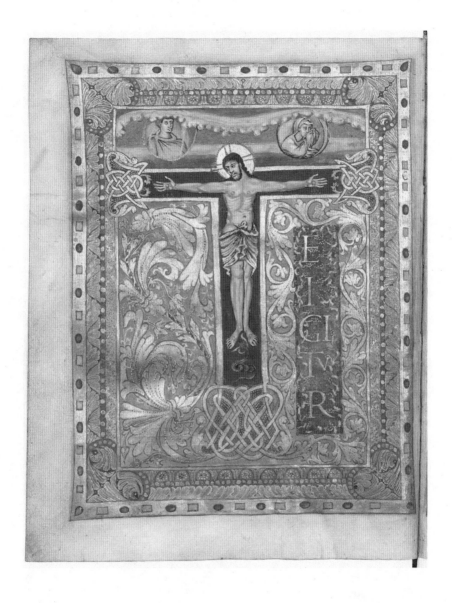

Fig. 44 Metz Sacramentary (9th cent.). Paris, BnF Ms. Lat. 1141, fol. 6v.

LE TIERS LIVRE,

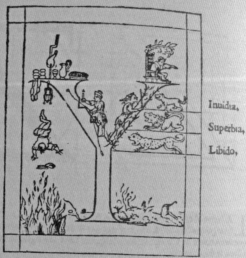

Inuidia,

Superbia,

Libido,

Frere Lu
cas Pa-
ciolus,

I En porrois dire beaucop daultres belles choses, mais pour ceste heure ie passeray oul-
tre, venant a deseigner & descrire
nostre derniere lettre Abecedai
re & Attique Zeta. Laquel
le Frere Lucas Paciolus
na pas mise en sa Di
uina proportione,
et la cause pour-
quoy il a omi-
se, ie ne le pu
is entēdre,
ne ne mē
soucye.

Fig. 45 Geoffroy Tory, *Champ Fleury* (1529), fol. 63v.

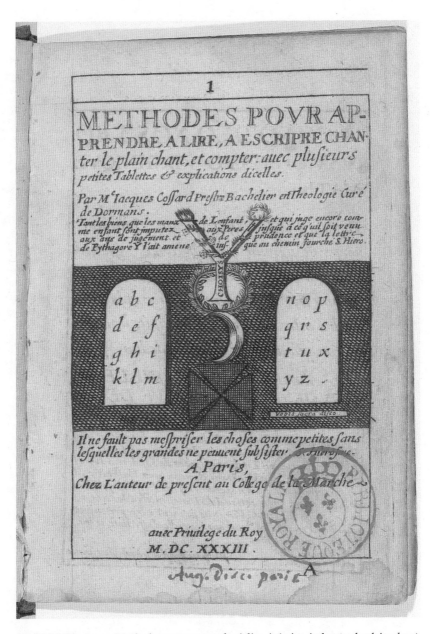

Fig. 46 Title page, *Methodes pour apprendre à lire, à écrire, à chanter le plein-chant et compter…* (1633).

Fig. 47 The Whore of Babylon, *Apocalypse Tapestry*, Angers, panel 64.

Fig. 48 Petrus Christus, *Virgin of the Dry Tree* (1462) (Madrid, Thyssen-
Bornemisza Museum).

Fig. 49 Graffiti, Berlin, Germany (2013).

THE LETTER AND THE COSMOS

1
Introduction

He sent for [Mrs. Penniman] to the library, and he there informed her that he hoped very much that, as regarded this affair of Catherine's, she would mind her *p*'s and *q*'s.

"I don't know what you mean by such an expression," said his sister. "You speak as if I were learning the alphabet."

"The alphabet of common sense is something you will never learn," the Doctor permitted himself to respond.

Henry James, Washington Square (ch. 19)

At the opening of the Book of Matthew in the Arnstein Bible in the British Library (ca. 1172) there is a large illumination in bright colours (predominantly red and blue) that takes up over half the page and is spread across the full width of the two columns of text. It depicts, as so many luxurious biblical manuscripts do, the evangelist writing his gospel in a book (fig. 2). Matthew is shown seated on a throne in the act of beginning his book, as is fitting for an illustration that accompanies the incipit. He holds his quill in one hand and in the other a knife for sharpening its point. We know that he is just beginning to write his gospel because we can see the manuscript page in front of him, and the only word he has written on it so far is the Latin "Liber" (Book).

The illumination is multilevelled, and is both clever and profound in its implications. It sets in play delightful reverberations between the individual alphabetic letter, the word, the book, and the world. The whole scene of Matthew on his throne is itself set into the midst of ornate tracery that turns out to be letters that also spell the word "Liber." The viewer gradually teases out the three large letters "L – I – b" and the smaller "e – r," at which point the delicate balance becomes apparent. Set into the word "book" is the evangelist Matthew who is writing the book in which the first word "Liber" is, in fact, written on the page before him. The macrocosm and microcosm become inter-changeable here: Matthew's activity in the real world is set within the alphabetic letters that spell the word "book," a direct allusion to the Augustinian notion that God wrote the "Book of the World" as well as the divine Bible. Within that divine alphabetic writing exists the "real world," and within that "real world" writers produce books that repro-duce the divine words. The book exists as so many alphabetic letters in which Matthew dwells, but also as an object in his hands and as alphabetic text in that book before him, and the result is a profound association of world, book, and alphabetic text. The world can be seen as a great alphabetic writing, analogous to what a writer inscribes, let-ter by letter, on a manuscript page.

What may have appeared self-evident to a twelfth-century illustrator steeped in the Augustinian tradition could only seem this way because of a powerful ideology that saw the created world as a vast writing that the *digitus Dei* or "finger of God" had inscribed. The alphabetic letter made up the macrocosmic world in which Matthew was seated, but also, to put it slightly differently, the letters were the lens through which one quite literally viewed Matthew and his writerly activity. The telescop-ing of levels is enticing: within the Arnstein Bible, which itself exists as an object within the Book of the World, we find the word "book" within which Matthew is depicted in the act of his real-life activity of writing the book in which the first word is indeed "book." Put yet another way: the word "book" exists within the book that Matthew writes, seated as he is within the word "book" inscribed into the Arnstein book-object in the real world. The five letters of the word "Liber" thus form both the smallest and largest units in this illumination, and they are linked by the visual representation of the book that is contained in, and also contains, the word "Liber."

What sounds a bit convoluted when spelled out in detail here is gracefully presented by the artist in an image in which the book is both an object and a five-letter construction. The illuminator assumes that the reader of the book (for of course all of this play on the book takes place within the Arnstein Bible, itself a book) will appreciate his artistry because he also assumes that the reader will view, as he does, the created world as a vast scripture in which God's Truths are articu-lated as surely as in the lettered Scripture that is the Bible. For both the illuminator and the reader in the twelfth century, the alphabet is an organizing principle in the world: that is to say, for the medieval Christian, God's Word is made Flesh in the person of Jesus, and as a result Jesus can rephrase the analogy between alphabetic letter and all of creation by stating, as he does near the beginning of the Book of Revelation, "I am the Alpha and Omega."

The Arnstein Bible is a good example of how the world has been seen as a lettered text and how the alphabet could be seen as analogous to Creation itself in the Middle Ages. But this analogy neither began with the Middle Ages around 500 CE nor did it come to an end a thousand years later, around 1500 CE. What the Christian illuminator expresses in the pages of the Arnstein Bible is merely one version of a long-standing view that goes back into ancient Greece and sees a profound relationship between alphabetic letters and the cosmos. What is more, this analogy between letter and world (or letter and cosmos) was destined to continue mutatis mutandis far beyond the Middle Ages, right into our own era.

Such, at least, is the thesis of this book.

I must confess at the outset that this book's thesis is surprisingly simple: namely that the alphabet[1] has expressed how people in the West see the world and its cultures while at the same time the world, and even the cosmos, has been seen as a kind of alphabet. For the many periods of the history of the West, letters speak the world, and the world speaks in letters. Since ancient Greek times, the peoples of Western culture have been –and they continue to be even in the twenty-first century – the children of alphabetic letters.[2] The alphabetic order, I shall maintain, permeates many domains of culture, including some that would seem, at first glance, to be quite unrelated to the alphabet.

This alphabetic way of viewing the world is a mindset of which we are often not even conscious. My concern here is not with the ways in which the introduction of writing affects a culture that has been illiterate hitherto. Marshall McLuhan (1911–80) addressed in *The Gutenberg Galaxy* (2011 [1962]) this question as it pertained to the introduction of alphabetic writing in ancient Greece and in more modern African societies; McLuhan's concern, like that of Claude Lévi-Strauss in his "Writing Lesson" (see endnote 7), is for how the thinking of an oral culture is changed by the introduction of literacy. My concerns are quite different for I am not addressing the oral/literate divide. Rather, my interest is in the way that, for the people who grow up in an alphabetic culture, it is second nature to conceive the world in terms of letters, from something as banal as seeing a fork in a road as a letter Y to considering it absolutely natural to put things in alphabetic order. Precisely because the alphabetic order permeates our daily world, we fail to notice it much of the time. This book is, in some ways, a making conscious of what people in the West implicitly know and partake of, though with only a partial awareness.[3]

Past eras of course knew other writing systems. The Egyptian hieroglyphics are probably the best known system that is neither a character nor an alphabetic system. There were, of course, other pictographic and pictogrammic systems, now extinct, and in fact both Chinese characters and alphabetic writing have their origins in pictogrammic writing. In the East, what began as more or less mimetic sketches were stylized early on as a character set by the Chinese. By the same token, the early Phoenicians formalized schematic drawings into letters. The Semitic scripts of both Hebrew and Arabic were similarly derived from the proto-Phoenician pictograms and gradually developed into alphabets of consonants (Hebrew and Arabic do not write vowels). The result is that in our modern world, every extant living language that is written down has been recorded using, with modifications, one of two systems: either ideographic characters based on Chinese or a lettered alphabet.[4] Languages written down for the first time in our own time, usually by linguists, are almost always recorded using the Western alphabet.

Curiously, the strengths of one system are the weaknesses of the other. Chinese characters, which have been exported to Japanese and other languages, may be pronounced very differently from one language to another and even among different dialects of the same language; but the kernel of meaning for the character remains the same, for which reason a text written in characters is more or less intelligible across cultures, but completely unpronounceable from one language or dialect to another. By contrast, alphabetic languages are pronounced in similar manners from one culture to another. The pronunciation of "a" or "o" or "t" or "s" will not change drastically. As a result a reader of one language can pick up a text from another language and sound it out for the most part. A speaker of English who has never seen Spanish or Dutch or Polish can sound out much of it at first sight, albeit with some mistakes. But as for the meaning, that person will not have the faintest idea what is being communicated.

One of the features that this difference highlights is that letters stand for sounds, whereas characters stand for things. There have been great debates as to whether letters reproduce the concrete world in some fashion, and in the next chapter we shall consider the Greek views on this topic. But the essentially aural nature of how letters signify is one of their key aspects. Almost any definition of the alphabetic letter in fact begins with this fact. Let us, for example consider the definition given by the *Oxford English Dictionary* (*OED*) for the word "letter":

> A character or mark designed to represent one of the elementary sounds used in speech; one of the symbols that compose the alphabet [...] Anything written; an inscription, document, text; a written warrant or authority; (pl) writings, written records (e.g. "By letters alone the actions of the past can be handed down to us with accuracy").

The first point of the definition is that letters represent the "elementary sounds" of a language, often what linguists generally call "phonemes" (i.e., the smallest units of sound in a language that affect meaning). Interestingly enough, the *OED* definition then moves on to letters as agents that store data in memory. Here the dictionary is returning, as we shall see in the next chapter, to one of the features that most astonished ancient peoples: letters can aid mankind by aiding one's memory and preserving one's memories in an external form – a kind of endless, early hard drive.

If we regress along the centuries, we find that the definition of the alphabetic letter is very much the same in earlier periods. The following is an English translation of the sixth-century CE writer Isidore of Seville's (560–636 CE) definition in his Latin work, *Etymologies*.

> 1. Letters are traces of things, signs of words, in which there is such power that without any voice the things said by absent people speak to us. They introduce words through the eyes not through the ears. 2. The use of letters was devised for the memory of things; they were strung together with letters so that they might not flee into oblivion.[5]

Amazingly enough, in 1500 years the definition has hardly changed. Letters permit words to speak without the intercession of the human voice. With letters, the aural now enters by means of the eyes, not the ears, for which reason people distant in times and places can communicate with one another. This ability to freeze words – essentially to freeze sound in a written form – is, Isidore realizes, a very powerful tool. In fact, Isidore suggests that what "speaks" is not the sign but the "things said" (let us remember that "loquor" is a deponent verb). Thus, the letter can triumph over the ephemerality of the spoken word. A thousand years later, the Renaissance French writer François Rabelais (1494–1553) returns humorously to this idea in chapters 55 and 56 of his *Quart Livre* (*Fourth Book*) in a comical scene in which words spoken in the cold of winter freeze in mid-air and then sound when they are unthawed the next spring. This is a humourous restatement of Quintilian's comment in his *Institutio Oratoria* that writing letters is like putting speech in a depository.[6] Many centuries after Quintilian, both Hernán Cortés, while conquering Mexico in the early sixteenth century, and Claude Lévi-Strauss who lived among the Nambikwara in Brazil in the twentieth recount how dumbfounded peoples without alphabetic writing have been at the ability of the lettered text to transmit an exact message over time and distances.[7]

What is more, Isidore, like the *OED*, also moves from the essentially aural nature of letters to their ability to retain items in the human memory. Marks that record sound in graphic form are a remedy for oblivion, a view that reverses Plato's take on writing in the *Phaedrus* (see chapter 2).

Isidore also makes reference to letters as containing "traces of things." He refers here to a debate, which, as we shall see, goes back at least to ancient Greece. What is the relationship between writing and the external world? Do letters somehow retain some elements or qualities of the world, or are they completely conventional? If this is a question that has dominated modern linguistic and philosophical approaches to language and writing, it also animated, as we shall see in the next chapter, debate in fifth-century BCE Athens.

Indeed, the question of the relationship between the letter and the world – that is to say, to what extent might there be an organic relationship between the alphabetic letter and the physical world – has occupied thinkers of both the Graeco-Roman and the Hebreo-Christian traditions. I have already alluded to the Graeco-Roman strain; let me here evoke the Hebreo-Christian one, which we will see in greater detail in subsequent chapters. If, as the beginning of Genesis tells us, God created the cosmos as a series of speech acts, this means that his language was at one and the same time the concrete world and its linguistic signifiers (oral sounds, written letters). God's language (and hence the alphabet), on the one hand, did not just represent the world (and his signifiers were certainly not viewed as arbitrary or conventional, as linguistic signs have been seen in the wake of the linguist Ferdinand de Saussure). God's speech *was* the world.

Not surprisingly there has been considerable debate as to what the original language of Creation was. For at least one and a half millennia, Hebrew was assumed to be the oldest language because it was the language of Moses. But was it also the language of Adam? Was there a language of Creation that predated Hebrew? What, then, was the relationship of the Hebrew alphabet to the concrete world: were Hebrew letters arbitrary, conventional signifiers or did they contain something of the real world in them? The answer to these questions could not be separated from the question of the relationship of Hebrew to the act of Creation. At the very least, if God spoke in Hebrew at the beginning of Genesis, it would have to have been a more perfect version of the language since the Hebrew known to the Jews was definitely not a language of divine Creation.

These background questions are important even though this book will be concerned primarily with the Roman alphabet that has come to dominate in the Western world. However, the concept that God's Creation has come to us in two forms, the divine text of the Bible and the "Book of the World," is one that has carried through two millennia and is still alive in our time. Beginning with the Greeks, we shall follow the path of alphabetical developments and the many meditations on the alphabet in Western Europe, leading up to our present day with special attention to the ways in which the alphabet has repeatedly been seen or used as a conceptual order to frame a view of the real world. The recurrence of this stance is more or less constant despite the many ways in which the details that manifest it vary with the ideologies and orientations of different centuries. One could cast this as a relationship of surface to deep structure in which the deep structure is the alphabet as a conceptual order and the surface manifestations the topical approaches at different moments in history.

For ease of organization, we shall move chronologically in the main. Temporal sequence, however, should not necessarily be seen as synonymous with a simplistic domino-like development, much less with "progress" of any sort. As we shall see, some early developments arch over many centuries. Chapter 3 will show how Roman "monumental" capitals have carried through Western culture from antiquity to the current day. The Carolingian minuscule is another alphabetic form that is still in constant use (somewhat altered) after over a millennium. We will detect after the medieval period a gradual secularizing of the conceptions regarding the alphabetic letter and its relationship to the real world, though the process is not without lurches and occasional returns to a theologizing of the letter. Renaissance humanism, for example, often shifts from considering the letter as a signifier of divine creation to seeing it as a bearer of the traditions of antiquity. But there is an ebb and flow of views over the course of the centuries. With the Counter Reformation of the seventeenth century, a renewed theological fervour occasionally turns to the alphabetic letter, setting aside the secularization of much sixteenth-century thinking and hunting for divine meanings and biblical origins for the alphabet. The Enlightenment then returns to a more secular mode, but we should not be surprised that some nineteenth-century Romantics revive a mystical approach to the alphabet as they do to many other phenomena. Even with secularization, alphabetic letters retain their role as a threshold phenomenon for one's entry into the plenitude of Western society; but the society is no longer defined in narrowly religious terms.

Let us therefore consider chronology as a convenient ordering for our material, every bit as meaningful (because so powerfully affirmed by the history of our culture) but also perhaps just as arbitrary as the alphabetic order itself. An earlier period of scholarship, including the important books of Gelb (*A Study of Writing*) and Havelock (*The Muse Learns to Write*), saw the alphabet as the culmination of a historical progression and as superior to all other forms of writing, the putative superiority due to an ostensible subtlety of expression (Havelock 11). Such a perspective has been challenged by more recent scholars, especially by those sensitive to the fact that similar arguments were used in the colonialist period to justify European superiority vis-à-vis indigenous New World culture (see, in particular, Houston 31–4). Indeed, the long-standing assumption that the alphabet radically changed human cognition and the organization of societies has been challenged, even occasionally by those who previously were proponents of such a view, as for example Jack Goody in his *The Domestication of the Savage Mind* (1977). Goody modified his early views and came to see graphic writing of any kind – and not necessarily alphabetic writing – as marking a seismic shift in thinking, and he argues that it may have influenced (or resulted from) other means of recording (lists, etc.). He argues as well that it had an effect on oral speech to some extent (76–7). Goody is rightly suspicious of arguments that categorize modes of communication as primitive vs. developed, closed vs. open, etc. He argues that alphabetical writing may have made matters easier, but the cognitive changes predate the invention of alphabetical letters themselves.

The imposition of an ideology onto chronology of course has a long tradition, whether the view sees a gradual decay from a Golden Age or

a progressive ascent from a stage of barbarianism.[8] Rather than acqui-
escing in any simplistic notions of either progress or decay, we will
proceed along a line that moves temporally in the main, but with the
full awareness that time, rather, is full of many loops even as it moves
forward. For that very reason, the developments regarding the alphabetic letter should not be seen as following along a straight line; the one
constant, however, is that the letter is repeatedly a lens through which
Western culture makes sense of itself and its world.

The World Made Alphabet, the Alphabet Made World

As has already been mentioned, the analogy between world and letter subtends this book. We will see in later chapters that this analogy comprehends
both antiquity's view of the alphabet as referring to the elements (Gr. *stoicheia*, Lat. *elementa*) that made up the physical world and the biblical notion
that the world is the Word of God made concrete text, for which reason the
Book of the World can be read as so many divine signs, just as the Bible can.

As a kind of introduction into the phenomena we will be investigating,
we might begin with some tangible instances in which letters are turned
into the world, and the world is turned into letters. Useful examples are
provided by a tradition at least half a millennium old that images alphabetic letters as actual buildings in which people might live and work.

In a perceptive essay, Erika Boeckeler has drawn attention to the
ways in which the "edifying" nature of the alphabet unites two realms
that to the modern mind may often seem quite distant the one from
the other: the alphabetic letter and the building ("Building Meaning").
In her article, Boeckeler is specifically concerned with a late fifteenth-
century northern European alphabet, German or Dutch, that draws
each letter as a piece of fanciful Gothic architecture. Such a treatment
of the alphabetic letter was conceivable because of the close relationship between architectural space and textual space in the medieval
imagination. The medieval Catholic Church, for example, articulated
an "edifying" text by virtue of its spatial disposition, which permitted its signifying features to be read by the faithful. Indeed, the Catholic churches stamped the shape of the cross on the ground, and as
one walked up the nave (i.e., a metaphorical ship) from the western
portal towards the altar at the eastern end, one moved closer, literally and spiritually, to Jerusalem, hence to salvation. It has also been
pointed out many times, most famously by Pope Gregory the Great
(ca. 540–604 CE), that pictures provided instruction to Christians

who did not know how to read alphabetical letters (this became the justification for stained glass windows in the great Gothic cathedrals). As Gregory put it, "Illiterate men can contemplate in the lines of a picture what they cannot learn by means of the written word."[9]

Architecture, then, could function as a signifying text for those who knew its "grammar." A mid-twelfth-century pontifical makes explicit the "edifying" relationship between alphabet and physical church in the directions for the dedication of a church, which instruct the bishop to trace first the Greek alphabet in the air with his crozier along one side of the church as he sings one antiphon and then the Latin alphabet along a second side as he sings another.[10] It thus did not require a great leap to arrive at a view of a building in alphabetical terms. Victor Hugo, in his novel about one of the greatest Gothic cathedrals, *Notre Dame de Paris*, articulates a quintessentially medieval view on the relationship between the alphabet and architecture:

> L'architecture commença comme toute écriture. Elle fut d'abord alphabet. On plantait une pierre, et c'était une lettre, et chaque lettre était un hiéro-glyphe et sur chaque hiéroglyphe reposait un groupe d'idées, comme le chapiteau sur la colonne. (Part 5, ch. 2, p. 143)[11]

> (Architecture began like all writing. It was first an alphabet. One planted a stone and that was a letter, and each letter was a hieroglyph and on each hieroglyph rested a group of ideas like a capital on a column.)

Nor is Hugo the only thinker to have seen a relationship between the buildings in which we dwell and the alphabet we use to express our ideas. In the Vatican, the *salone sistino*, which supports the great library reading room above, depicts on its pilasters the creators of particular letters and scripts, culminating in the final pilaster on which is depicted Jesus, who is, we have seen, "the Alpha and the Omega."[12] Indeed, there has been a whole stream of architectural designs, some more elaborate than others, consciously designed to evoke alphabetic letters.

In fact, to see buildings as alphabetic letters, or alphabetic letters as buildings, remains a common phenomenon in our current world. A quick perusal of the internet or a local bookstore's shelves will immediately turn up a large number of ABC books that "find" the letters in the forms of architectural details: peaked roofs that form "M"s and "N"s and "V"s, etc. (see, for many examples, Heller and Anderson). Similar are alphabets made up of topographical shapes of shrubs and fences and rivers as seen from above. It is surely significant that photographer after photographer should "discover" the alphabet in the world, both natural and man-made, around him or her, even in the full knowledge that there was likely no intention to reproduce alphabetical letters in the photographed shapes.[13] Such discovery is a low-level instance of how the alphabet conditions our view of the world and turns the world into a lettered text.

More telling are the examples in which people have engineered letters specifically with architectural constructions in mind, and even more striking are those who have designed actual buildings in the shape of alphabetic letters. In the 1529 volume *Champ Fleury* by the great French typographer Geoffroy Tory (ca. 1480–1533 CE), for example, Tory remarks that lettristic forms are often reproduced in buildings' shapes, citing as an example the "O" of the Roman Coliseum (we shall examine the *Champ Fleury* in greater detail in chapter 5). Tory then goes further to propose that certain letters can form platforms for theatres and other buildings. He draws a rudimentary house with a capital "A" as the gabled roof, and the "K" as the stairs to the second level, etc. (fig. 3). Geoffroy sums up his view by saying that "nos lettres Attiques veulent sentir l'architecture" (fol. 19r: our Attic letters would make us perceive architecture).

The art historian Henri Focillon has stated that "No art is closer to architecture than typography" (cited in Biggs 53), and Tory's drawings and his professional orientation as a typographer would seem to express this view. After all, it is relatively easy to see letter shapes in existing buildings or to draw letters as architecture, as both Geoffroy Tory and Antonio Basoli in his nineteenth-century *Alfabeto pittorico* (1839) have done.[14] More astonishing perhaps is that architects themselves have intentionally designed buildings in the shape of alphabetic letters. One can legitimately ask whence comes the desire to stamp the alphabet literally (in both senses of the word) on the ground. Why this need to write an alphabetic text on the face of the earth? Is it simply a caprice on the part of architects?

Were we faced only with the instance of John Thorpe (1565–1655?) who made a rudimentary drawing and floor plan of a country house in the shape of his initials, an "I" and a "T" (in the sixteenth century "I" and "J" were not yet fully distinguished), we could dismiss the phenomenon easily enough. But there have also been more sustained and more serious approaches. Is it simply that "Of all arts, architecture is most akin to typography," as the director of the Gutenberg Museum,

Helmut Presser, has remarked? (quoted in Biggs 7) The Jesuit Anton Glonner (1723–1801) designed a college for novices that consisted of three buildings in the shape of IHS (i.e., the first three letters of Jesus's name in Greek) (fig. 4). The "S" contained the schoolrooms, while the "H" housed the kitchen, dining room, and sacristy (Conrads and Sperlich 173). While only a single drawing with scant commentary is extant, the intention is clearly to create a school in which the material taught in the classroom (Jesus's teaching) would be echoed by the very spaces the novices inhabited and in which the namesake of the Jesuits would literally house the members of that order. Macrocosm and microcosm, world and letter would be intertwined and even interchanged, and the Jesuit students' world would be mapped visually as a divine text. The Jesuits would quite literally dwell in Jesus by dwelling in his letters.

The seventeenth and eighteenth centuries saw two more elaborate projects, both of them centred in the baroque period and infused with a baroque aesthetic. In celebration of Louis XIV's dissolution of the regency and assumption of full regal power in 1661, the French architect Thomas Gobert created and published *Traité d'architecture* which contained the plans of twelve churches or chapels in the shape of the letters that formed the phrase "Louis le grand" (Louis the Great).[15] Characterizing his studies as a "jeu d'esprit d'architecture" (an exercise in architectural wit), Gobert explained that because the letters were not symmetrical in and of themselves, the buildings all consisted of a letter and its mirror image, thus achieving symmetry (fig. 5). Curiously, the result is that the shapes are not immediately recognizable as letters. Nor did Gobert expect all twelve churches to be built together, expressing the entire phrase. Nevertheless, he suggests that his designs could be of utility for the design of other churches and chapels in France. The result, of course, would be to inscribe the letters of the king's name and title all across France. If the French baroque, as has often been noted, was an aesthetic that served and promoted the national state and royal power, this proposal to spread the letters of the Sun King's name across the face of the nation associates alphabetic domination with the larger political program of governmental control, instituted by Cardinal Richelieu with the founding of the Académie française (1635), of the French language and linguistic productions. In Gobert's project, "L'état c'est moi!" takes on a concrete form. But the project also anticipates the kind of potential inherent in alphabetical letters that will come to the fore in the twentieth century with the Oulipo movement in France, since it uses the letters almost as catalysts for architectural creation rather than for any recognizability in the final creations, since the mirror doubling makes the letter shapes hard to perceive.

The other baroque architect to form a similar project is the eighteenth-century Johann Steingruber who designed a series of buildings in the shape of every letter of the alphabet and then printed engravings that, like Gobert's, illustrated both the plans and the elevations of the buildings. Steingruber was interested in the practical problems posed for an architect when each letter was translated into a three-dimensional mansion: where to put the kitchens, the stairways, the bedchambers, etc. In the case of a few letters ("W," "Q"), Steingruber made two different designs, determined to work out details of a practical order that the first version did not fully resolve (fig. 6).

Steingruber was clearly fascinated by the architectural challenges of making the letters work as practical buildings. He takes pains to emphasize that he did all the work – and it was considerable – during his own leisure time, and he suggests that the buildings could be of interest to clients who might want mansions in the shapes of their initials. Latent in this comment is again the idea of stamping one's dominion over the natural world by imposing one's alphabetic letters on the terrain, making the earth into a text of the self. Steingruber even comments that the full effect of the buildings would only be visible from a tower or other high place.

Perhaps the most serious attempts to make a terrain speak alphabetic letters through architecture are from the twentieth century, and they return to the Hebrew alphabet. The Polish-born, American Jewish architect, Daniel Libeskind, has designed two museums around Hebrew letter shapes: the Danish Jewish Museum (2003) and the Contemporary Jewish Museum in San Francisco (2008). Libeskind consciously returns to the ancient analogy that subtends the Hebrew, Greek, and Latin alphabets and that sees the structure of the world and that of the language and alphabet as being the same. In all three languages, the letters are also numbers, so that the mathematics that rules the cosmos inheres in the letters as well. The Danish Jewish Museum is structured by the four Hebrew letters for "Mitzvah," meaning "obligation" or "good deed" or "deeply felt reaction," which, for Libeskind, characterize the generally positive experience of Danish Jews during the Second World War.[16] An early watercolour made by the architect himself depicts the word becoming the floorplan of the museum (fig. 7). Libeskind himself has commented that "The organizing principle of the Danish Jewish Museum is the concept of Mitzvah itself in its deep ethical meaning

[...] The museum takes the tradition of writing, reading and memory as the overall matrix of organizing the exhibition space" (Libeskind, "Mitzvah" 41).

The Contemporary Jewish Museum in San Francisco is designed in similar fashion around Hebrew letters, this time the letters for "L'Chaim" meaning "To Life." Libeskind was inspired by the Hebrew phrase "L'Chaim" because it seemed to him fitting for application to the role the substation played in restoring energy to the city after the 1906 earthquake as well for the museum's mission to be a lively centre for engaging audiences with Jewish culture. The architect based the extension's conceptual organizing principles on the two symbolic Hebrew letters comprising "chai" (life), the "chet" and the "yud."[17] As the architect explains, "The new CJM [Contemporary Jewish Museum] building is based on unprecedented spaces created by the two letters of the *chai*: the Chet provides an overall continuity for the exhibition and educational spaces, and the Yud, with its 36 windows, located on Yerba Buena Lane, gives a new identity to the Jessie Street Power Substation" (Libeskind, "Contemporary" 107).

The lettristic floorplans of Libeskind's museums are, of course, not readily apparent to the casual visitor. What is important, however, is that they reproduce the concept that objects in the world and alphabetic letters can be analogous. In Amsterdam, a recently designed "alfabet-gebouw" (alphabet building) deliberately employs the alphabet to frame one's view of the world. The windows of one façade are in the shape of twenty-four alphabetic letters ("I" and "Z" were left out for aesthetic reasons, allowing for the neat ordering of four stories with six windows each). The result is that one quite literally sees the world through the lens of the alphabetic letters (fig. 8).

Alphabetic letters have been with us now for almost three millennia. They have gone through many changes in terms of their shapes, their deployment on the page, and the technologies that produce them. As subsequent chapters will show, they have often been infused with moral qualities. As my readers will be aware, to this day "penmanship" is taught in schools, almost as a subcategory of "citizenship," or at least this has been the case until recently. In North America, grammar school classrooms still often have the alphabet displayed as a kind of cornice around the front of the room, just above the blackboard. To learn to write and to form one's letters well is a key part of a civic education: basic literacy – that is, knowing how to read and write letters – is the price of entrance into full participation in the culture.[18] Even in an age in which most writing is now done on digital devices, in which hundreds of fonts are available to a person, and in which the real encoding is entirely numeric, learning how to form or use majuscule and minuscule letters properly is nevertheless seen as a key expression of one's membership in a civilized, human order. The "human" qualities of letters are evident in the very terminology we use to describe them: letters have a "body" and "feet" and "shoulders" ("the shoulders of an R," for example). And different letters have different connotations for people. In English, "q" and "k" have the same sound, but they are definitely "felt" very differently, in part because of their different origins and histories. "K" was a late entry into Latin and was used for very few words. "Q," or rather "qu" since, as every school child knows, "q" is always followed by an unpronounced "u," evokes the Latin substratum, and it matters little whether an individual reader consciously knows this fact or not, because the clusters of words that have a "qu" are, in aggregate terms, different from those that have a "k." Similarly, "Amerika" with a "k" has a very different ring for North Americans than "America" does, despite the fact that the "k" and the "c" sound the same in this case. It is therefore no surprise that many language groups, beginning with English, have proven resistant to programs of orthographical reform. Speakers of English have almost a perverse pride in the eccentricities of their orthography; foreigners who have slogged through the frustrations presented by the tenuous relationship between English orthography and pronunciation are inevitably amused by such visual puns as "ghoti" in which a conceivable pronunciation could be "fish" ("gh" as in "enough," "o" as in "women," "ti" pronounced "sh" as in "nation"). The fact that this example no doubt brings a smile to readers rather than provoking frustration speaks volumes about the ways in which our cultural identity (which is to say, our view of our world and our place in it) is linked to how we use our letters.

No wonder, then, that different historical periods, languages, and cultures have fretted and obsessed over their letter forms, their orthography, and their writing tools. This book is not intended as a text in paleography or a history of letter types, though we shall often have occasion to look at how letter forms have changed and how certain forms (or fonts) have come to be favoured. We shall consider why certain letters have been re-formed and deformed, fetishized or avoided, all because of what they might seem to speak about our world, far beyond the simple phonetic value attached to them.

Nor will we look very much at alphabets apart from the Latin one, despite the fact that some other alphabets are in wide circulation today. This limitation is due in part to the need to examine a corpus with clear boundaries, but also due as much or more to the intellectual and linguistic limitations of the author. The Semitic alphabets, particularly the Arabic and Hebrew ones, have their own histories. The Cyrillic alphabet used for many Slavic languages, traditionally attributed to Saints Cyril (ca. 827–69 CE) and Methodius (ca. 820–85 CE) as a result of their mission to the Slavs in 862, is based on the Greek alphabet. In Korea, the Hangul alphabet was developed by the fifteenth-century monarch Sejong (1397–1450), and is still used; made up of fourteen signs for consonants and ten for vowels, the Hangul alphabet constitutes "one of the most scientific writing systems ever invented" (Meggs and Purvis 32). In Iceland, the Latin alphabet is supplemented by the "ð" (the "eth") and the "þ" (the "thorn") that represent, respectively, the voiced and unvoiced English pronunciations of "th" and which come from earlier runic writing. No doubt one could pursue the ways in which these alphabetic letters have been instrumental in how the peoples who use them conceive of their world.

For historical reasons, nevertheless, we shall begin by glancing at the Phoenician and Greek scripts that preceded Latin letters. The Greeks, in particular, although they were only partly responsible for Latin letter forms, were key influences for how the Latins and subsequent Western thinkers saw their alphabets. For this reason our story must begin with the first writing of Phoenician and Greek culture. The Greeks, as is well known, were forever looking over their shoulders at the Egyptian world. They knew of the long history and the grandeur of Egyptian civilization, and they knew of hieroglyphic writing. But when it came time for the muses "to learn to write," as the classicist Erik Havelok put it in *The Muse Learns to Write* (1986), they turned to the Phoenicians who had developed an ingenious graphic system for recording not things but sounds.

Our investigation must begin, then, with the origins of writing that first gave birth to letter forms of various sorts, and the development of Phoenician and then Greek writing.

2

Ancient Greek Letters

Origins

The origins of alphabetic writing are shrouded in what the French call "the night of time" and, as a result, have been the subject of much mystery and inquiry. We know, of course, that alphabetic cultures were preceded by oral ones, though inevitably we only have access to oral cultures at the point when they become recorded – either through writing or, in more modern times, aural media – which also means that we only have a mediated version of orality because it has always already been taken down in some other form (writing, analogic/digital recordings, etc.). For early civilizations we thus have a textualized version of an oral culture – what we might think of as a reconstructed orality. In short, while oral cultures may have left traces in later written cultures, we are always dealing with written recreations or imitations or echoes of prior orality.

Historians have been able to trace some of the developments that led to early alphabetic writing. The Egyptians had some phonetic symbols, hence "letters" of a sort or at least a representation of syllables, that they used alongside their hieroglyphs: an inscription, for example, from about 330 BCE phonetically writes "Alexander" – a reference either to Alexander the Great or his son – in the course of a hieroglyphic text. But by that time, alphabetic writing was already well developed in numerous parts of the Middle East and the Greek world. It seems likely that alphabetic writing was first developed around 1500 BCE. Cuneiform writing, with its wedges imprinted into wax, was first invented around 3200 BCE in Uruk in Babylonia as the southern part of Mesopotamia was called, but this was not yet an alphabetic script; over the course of the next millennium the cuneiform syllabary was adapted to other languages in the Middle East. Then sometime around the thirteenth century BCE at the royal city of Ugarit cuneiform wedges were adapted for alphabetic writing. Around this time so-called linear letters (because they are formed of lines not wedges) were also developed by the Phoenicians in modern day Lebanon. It is hard to establish which of the two alphabetic systems came first or to what extent they may have influenced each other: cuneiform or linear. While cuneiform letters were better suited to making impressions on wax or stone tablets, linear letters were better for writing with ink on papyrus. Since papyrus was biodegradable, this difference may explain the survival of more (or of earlier) cuneiform writing than of linear writing. Other alphabets were developed for other languages between, roughly, the tenth and the fifth centuries BCE, including Aramaic, Hebrew, Arabic, and Greek.[1]

We cannot know what alphabetic writing "felt like" for the people who first used letters. The earliest epic known to the West, *The Epic of Gilgamesh*, was written in a cuneiform script developed for the Babylonian language (now extinct) between 1300 and 1000 BCE. A few centuries later, the alphabet that was to have extraordinary importance for the subsequent history of the West – that is, the Phoenician alphabet – was being used to record not only accounts and legal documents, but also myths and legends. Did the scribes who wrote these texts have the sense that the ability to record speech in a durable form gave to human beings an extraordinary extension in terms of their power and reach? Did they sense at all that they were embarking on a new period in terms of human culture, much as people did in the decades following the invention of the printing press in the late fifteenth century or, more recently, the way people have viewed personal computers and the internet as they have become important features of our daily lives in the twenty-first century? Did the fact that people no longer had to store every important item in their personal memory but that, rather, they could store information, ideas, and stories in communal texts from which the data could be retrieved later on with perfect accuracy stun them with the power that inhered in letters? Or did they, instead, take it all in stride as simply a self-evident aspect of their daily lives? After all, the fact that a few dozen marks should be able to freeze speech and thought – and do so for people who speak vastly different languages – is truly extraordinary. Ideas and pronunciations that have been encrypted according to the system of alphabetic letters can be decoded and reproduced by anyone who knows the language and the lettristic system, even across large swathes of space and time.

On the other hand, perhaps the first peoples to manipulate letters did not consider alphabetic writing terribly significant, viewing it as simply one utilitarian feature and less crucial for survival than agricultural advances, say, or natural phenomena? Such may have been the case if writing developed gradually. In any event, the past is silent when we ask it these questions. We can see the peoples of these early writerly cultures using the alphabet in increasingly creative ways, but we do not know how they thought and felt about the spreading uses of their letters.

Greek Letters

With the Greeks things change. The Greek alphabet was derived from the Phoenician one, which has made the Phoenician alphabet the fount for Western letters. Sometime between the twelfth and the eighth century BCE, the Greeks adapted the Phoenician alphabet to suit their language, creating an alphabet of twenty-four letters in which in general each letter represented a phoneme or minimal unit of sound:

ΑΒΓΔΕΖΗΘΙΚΛΜΝΞΟΠΡΣΤΥΦΧΨΩ

By putting together the letters in different combinations, as the Phoenicians had done with their own alphabet, the Greeks could represent the sounds of their words. They made some modifications in terms of letter forms and distribution since they had some sounds that the Phoenicians did not (and because Phoenician had some sounds that Greek did not have, they could redeploy some letters). The most notable change the Greeks made was to redistribute certain letters in order to represent vowels, departing from the Semitic alphabets that, down to our day, represent only consonants.

Interestingly, it seems that the Greeks wrote down their greatest narratives almost as soon as they had the alphabet. At some point during the eighth and seventh centuries BCE the most famous works of Greek culture of the time were committed to writing, especially the two great epics by Homer, the *Iliad* and the *Odyssey*, as well as the two works of Hesiod, *Works and Days* and the *Theogony*. We do not know what other, more mundane texts may have been written as well, but it is surely significant that the Greeks saw an immediate need (or had the strong desire) to inscribe the two great oral tales that "Homer" (whoever he was or they were) had composed orally.[2] Indeed, the Homeric epics are models of "mock-orality," reproducing what are almost surely vestiges or imitations of earlier oral composition, even though the stories were now being inscribed on papyri. Homer's epics make no direct mention of writing, but the power and artistry of the works, with their delicate use of recurrent themes and motifs, were almost surely due in part to a certain amount of reworking in written form. At least one specialist has gone so far as to suggest that the Greek alphabet was actually developed in order to write down the Homeric epics.[3]

As one may expect, modern critical debates about the composition and authorship of the Homeric poems have been lively. Just as we will never know to what extent the Homeric texts as we know them are the result of reworking in a written format, so also it is hard for us to discern to what extent they were written down because they were canonical or they became canonical because they were written down and could be read repeatedly. In any event, the earliest fragments extant date from half a millennium after Homer lived, and the oldest complete manuscripts are from the tenth century CE. For our purposes here, what matters is the obvious realization that the alphabet could be used not just to record but also to polish, edit, and reproduce the products of the human imagination. The scribes pried loose the great epic tales and the finest poetry from the bards, and the products of the throat that sang became those of the hand that wrote. This was a seismic cultural shift. From this point on we can speak of a literary "text": the chanted song became a tangible object that existed outside of the human body and to which any voice could give utterance, provided one knew how to read. Literacy would begin to assert itself as a powerful tool; to be able to read the alphabetic text was to have a measure of social dominion. Alphabetic letters were becoming agents of social power.

The writers that gave us the *Iliad* and the *Odyssey* did not discuss the power of lettristic writing per se, preferring to maintain a fiction of orality. The closest Homer's poems come to acknowledging writing is in the reference to graphic signs in the embedded Iliadic tale of Bellerophon in which the sealed tablets he carries contain signs (*semata*) that tell the receiver to put him to death (*Iliad*, Bk 6, l. 168). We cannot know, however, if the reference to *semata* would have denoted alphabetic writing or not. Similarly, Hesiod, in his *Theogony*, does not reflect specifically on the role of alphabetic letters either, though he appears very much as a writer and he presents himself as the receptor of the divine messages relayed through the muses, placing the authority of his alphabetic writing on the same level as that of sacred kingship (*Theog.* 22–8).

In the classical period, fifth century BCE, Greek writers begin to write about their own writing – that is, about their own letters. What we find is an already highly developed and nuanced reflection on the origins, power, and uses of alphabetic letters. Concurrent with this metacritical discourse, a view emerges that associates the Greek alphabet with concepts of the cosmic order and human civilization. A bit of backstory is in order here.

Greek letters were called *stoicheia*, which was also the Greek word for the elemental particles or atoms that made up the cosmos. In the use of this term inhered the idea that alphabetic letters were much more than just convenient graphic signs: rather, they were viewed as the building blocks of the cosmos, quite literally as "elemental." (The Latin term for *stoicheia* was, indeed, *elementa*.)[4] For the Greeks, the term *stoicheia* was usually used to mean both elements and letters, though the original reference was, in fact, to alphabetic letters, the reference to atomistic particles coming later (Snyder 33). The full alphabet – originally eighteen letters to which were added four or six more – was therefore also a kind of compendium that constructed the cosmos. Indeed, the analogy between the elements and letters was a long-enduring one, beginning very possibly with Leucippus and Democritus (ca. 460 BCE). Aristotle (384–322 BCE), in his *Metaphysics*, refers to the analogy between atoms and letters, suggesting that atoms can combine in different ways to make different forms just as the letters A and N can (985b: 16–19). The notion reappears in Cicero (106–46 BCE) and is extensively used by Lucretius (99–55 BCE) in his *De Rerum natura*.[5]

What is more, in Greek, as later in Latin, the letters were also numbers.[6] We should remember that for the ancient Greeks the cosmos was seen as ruled by certain basic mathematical ratios. The sixth-century BCE mathematician Pythagoras is reported to have claimed that "all is number," and whether the attribution is correct or not, the statement expresses very well the Greek view of the cosmos. Excelling in geometry, the Greeks were astounded to discover, for example, that basic ratios seemed to rule the world around them. In music, which was a branch of mathematics, the octave, fifth, and fourth proved to be the results of very simple ratios: for example, a plucked string, when pinched in the middle, was exactly an octave higher, meaning that the ratio between any two octaves was always 2:1, the waves of the higher octave being exactly twice those of the lower one. A perfect fifth was a ratio of 3:2, and so forth. Pythagoras philosophized that the eight known planets therefore corresponded to the tones of the scale and that their movements created a "music of the spheres" which humans no longer noticed, just as after a while one does not hear the daily crowing of the same rooster each morning. It seemed logical to Pythagoras that the universe was ruled by the same numerical order as the one found in the sounds of our world. His theory of the music of the spheres had enormous longevity and was accepted well into the seventeenth century CE.

If alphabetic letters were both elements and numbers, the complete alphabet was analogous to the whole cosmos.[7] The alphabetic order contained the building blocks of the universe. This view was assimilated to the broader Greek outlook on the world, and served to underpin attitudes towards not only the physical cosmos but also other peoples. Half a millennium or so after Pythagoras, the writings of the Epicurean Roman poet and philosopher Titus Lucretius Carus (99–55 BCE) were still infused with this idea. In the one extant work by Lucretius, his *De rerum natura* (On the Nature of Things), he proposed that atomic rearrangement is analogous to a reordering of the alphabet. In Cicero's *De natura deorum* the stoic satirist Quintis Lucilius Balbys (fl. 100 BCE) mocked Lucretius's ideas by suggesting that, according to Lucretius, if untold quantities of the alphabetic letters were jumbled up and then dumped out on the ground, the result would be a readable copy of the *Annals* of Quintus Ennius (239–169 BCE).[8]

To enter the world of the alphabet was therefore, beginning with the Greeks, to enter the order of the cosmos – to enter an ordered universe. Moreover, the individual letter was part of a compendium, an all-inclusive structure, which was the alphabetic universe. Among the Greeks we thus encounter for the first time the view that alphabetic letters provide a means of apprehending the world, of conceptualizing the cosmos and one's place in it. The alphabet, adapted from Phoenician letters, permits the Greeks to write down their language, and to write in Greek necessarily has important implications for Ionian culture. For the Greeks, to be civilized is to speak Greek; "barbarians" are, by definition, people who do not speak Greek. Thus for the Greeks, their letters are, at one and the same time, more civilized than other scripts, and they also have a civilizing dimension.

By the time the Greeks begin in the fifth century BCE to write about their own writing, they are fully aware that the medium they are using to carry on their discussions is also the medium they are in fact discussing. This self-consciousness surfaces wittily in some of their writings. One play from the period by the writer Kallias, usually titled in English the *ABC Show* (the Greek title is *Grammatike Theoria*), has a chorus comprised of all the letters of the Ionian alphabet. Only fragments of the play have survived, but among the extant parts are dialogues between characters in which they discuss and pronounce the letters of their alphabet.[9] The Greeks also investigate the power and functions of their alphabetic system as well as the origin of their letters. The underlying question that they need to address is: are letters divine in origin or are they a human invention?

Greek texts reveal that on the one hand the Greeks are aware that their alphabet derives from the Phoenician one while on the other they consider it a divine gift that surpasses human talents for invention. The earliest Greek source on the origins of alphabetic letters is Herodotus (ca. 484–25 BCE), considered the West's first historian. In his great work, *The Histories* (the word "history" in Greek meant "inquiry"), Herodotus considers, albeit briefly, the Phoenician origin of Greek letters (Herodotus, 5.58). Herodotus's basic theory that the Greeks took over and modified the Phoenician alphabet is still the accepted theory today regarding the development of Greek letters.

Along with a historical explanation, however, the Greeks put forth several myths regarding the invention of their alphabet. There are legends regarding the Phoenician Cadmus who supposedly gave the alphabet to the Greeks, and Greek writers, including Herodotus, take these up. Indeed, Herodotus backdates Cadmus's role to an impossibly early period. There is another legend that confuses one tale of Cadmus and a cow with the tale of the beautiful girl Io (*Iω* in Greek), who is turned into a heifer. There are many versions of the tale among the Greeks, and it is taken up again in Roman culture. In most versions Zeus, having ravished Io, changes her into a heifer at the moment Hera, his wife, becomes suspicious about her. Hera then places the heifer under the watchful eye of the hundred-eyed Argos whom Hermes (or another god) kills, which sets Io off wandering.

Ovid, in his *Metamorphoses*, adds a new dimension to the tale. In the great Roman poet's version, Io, in a cow's form, has an encounter with her father, who has been looking for her. Unable to use her voice (she just lows when she tries to speak), she stamps out her name in the sand

with her hoofs. Lettristic signs that capture speech thus substitute for
orality, the hoof (analogous to the human hand) eliding the mouth as
the source of linguistic communication. Io's ability to write her identity
alphabetically becomes the reaffirmation and communication of her
essential humanity, despite her animal form.

Naturally, an overly logical approach to Ovid's tale would point out
that in order for Io's father to understand her marks in the sand, the
grammata or letters would have had to exist already. But myths are not
about rational explanation. They are about explaining phenomena that
seem to surpass the human dimension – such as something as powerful
as the alphabet. In the legends, letters are a gift in one way or another
from the gods. This is why the Greeks could investigate at one and
the same time the introduction of letters as a historical question while
also approaching the origin through the medium of legendary tales;
the two tracks of inquiry are not contradictory because they are not in
competition. Herodotus, as a historian, looks for the evidence of the
real Cadmus and marshals data to determine when the introduction
of Phoenician letters into the Greek orbit took place. He situates Cadmus's arrival among historical wars and other events, telling of how
Cadmus and other Phoenicians finally were taken in by the Athenians
to whom they gave "among many other kinds of learning, the alphabet [γράμματα], which had been unknown before this, I think, to the
Greeks" (5.57.1–58.2). Herodotus goes on to discuss how the Greeks
altered the form of Phoenician letters, adapting the letters to their own
language. The Cadmus legend, by contrast, casts Cadmus as a semi-
divine being who gives the means for a kind of communication that
bypasses the voice. Or to be more precise, the letters compensate for
the voice: they were invented as a purely graphemic replacement for
the lost voice. As Isidore of Seville (560–636 CE) will express matters
at the end of the sixth century CE in his *Etymologies*, letters have great
power such that "without any voice the things said by absent people
are spoken to us."[10]

Both the Cadmus tale, in which letters pass from gods to a human
consciousness, and the Io story, in which an inner humanity, trapped
in an animal's body, is expressed through letters, see the alphabet as a
key tool for human communication. Letters give a graphic voice to the
mute, compensating for a voice that for whatever reason is absent; they
reunite father and daughter, reaffirming and re-establishing the social
bonds; and they communicate the essential humanness that remains
despite Io's superficial transformation into a bestial shape. The essence

of humanity is seen as part of Io's interiority, and the set of alphabetic symbols becomes the means by which her humanity is exteriorized. In other words, the ability to manipulate lettristic signs is both the proof and definition of one's humanity.

Greek culture also turns back to the Egyptians for another of its theories regarding the origin of letters. Just as Greek sculpture derives from Egyptian statuary, so also writing, the Greeks posit, may have come from the Egyptians. Certainly, the Greeks were fascinated by hieroglyphic writing and they were well aware of how different it was from their own alphabetic script. As a result, there was little likelihood, as they knew, that the historical roots for the Greek alphabet lay in Egyptian culture. But, again, mythic explanations are of an order different from that of historical investigation, and the mystery and fascination of the earlier Egyptian world was, for the Greeks, a good source for tales of divine origin. The most common myth is that of the Egyptian god Thoth or Theuth who gives letters to man as a means of holding things in memory. Thoth is the scribe for the Egyptian gods and is associated with Hermes, the messenger god of the Greeks. As such, he is the perfect vehicle for the transmission of writing, for what does writing do if not transmit messages? When he gives mankind writing, he gives man the means of holding things in memory.

The great fifth-century BCE philosopher Plato famously turns around the myth of Thoth in his *Phaedrus*, arguing that Thoth's gift is a recipe for forgetting, not for remembering, because rather than internalizing knowledge mankind will now become dependent on external signs. This tale has had much currency in late twentieth-century philosophical circles.[11] The importance for us here is that Plato's view nevertheless still encapsulates a view of the alphabet as a divine creation handed down from distant and ancient sources. It betrays as well a certain distrust of writing because writing is seen as external to the self. Pre-writing culture could only be maintained by the internalization of information and poetry: the oral bards were undoubtedly masters of memory. What they knew became housed in their physical selves, and this corporeal view of what it is to *know* will continue to vie with alphabetic letters for many centuries. In the late 1500s, the French philosopher Michel de Montaigne will still claim that one only truly knows that which one has "made one's own" (*faire sien*).[12] Montaigne will even argue that when one has lived with a poem or a work for a long time, the text sometimes becomes so much a part of a person that one alters a word here or there without realizing it – proof, for Montaigne, that one has fully internalized the work and "knows" it profoundly. As lettristic writing displaces earlier oral culture, memory comes to be cast in alphabetic terms: remembering is repeatedly compared to writing on wax tablets by Cicero, Quintilian, and in the anonymous *Ad Herennium*.[13]

Plato also considers the nature of alphabetic letters in his *Cratylus*, concerning himself here less with the historical dimension of the alphabet's origin and returning to the relationship of letters to the external world and the cosmos. In this Platonic dialogue, Cratylus and Hermogenes square off, presenting two different views of alphabetic letters with Socrates as moderator and judge. Cratylus takes an essentialist, atomistic view, arguing that the letters do not simply signify the things of this world; rather, Cratylus argues that there is an organic bond between words and what they mean. For Cratylus, letters are "motivated."[14] Hermogenes, on the other hand, argues that letters are entirely conventional. At issue is whether the letters are simply arbitrary signs of the world around us or whether there is some sort of tether that ties them to the ambient physical world. Alphabetic writing, in the moment of inscription, turns language into a concrete artefact, making it part of the material world. But does this mean therefore that a kernel of the world is contained in each letter in some elemental way? Or do letters simply represent speech sounds, there being no bond other than a consensual one between letter and world?

This question will continue to be debated over the course of many centuries. Curiously, Socrates (and hence Plato) gives a mixed response. If letters are linked to the things they stand for in some elemental way, perhaps by a process of mimesis, Socrates says, then the better they signify, the more they will resemble the things they represent. But according to this line of reasoning, he argues, the best or most accurate letter would have to completely reproduce the thing for which it stands, in which case it would no longer be a letter, having reproduced the object in its entirety (the twentieth-century Argentine writer Jorge Luis Borges picks up this idea in his essay about a map so detailed that it reproduces every phenomenon of the world it represents, which means it finishes by reproducing the world). As Socrates states, "how ridiculous would be the effect of names on the things named, if they were always made like them in every way! Surely we should then have two of everything, and no one would be able to determine which were the names and which were the realities" (Plato, *Cratylus* 432d).

Rather, Socrates says, the resemblance (or imitation) between letter and material world is only partial, and letters are largely conventional.

But the attraction of similarity (*homoiotes*) alone is not sufficient, he adds, and so "it is necessary to use in addition this common/vulgar (*phortikos*) thing [called] convention (*suntheke*)" (*Cratylus* 435c). Thus, even though letters are largely conventional, there is still some trace of the elemental world contained in them. In other words, for Socrates letters have a limited motivation. Socrates considers several letters in which the trace of the world can, he claims, still be perceived, as for example in the letter "rho" (written "ϱ" in Greek and pronounced like the trilled "r" of Spanish or Italian). The "rho" contains, he says, a mimetic trace of movement, as is evident in the motion of the tongue as it trills. No surprise, Socrates then concludes, that it appears in words denoting motion of one kind or another: *tromos* (trembling), *traxis* (rugged), *thranein* (crush), etc. (*Cratylus* 426 d–e).

Socrates's view thus sees alphabetic letters as still "speaking the world" in an elemental way, though only to a limited extent. The real world is partially contained in each letter, and that partiality is compensated for by conventions of meaning. In Socrates's compromise view – for it is a compromise – we see the beginnings of a long tradition that will conceive of letters as somehow expressing the world, because containing some trace of it, and that will view the world as an alphabetic compendium of sorts. And, like Michel de Montaigne some two thousand years later, Socrates argues that even if one occasionally gets some aspects wrong by "the occasional substitution of a wrong letter" or the omission of a right one, the meaning will not necessarily be affected. So long as "the general character is preserved, even if some of the proper letters are wanting, still the thing is signified" (*Cratylus* 433a). For Plato, the alphabet also becomes a model for understanding the universe. In his dialogue *The Statesman*, Plato argues that if one tries to understand the world the same way one reads "the letters with which the universe is spelled out," one can make proper judgments by considering the elements of the world as "the long and very difficult syllables of everyday existence" (278d).

Half a millennium after Plato, Plutarch (46–120 CE) returns to the relationship between the letter and the world in his essay on the large E (the Greek epsilon which was both named and pronounced EI) engraved since time immemorial at Delphi, the "navel" of the world and source of enigmatic oracles. The Delphic epsilon was inscribed in stone, along with the celebrated injunctions to "know thyself" and to avoid excess. For Plutarch, then, this E has not been placed at Delphi by chance. Why an E, he asks, and what can it mean? Since the very stone of one of the most sacred places in Greek culture offers up a key letter of the alphabet, it is therefore, for Plutarch, important to try to understand what the lettristic inscription wishes to say, just as one does with the injunctions and the ambiguous responses the oracle is famous for giving.

In other words, for Plutarch this single letter E can tell us about our world and our lives. It must, he believes, mean more than just its value as a conventional letter. He puts forth various explanations without championing any single one. Because the Greek letters were also numbers (and as we have seen, numbers, for the Greeks, were considered the binding forces for the universe), he considers the E's position in the alphabet. The epsilon is the fifth letter (as is our modern "E," which comes from the Greek letter), and the number five, he says, is of great importance in mathematics, philosophy, and music. Might the letter's meaning be found in the associations of its numerical value in various disciplines? The epsilon is also the second of the Greek vowels, and the sun (i.e., Apollo) is, for Plutarch, the second planet. Is that the source of the letter's meaning? Or does the epsilon's signification derive from the pronunciation EI? "EI" means "if" in ancient Greek, in which case the letter perhaps refers to the queries of the seekers who come to Delphi to ask if they should take a particular course of action or if they will meet with success. The word "if," Plutarch reminds his readers, is also key to the construction of the premises of syllogisms. Taken another way, "EI" is the second-person address of the verb "to be," hence "thou art." Is the E representative of the seeker at Apollo's temple at Delphi who addresses the eternal deity with the affirmation, "Thou art"?

The point is not the rightness or wrongness of any of Plutarch's speculations (I have only given some of them). What matters here is his attempt to get the alphabetic letter to utter something more than simply its semiotic value as a letter; he is looking for a deeper, shrouded meaning, through which the letter would somehow speak or encapsulate the world. The letter, because of its numerical and elemental characteristics, might form a bridge between the alphabet and material reality, especially at Delphi where enigmatic speech relates to the things of our world. The alphabetic letter somehow speaks the world while the world also, at Delphi, speaks the letter E.

In a sense, Plutarch is doubling back to a view expressed by the Greek play *Prometheus Bound*, which was composed, like Plato's dialogues, in the classical period, most probably by Aeschylus (525–456 BCE).[15] Traditionally, Greek myth had seen Mnemosyne ("Memory")

as the mother of the nine muses, hence the source of Greek poetry.
Legend had it that Zeus slept with Mnemosyne, who gave birth to the
virgin muses. In Aeschylus, however, the alphabet is described as a
"memory, Muse-mother," making it the source of poetry and associating the cultural memory with the act of lettristic writing. Moreover, in
the play it is Prometheus who gives writing, along with fire, to humans,
which is to say that Prometheus gives the tools for creating civilization to the Greeks. His gift of the alphabet is of a piece with his theft of
fire – an audacious act that gives humans a new degree of mastery over
their world. Letters can now be used to reveal, yes, but they are also a
powerful means for equivocation and hidden meanings (as with the E
at Delphi). Prometheus, after all, is one who repeatedly hides things.

As this chapter demonstrates, the Greeks set forth a view of written letters that sees an analogy between the alphabet and the world.
The alphabet corresponds to a universal order and expresses the whole
cosmos while it also exists in this world and is a powerful tool for re-
creation, beginning with the recording of the Homeric world in the two
great epics *The Odyssey* and *The Iliad*. The implications of these early
developments are enormous for subsequent Western culture because
the Greek view first implants the notions that alphabetic letters are
more than merely communicative. Despite major shifts in culture and
religion over the course of the next two millennia, the conception of the
alphabet as both corresponding to the cosmos in which humans dwell
and also expressing the very essence of what it is to be human or civilized will reappear again and again. The Christian world will take over
many of these attitudes towards the alphabetic letter, making them key
tenets of the Christian view of both the world and letters. After the
sixteenth century, early modern society will modify and adapt these
long-standing views, without eliminating them. The Greeks thus stand
as the seminal creators of a worldview that sees our reality and our
humanity as bound up by and in the alphabet.

3

Latin Letters and the Enduring Influence of Roman Scripts

Que l'alphabet est la meilleur possession que nos ancestres nous ayent laissé.

Honorat Rambaud

Let us begin our investigation of Latin letters with the famous text carved into the base of Trajan's Column in Rome. The column, near the Roman Forum, is a popular tourist sight, and most guidebooks to Rome discuss the detailed reliefs that gradually ascend the column, wrapping around it, in which the Spanish-born Emperor Trajan's victory over the Dacians (in what is modern-day Romania) is depicted. The column is an artistic marvel, and there are ongoing debates regarding exactly how the carvings were executed shortly after 110 CE.

Most tourists do not pay much attention to the pedestal supporting the column (fig. 9). The information chiselled in Latin on the pedestal is also explicated by most guidebooks for those who might be interested. However, one of the remarkable aspects of the inscription – and this is quite evident in figure 9 – is that a twenty-first-century person has absolutely no difficulty in reading the inscription. Nearly two thousand years have passed since this text was chiselled in stone, and yet almost any observer who speaks a language that is written in the Roman alphabet can make out the words with no problem. They stand out as though they were carved yesterday, and one hardly needs a knowledge of Latin to get the gist of the text: "SENATVS POPVLVSQUE ROMANVS IMP CAESARI DIVI NERVAE F..." The casual viewer will know that "CAESARI" must be "CAESAR," so that even without knowing anything about the dative case in Latin, s/he will know that the inscription concerns in some fashion the emperor and the Roman senate

("SENATVS"). Furthermore, even a modern viewer might well realize that "TRAIANO" has something to do with Emperor Trajan and such a person will probably surmise that "AD DECLARANDUM" has to do with a declaration of sorts. Obviously, then, one can surmise that the inscription says something about Emperor Trajan declaring something, perhaps to the senate, or maybe the senate is declaring something with (or to?) Emperor Trajan. Not even the "V" where we would expect a "U" in "SENATVS" will hang up many modern readers. One does not need to know that Latin and the vernacular languages had only the "v" for many centuries, and a consistent distinction between both "u" / "v" and "i" / "j" did not come about until after the Renaissance.[1]

Considering that this is an inscription in a language that most modern readers have never studied and that the writing is almost two millennia old, it is remarkable that we can make it out with such ease. But then, if we look at the letter forms, they look surprisingly modern. We have in fact seen these letter types countless times all around us in the modern world. Those capital letters with the handsome serifs are part and parcel of our daily lives. That is to say, the letter forms the Romans were using two thousand years ago are still with us, remarkably unchanged. Paleographers call them "Roman capitals" or "monumental capitals," the latter name being very à propos because one of the most common uses of these letter forms is for monumental inscriptions on buildings and memorials the world over. The inscription on the front of the United States Supreme Court building "EQUAL JUSTICE UNDER LAW" is chiselled in Roman capitals that reproduce Emperor Trajan's script almost perfectly except for the concession to modern sensibilities in the use of "u" and "j" in place of "v" and "i" (fig. 10).

The same is true for the gilt letters proclaiming "NEW YORK STOCK EXCHANGE" on the front of the famous Wall Street Building. Nor will it come as a surprise that most of the inscriptions on the Arc of Triumph in Paris, including the names of celebrated battles, French victories, and famous generals are carved, for the most part, in monumental capitals. And so it goes for countless other governmental buildings and memorials. Moreover, modern societies are merely continuing the Roman practice of alphabetic writing in public spaces. One of the features of Roman cities was the ever present textuality in their public spaces (squares, streets and alleys, walls, etc.), whether it was a matter of stone inscriptions, scrawled graffiti, or painted letters (Petrucci, *La Scrittura* 3).

Now, one of the extraordinary features of monumental capitals is the pure durability of this roman script. The Romans adapted their monumental capitals (*capitalis quadrata*) for literary texts of which "[t]he highpoint of refinement was reached with the writing of whole codices of Vergil" (Bischoff 59; see also 59–61). In two thousand years we have hardly improved on the clarity and sense of order Roman capitals give us; in the sixteenth century, Francesco Torniello (1490–1589), for example, will find it natural in his *Opera del modo de fare le littere maiuscole antique* (1517) to go back to Roman capitals as the models for his letter types. The Times New Roman font in every computer, which was developed in 1931 for *The Times* of London and is now used ubiquitously for the documents we spit out, is based on the same script; its majuscule letters are virtually unchanged from the time of the Roman emperors.

Now, there is nothing inherent in these letter forms that make them more ordered or stately than other fonts: a nice italic or a simple sans serif script could do the job just as well. But we attribute these qualities of stability and monumentality to Roman capitals with their delicate serifs. Why is that? Why do inscriptions on buildings invariably revert to the same script, and why do we use them for the majority of our documents?

The answer lies, of course, in political history more than in any qualities inhering in the letters. Quite simply, these are the letters that the Romans themselves chiselled on buildings throughout their empire. For that reason, to this day Roman capitals signify monumentality in the Western consciousness. Roman capitals were produced by a great civilization that ruled over much of the known world, and thus great civilizations – or civilizations that wish to see themselves as great – feel obliged (or entitled) to inscribe Roman capitals on their monuments and buildings. The equation aspires to be reciprocal: if a great civilization wrote in Roman capitals, then to write in Roman capitals is to be a great civilization. Culturally, the letter shapes speak the grandness and grandeur of a people. As a result, the name of President John Fitzgerald Kennedy carved into granite in the Kennedy Memorial Park in Cambridge, Massachusetts, must necessarily be written in monumental capitals. No other script would do. And so it goes for many thousands of other inscriptions.

Clearly, the cultural meaning of letters is often greater than what they simply mean as letters. The phenomenon at play here is different from the Greek notion that letters are numbers and thus are related to the cosmic order, though that notion is also picked up by the Romans. Here it is the very forms of the letters that matter. By its use of certain letter forms, a culture states both its place in the world and how it conceives of itself and others. The state proclaims its power and seriousness (what the Romans called *gravitas*) through these letter forms; in a later chapter we shall see that some modern artists proclaim their status and contest traditional conceptions of the world through the use of very different letter forms (who ever heard of a graffiti artist writing his "tag" in Roman capitals?). Moreover, the whole culture participates in this monumentality without consciously realizing it. Precisely because the monumentality of Roman capitals is so internalized we are hardly aware of the effect (and even less of the origins) the letter forms have when we see inscriptions on buildings and memorials. We simply think of the inscriptions as stately and somehow fitting for a government's serious pronouncements.

Roman capitals also have a second use as a "display script" in many books. We are all familiar with the oversized lettrine that opens each chapter of a book. These letters are often Roman capitals. But the modern world is hardly the first era to realize the value, culturally, of making use of Roman capitals as "display scripts" in their books. Charlemagne (742–814 CE), who was determined to revive the Roman Empire in a Christian form and had himself crowned emperor by Pope Leo III on Christmas day in the year 800, understood very well the cultural signification of Roman capitals (Bischoff 60). Not that Emperor Charlemagne could read and write very well. His biographer, Einhard (ca. 775–840 CE), says that Charlemagne tried to learn to write and kept wax tablets under the pillows of his bed so that he could practise forming alphabetic letters during his leisure time, "but although he tried very hard, he had begun too late in life and he made little progress" (Einhard, Bk III: 25 [79]). Nevertheless, Charlemagne, or at least those in his entourage, understood the role of Roman capitals in connoting grandeur.

In fact the Carolingians' sensitivity to the political meaning of letter forms predates Charlemagne. His father, Pepin the Short (d. 768), first of the Carolingian line, was conscious of how precarious his claims to the throne were initially, and he sought to buttress his standing as King of the Franks (*Dux et princeps Francorum*) by exploiting Pope Stephen II's weaknesses and having the pope also anoint him as *Patricius Romanum* (Patrician of the Romans), giving him religious as well as secular authority. Along with this moral sanction from the pope came a whole library, supplied by Stephen's successor, Pope Paul I (757–67). The stage was set for an enormous amount of scribal work, carried out largely at the monastery at Corbie, which led to the development of a new script called the Carolingian minuscule. The copying of texts with these new letter forms became one of the "proofs" of the high level of Carolingian civilization, the alphabetic letter serving as the footman to proclaim Carolingian culture as the inheritor of Roman civilization.

Charlemagne seized his brother Carloman II's (751–71 CE) part of the Frankish lands after the latter's death, driving Carloman's widow and sons into exile. He also needed to buttress his position as king over all the Franks. One means of doing so was to promote a unity in terms of administration and religion. At Corbie, Charlemagne's scribes undertook the publication of an enormous version of the Old Testament. In terms of propaganda the meanings were clear: Charlemagne was a new King David. Indeed the leader of the literary circle at Charlemagne's court, the erudite Englishman Alcuin (ca. 740–804 CE), regularly referred to Charlemagne as "David." The cost of such an undertaking was enormous, and according to Stanley Morison, the twelve projected volumes that "served no liturgical or parish purpose" required the work of "several monks for a number of years, and a great mass of vellum" (130). The official (and officious) nature of the text as a grand statement of the political Carolingian order is attested to by the fact that the letter type chosen was the slower-to-write but clearer and more stately Carolingian minuscule, rather than the former Luxeuil minuscule that had flourished under the Merovingians and was faster to write, though far less clear. The change in alphabetic letters connoted a change of political dynasty and a message of power, unity, and clear order (see Bischoff 112–17; Morison 128–34).

With his assumption of the mantle of Roman emperor, Charlemagne consciously sought to emulate his predecessors in antiquity. Since the earlier Roman emperors were expected to foster intellectual activities and the arts, Charlemagne oversaw the school at his court in Aix-la-Chapelle (Aachen) in which intellectuals and poets gave themselves Latin names and composed poetry in Latin. Alcuin, as head of this court school, was now to oversee the promulgation of an authoritative Latin Bible. Charlemagne was a Christian Roman emperor and so he devoted himself to Christian letters. When he came to power, there were multiple versions of the Latin Bible, a situation it was up to Alcuin to rectify.

The result was a standardized biblical text that was intended to be exemplary of the stability and order Charlemagne's rule wished to offer (it should not be forgotten that the Carolingians came to power by overthrowing the Merovingian dynasty). The standardized Bible was then promulgated through a series of sumptuous manuscripts, which were designed to demonstrate the heights to which Carolingian culture could not only aspire, but which it could actually achieve.

Figures 11 A and B show one of the sumptuous biblical manuscripts created at Charlemagne's court in the late eighth century. Known as the Coronation Gospels because the manuscript was created to celebrate Charlemagne's coronation as emperor (tradition has it that the manuscript was found in Charlemagne's tomb when Emperor Otto III (980–1002 CE) opened it in 1000 CE), the book is a magnificent display of the heights to which Charlemagne's court aspired. The beauty and stateliness of the book is evident in both its images and in the disposition of its text. The cost in terms of time and resources must have been enormous, and only a great king could support such expenditures for a text that had symbolic value above all.

The world view of this new "Roman" empire is summed up admirably in the style and disposition of the alphabetic text. The two manuscript folios in figure 11 (fol. 76v and fol. 77r) face each other when the book is open, creating a perfect balance between man and text. Art historians have long appreciated the portrait of Saint Mark as well as those of the other evangelists in this manuscript; the consummate artistry and the sense of philosophical wisdom that the image conveys hearken back to classical models, probably Byzantine imperial art. One critic has pointed out that the portrait on the page looks like the sort one might have found on a wall in a villa of the Roman Empire (Gaehde 1977). Of the same dimensions on the facing page is the beginning of the Gospel of Saint Mark, and the text, written in gold ink, is set out with the same balance, proportion, and serenity that we find in the portrait, and the rectangular space it occupies matches that of the portrait of Saint Mark. Moreover, behind the gold letters the page has been dyed with "Phoenician purple," the very emblem of royal prestige and power dating back to antiquity.

This correspondence is significant because the evangelists were writers above all. The man and his written work are equated here, an equation that is recurrent in Christian culture (I shall come back to this). For the moment, I wish simply to concentrate on the letter forms. What I wish to emphasize here, however, is that the initial word "(I) NITIUM" is written, except for the "I," in none other than (slightly modified) Roman monumental capitals – the same forms we find on Trajan's Column and on the United States Supreme Court building.

The Carolingian scribes who made this book understood, in the same way that modern American architects did, that to double back to Roman capitals was a way of evoking classical seriousness and grandeur. We enter Mark's Gospel under the archway, as it were, of Roman capitals, and the *gravitas* of ancient Rome is transferred to the Christian gospel. It will come as no surprise that each of the four Gospels in this manuscript begins with Roman capitals. In fact, the forms of the letters, the ink used, and the textual disposition are all designed to convey Carolingian grandeur and control: they broadcast Charlemagne's power and empire. The incipit above the "INITIUM" is written in the other major non-cursive script bequeathed by Roman antiquity – what are called "rustic capitals." The rest of the page is written in a highly readable set of uncials. The page enacts a kind of *translatio* from the imperial culture of antiquity to that of the Christian Middle Ages as a passage from one set of letter forms to another, all while maintaining continuity by using the imperial purple for the page and ink made with gold for the text.

Nor is this the only example of the Carolingians' conscious use of Roman scripts as a way of imprinting their notion of empire on their times (in 814 Charlemagne finally succeeded in getting Byzantium to recognize him as emperor). They also used them, for example, in similar fashion in the Golden Psalter of Charlemagne. More important, following Gregory the Great, Roman capitals were used for public display texts in stone as well; the great stone epitaph Charlemagne sent to Rome after the death of Hadrian I (after 795) is carved in impeccable Roman capitals (it is still visible in the portico of St Peter's).

The three soundings of Roman capitals that we have taken – from Trajan's Column, a late eighth- or early ninth-century manuscript, and a modern American building – demonstrate not only the endurance of one particular letter form (Roman capitals) but also the ways in which letters can come to mean much more than simply the sounds they stand for. The very shape of letters becomes deeply involved in history, in ideology, and in the ways in which a culture represents itself to itself and to others. That different geographical areas or time periods should become attached to certain forms of letters is entirely understandable. In the pre-modern world one would expect Irish scribes to have developed scripts that were different from those favoured by writers in southern Italy, as was in fact the case. Many centuries later, however, we continue to use Irish letters for book or pub names when they have to do with Ireland, even though most of what is written about and/or in Ireland has long since abandoned Insular scripts. But certain letter forms still say "Ireland" to us.

Moreover, the several alphabets currently in use in Western culture will probably never be standardized as one, largely because of historical and cultural values, including national pride. Greek has retained the ancient alphabet used to write down Homer's epics. The Russians and Bulgarians have also kept the Cyrillic script devised by Cyril and Methodius around 862 CE when, according to tradition, they adapted the Greek alphabet in order to record Slavic speech. Russia, while it reformed somewhat its alphabet after the Bolshevik Revolution, would never consider giving up the Cyrillic alphabet; that is to say, its identity is bound up deeply with the Cyrillic letters. But some Slavic languages such as Czech were written in Cyrillic at first, but then switched to Latin scripts, and their decision to go with Roman letters is undoubtedly associated with a desire to be oriented more towards western Europe than eastern Europe, which is to say Russia. Moreover, the distinction between Serbian and Croatian is largely one of alphabetic forms, not of grammar or vocabulary. The decision of the Serbs to embrace the Cyrillic script is part of an orientation towards the Slavic world and a long-standing alliance with Russia, whereas the Croatian use of Latin letters emphasizes historical roots with the Hapsburg Empire and western Europe as well as connoting an opening towards adjacent countries (Italy, Slovenia, Austria) and participation in the European flow of money and tourists.

Letter forms thus "speak" a particular culture or nation or historical period. Over the course of the past few thousand years most language groups have been deeply attached to the form of their letters, seeing in them a source of their identity and an expression of their world view, and such attitudes continue today. The German double "s" – ß – looks strange and antiquated to non-German speakers; and indeed it is antiquated to the extent that it links the old "tall s" (ſ) found in books of many languages in earlier centuries with our modern "s" (s) in a single letter. The Germans could just as easily write the "ß" as "ss," and occasionally they do this, but in the main they prefer to retain the "Germanness" of their distinctive ligature. However, as Germans increasingly adopt "ss" for "ß" this becomes a way of stating their modern-ness and their adherence to contemporary European and global values rather than purely Germanic ones. So, too, the Icelandic "thorn" ("þ") and "eth" ("ð"), drawn from early medieval runic writing, express the sounds that "th" covers in English. Since Icelandic has both the "t" and the "h," it could dispense with the two runic letters, but in doing so Icelanders would feel that their whole ethos was being undermined. Much the same could be said of the Danish "ø" which somehow speaks Danish-ness or the Czech "ž," though at least these have distinct phonological values. Even languages that have no distinct letters are deeply proud of their complex systems of accents and diacritical marks. Learning where dashes, apostrophes, accents, and cedillas go in a particular language is part of the whole ritual of indoctrination into its culture.

Letter forms can thus come to be felt as nationalistic, almost as emblems of a culture; a language's orthography, to which letter forms are often deeply related, can have many of the same connotations. Woe to the person who would tamper with a language's orthography, no matter how illogical it might be. Even countries that are relatively accepting of orthographical reforms hold referenda, canvas opinion, and appoint grand commissions before proposing even the slightest changes. Native English speakers are notoriously proud of the absurdity of their spellings and consider the mastery of them a key aspect of a child's education and a rite of passage for foreigners hoping to succeed in an English-speaking society. Every English-speaking grammar school student learns the rhyme "'i' before 'e' except after 'c.'" Because English has become the "lingua-franca" of the modern world, it would of course facilitate matters if the spelling were made more phonological. But hackles go up the moment anyone makes this suggestion. To be sure, even advanced foreign students of English take pride in the quirks of English orthography, once they have mastered them. I have already mentioned, in my introduction, the glee with which advanced students learning English as a second language take down the spelling "ghoti" for "fish." They are delighted to be "in" on the joke and anxious to show it to their fellow countrymen struggling with English orthography.

French is another western European language with some rather strange spellings, and one in which the heritage of Latin letters and the deep substratum of the Latin language have loomed large in questions of French orthography and national identity.[2] In the sixteenth century, grammarians carried on acrimonious debates regarding their spellings and in particular whether French orthography should show the Roman past in its forms or not. On one side of the debate were the "etymologizers" who proposed adding unpronounced letters from Latin to French words in order to show the Latin roots of French words. This attitude was part of the larger Renaissance reverence for, and recovery of, its

Graeco-Roman heritage, and these grammarians conceived of French as bearing the weight of ancient Rome in its letters. Letters, according to them, should reveal the greatness of their Roman past each time French words were committed to paper. During the sixteenth century, many of these Latinized spellings took hold, and although most of them have since been abandoned, a few of them still remain in the modern language. For instance, the French word for "time" is, to this day, "temps." The "p" is not pronounced at all (nor, for that matter is the "s" – plus the "m" is completely nasalized – but that is simply part and parcel of the eccentricities of the language). Prior to the sixteenth century the word was written "tems." But Latinists knew that the word came from "tempus" in Latin, so they added an unpronounced "p" to recall the word's Roman past.

The series of debates in France is worthy of a small digression. To be sure, there was a certain absurdity to the whole project of adding letters from Latin. After all, the "p" in "temps" would only recall the Roman past to a person who already knew the Latin word, and if one knew the Latin root, one did not need the "p" in order to be informed of it. What is interesting for us is that certain intellectuals should have been so attached to the alphabetic letters of the occulted Latin substratum in French words that they would want to resuscitate some of the letters and include them in French words. The project suggests a deep attachment to Latin letters in the most literal sense even though, as one contemporary grammarian, Charles de Bouvelles (1475–1566), pointed out at the time, this would lead to the conclusion that the most "pure" French was in fact simply the Latin language (discussed in chapter 5).

Besides, the etymologizers sometimes got matters wrong. The modern French word for "weight" is "poids," in which the "d" is not pronounced (neither is the "s"). Sixteenth-century Latinists added the "d" because of the Latin word for weight, "pondus," and the "d" has stayed in the word. But, as specialists of the French language love to point out, the etymologizers of the 1500s in fact got it wrong: "poids" came from another Latin word – "pensum," also meaning "weight" – so there was not really any "d" to add. No matter: the word gained a "d," and the "d" has remained ever since, in part for the practical reason that it distinguishes the word from the homonym "pois" (English "pea").

Against the etymologizers in the mid-1500s stood the reformers, led by Louis Meigret (they were even referred to as "Meigretistes"), who sought instead to render French spellings more phonetic along the lines of Italian and Spanish. They wanted to reform the alphabetic letters in various ways, from adding small diacritic marks to creating entirely new letter forms. The reformers were not a unified group, and there was constant infighting. Indeed, they wrote more treatises against each other than against the etymologizers. When one grammarian, Guillaume des Autels, published under the near-anagrammic pseudonym of Glaomalos de Vezelet an attack on the most important of the reformers, Louis Meigret, Meigret came back with a rebuttal in which he accused Des Autels of "arrogance in foolish rants, axioms, angry words and insults." Des Autels then turned around and in 1551 published his *Replique de Guillaume des Autels aux furieuses défenses de Louis Meigret* (Reply of Guillaume des Autels to the Furious Defences of Louis Meigret) in which he claimed: "I do not know who this Meigret is, except that I have been told he is one of these trivial and vulgar translators who do not know how to do anything except to shatter our eardrums from one day to another with their foolish versions, or should I rather say perversions."[3]

Of all the programs of reform, Meigret's was undoubtedly the most important. In 1550 he convinced a publisher to publish his most recent treatise using his reformed orthography, which included the addition of cedillas and accents for letters that formerly did not have them and the elimination of some letters. To print the book with the altered alphabetical letters represented a financial outlay on the part of the publisher since new letter type had to be cut. The economics of alphabetical reform played a key role in the acceptance or rejection of orthographical changes in this period. The scribal freedom to choose or change letter forms in a preprint culture would only have affected a single book at a time; but printers had to print numerous copies and then sell them to readers. If a printer embraced a radical departure in terms of letter forms and the public did not take to it, he risked financial loss.

Some of the more radical proposals therefore stood no chance of widespread adoption, either because they were too ungainly, too expensive, or both. One grammarian, Jacobus Sylvius (Fr.: Jacob Dubois) (1478–1555 CE), proposed a two-tiered system in which both the French word and the Latin word would be able to be reconstructed. For example, the French word "chevaucher" (to ride on horseback), coming from the Latin "cabalcar" would appear as:

```
h e v    u  h e
c  a b a l c a  r
```
[4]

By going back and forth between the words, one could read both the French ("chevaucher") and the Latin ("cabalcar"). To read a whole book printed in this fashion, however, would be a dizzying affair, and to print such an alphabetical text would be needlessly complicated – and expensive.

If Sylvius/Dubois's system was the most extreme Latinizing proposal, the most extreme revised orthography was the one proposed by Honorat Rambaud (ca. 1516–86 CE) who ended up creating a whole new alphabet for French. He printed his book in a *face-en-face* edition with the text in traditional French letters on one side and in his proposed alphabet on the facing page (fig. 30). Rambaud's proposal may have rationalized French letters admirably, but, as one can see immediately, he abandoned almost completely the Latinized alphabet inherited from Rome. Rambaud's French no longer looked "French" at all. In abandoning the familiar Latin letters his spellings lost their grip on a sense of what European culture was and how it represented itself in the world. A whole world view was at risk in such a radical change, and the "Frenchness" of French identity was completely erased.

Indeed, this was the problem with the reforms in general. The great complaint against the reformers was not a philological or linguistic argument. Rather, it was that they denatured the French language, robbing it of what people called the "naive French grace" (naive grace française). In other words, something of the French identity and the French world view was felt to be lost if the spellings and letter forms departed too much from the heritage of Latin letters. The traditional letters and spellings contained for people something of the "Frenchness" of their country and culture, and this had meaning for them far beyond the primary role of letters as representing sounds.

That certain traditional combinations of letters – that is, certain spellings – could be seen as somehow expressing a people and its culture meant two things. First, that the letters carried the weight of the past and were seen as the filial result of many centuries of writing. National identity was bound up with and expressed by the letters handed down from Roman antiquity. Second, that cultural tradition trumped practicality. Despite some grammarians' concern that French needed to have a more rational orthography in order to compete with Italian and Spanish, which were written phonetically in the main, their reforms were rejected. At issue was the question of a country's place in the world. Was the essence of France to be found in the particularities of its spellings? Or should French make itself more accessible to foreigners?

Would people in foreign lands choose to learn French if the spellings were so chaotic? After all, Spanish had already spread throughout most of the New World, and Italian was considered a superior language for philosophy and literature in the sixteenth century. Decisions about which letters should have accents, or be added or eliminated from the language, were intimately tied to global politics and the jockeying for dominance in the world.

In the Roman world there had been a close alliance between the extension of Roman power and the spread of the Latin language, or at least this was the view of Europeans in the fifteenth and sixteenth centuries. Antonio de Nebrija, in his *Gramática castellana* of 1492, famously remarks that in Roman times "the language always accompanied the empire; and it followed it in such fashion that together they began and grew and flourished, and later together they both collapsed."[5] At the time Nebrija penned this sentence, the voyage to the New World was still in the future, but the spirit of empire was very much in his mind, whether he was thinking of Africa or some new version of "the East." A few decades later, the important French printer Geoffroy Tory in his treatise on letter forms, the *Champ Fleury* (1529), not only reiterates Nebrija's claims, which he may have read, but extends the arguments that yoke empire and language. The Romans, Tory claims, prospered more and obtained more victories by means of their language than by means of arms. "[T]he Romans ... had dominion over the greatest part of the earth [and] prospered more and had more victories by means of their language than by their lances."[6] So, argues Tory, should the French do as well, for which they need, as he says, to regulate their language and put it in order.

The worries that France would lose out to other languages with more phonetic orthographies proved unfounded as became clear over the course of the next century when France's stature and military might grew until France was the pre-eminent power in Europe. By the late eighteenth century, French was well ensconced as the international language of diplomacy, learning, and science, and it was employed at most European courts, including Russia, even though the orthography had not been reformed. In 1782 the Academy of Berlin held an essay contest for which the subject was, "What has rendered the French language universal?" which in effect took French's universality as a given.[7] This situation was to continue until the late nineteenth century when the power of the English empire made English, with its even more bewildering orthography, the rival for linguistic dominance. Finally, with the increasing power of the United States in the twentieth century and its supremacy following the Second World War, English became the universal language we know it to be now.

It is by now quite clear that the forms of our letters – that is, our typefaces and our scripts, as well as the way we put our letters together – are key features for the expression of our world views. With the shape of our letters and the way we combine them into words we reinforce to ourselves and to others a sense of who we are as a culture, which is why each language is highly attached to the peculiarities of its alphabet and orthography. And in our choice of scripts we also reaffirm how we conceive of the world: what we find important both in our past and our present day. In a subsequent chapter we will look at how modern writers and artists have used letter forms to suggest that our relationship to the cosmos has changed in recent decades and as a result new lettristic expressions are in order.

For the moment I wish simply to consider the script that we make use of on a daily basis when we type or read or even print by hand lower case letters in English (or in most of the other major European languages). We have already seen how we make use in books and on buildings of Roman capitals to suggest monumentality. But the letters that we learn to print in primary school (I am not speaking of cursive here) or the letters that make up the text of this book are for the most part lower case, so they cannot be Roman capitals.

As it happens, our modern lower case letter forms are taken, with only slight changes, from the letters of Latin texts in the Carolingian period – that is to say, the period of Charlemagne and his successors in the eighth to the eleventh centuries. The script that was developed at Charlemagne's court, called "Carolingian minuscule" or occasionally "Caroline minuscule," is characterized by order and clarity. It is based on a series of rounded forms with trailers that rise above the body of the letter (as for a "d" or a "b") and ones that hang down below ("p," "q," etc.). We are so accustomed to these letters that they seem unremarkable.

The Carolingian minuscule was created at Charlemagne's court as part of the intellectual activity that also addressed, as we have seen, the standardization of the biblical texts. To a standardized Latin Bible corresponded a standardized script that would be employed throughout Charlemagne's empire. In the creation of these letter forms, the Carolingians also sought to differentiate themselves from the Merovingians who had ruled before them.

A quick historical excursus is perhaps in order here. The Frankish Merovingians came to power in the fifth century, during a period for which the outmoded and derogatory term "Dark Ages" may never-theless well apply. After the Germanic tribes swept through Europe, raiding and pillaging, intellectual activity waned; indeed, the intel-lectuals who continued to work in monasteries were well aware that knowledge was being lost, but they were powerless to halt the decline. The bloodline, also Frankish, that would later become the Carolingi-ans traditionally supplied the seneschals to the Merovingian kings, which meant that they were the Merovingians' right-hand men who ran the kingdom when the king was absent and oversaw the day-to-day affairs of the palace. As one sees in much medieval literature, the seneschal was also a dangerous figure because, if he shifted his allegiances away from the king, he was the most likely person to be able to engineer a coup d'état. This is in fact precisely what the Caro-lingians did. As the real power behind late, weak Merovingian kings, the Carolingians succeeded in replacing them and ensuring the con-sent of the pope in the process. The term "Carolingian" goes back to Charlemagne's grandfather Charles Martel (686–741 CE), who gained fame for having halted the advance of the Muslim forces at the Battle of Poitiers in 732; the attribute "Martel," which in French meant "ham-mer," was added to the name Charles ("Carolus" in Latin) because he "hammered back" the invading Muslims, preserving Christianity. Charles Martel's son, Pepin the Short (714–68) then officially seized power, doing away with the Merovingian line, and he had himself crowned king in 751. Charlemagne assumed power in 768 and was crowned emperor, as we have already seen, by Pope Leo III (d. 816) on Christmas day, 800.

Merovingian writing was a mess, to put it bluntly. The letter forms were not standardized, and in fact scholars distinguish several distinct areas by differences in the writing. Moreover, the script was difficult to read, lacking clarity and order on the page. A glance at a Merovingian manuscript such as the Luxeuil Lectionary is sufficient to demonstrate this. Gone, to be sure, is the stateliness of Roman capitals.

Charlemagne and his court, when they revived, after a fashion, the Roman Empire, had an interest in reforming the written scripts as well. By developing a new script that was clear, concise, ordered, and pleas-ant to read, the Carolingians showed themselves as superior to the Merovingians and worthy heirs to the great Roman civilization. This was one element among many that served to convince themselves and others that they held the same sort of status as their Roman anteced-ents (in truth, Charlemagne's empire was quite small compared to the

Roman Empire at its height). To be able to create noble letter forms and then use them for important intellectual activities was part of being "Roman," hence an important element in achieving legitimacy for Charlemagne's empire.

Most literary and clerical texts during the Carolingian period were written in the Carolingian minuscule. So, too, were many documents, letters, etc. from the period. In fact, over the course of over three centuries – that is, until the development of Gothic scripts – the letter forms hardly changed at all.

How, then, did the Carolingian script become the letters of choice for the modern world?

In a later chapter we shall glance at the Gothic writing of the late Middle Ages. For the moment, what is important to bear in mind is that in the fifteenth century, when humanists were fomenting what we now call the Renaissance, they wished to do away with writing that they considered "medieval," which meant, for them, "unenlightened." They therefore rejected Gothic scripts – indeed, the term "Gothic" to refer to late medieval writing was a derogatory one invented by the Renaissance humanists – and instead they turned to Carolingian writing. Quite apart from the qualities of order and clarity that the Carolingian minuscule possessed, what made it the script of choice for the humanists was that they in fact thought – erroneously – that it came from Roman times. Thus, in the mistaken belief that the Carolingians, in reviving the Roman Empire, had also revived a Roman script, the humanists, who also saw themselves as returning to and giving new life to classical antiquity, adopted the Carolingian minuscule as their preferred script. With the invention of the printing press the Carolingian letter forms then became widely distributed, and for lower-case letters they have been with us ever since.

We have circled back to the argument with which we began this chapter when we considered Roman capitals and monumentality. The pseudo-Roman Carolingian forms were chosen because they seemed to the humanists to "speak" enduring Roman culture. The letter forms uttered a bond between fifteenth and sixteenth-century humanism and ancient Latin writers and thinkers. The recovery of classical writings, art forms, and architecture was announced visually by the adoption of a resuscitated script they also believed to come from antiquity. To write treatises in Carolingian letters was, in the humanist mentality, to take on the robes of the great philosophers, historians, and poets of the Graeco-Roman world. It does not matter that they were mistaken. What is important is that they believed that the letters spoke those values and uttered a world view that the Middle Ages had smothered under Christian teaching and Gothic letter forms. The renaissance in thinking mirrored a renaissance in letter forms, and the renaissance of letter forms was seen as mirroring in turn a renaissance in ways of thinking and attitudes regarding the world.

4

Christian Letters: The Middle Ages

Somebody said once or wrote, once: "We're all of us children in a vast kinder-garten trying to spell God's name with the wrong alphabet books."
Tennessee Williams, *Suddenly Last Summer*

From early in its history Christianity has been deeply involved in questions of the alphabetic letter. To begin with, Christianity, like the other two great monotheistic religions, Judaism and Islam, is a "religion of the book," which is to say, a religion that is self-consciously aware of its status as writing. The opening of the Gospel of St John is often cited as evidence of Christianity's bookishness: "In the beginning was the Word, and the Word was with God, and the Word was God." The first part of the statement sees an origin of the cosmos in the Word, referring back to God's creation of the world as a series of speech-acts in which the words he uttered became created entities instantaneously. The second part follows from the first, since clearly the Word was with God. But the third part is truly extraordinary. The Word *was* God. This statement declares God to be an active linguistic presence that speaks the cosmos in a language for which utterance and concrete reality are coexistent.

God is thus utterance, and in the medieval view both the world and the Bible are his word made concrete texts: along with the Bible stands the "Book of the World." For the Middle Ages, either of these two books could be read for one's salvation, and for this reason one did not have to be literate in order to be saved (indeed, how many people knew how to read and write in the Middle Ages is a hotly debated topic).[1] Saint Augustine (354–430 CE) recast Platonic views that saw the things of this

world as imperfect articulations of perfect, divine concepts. He argued
that this world should be viewed as so many signs, all of which could
lead the Christian to God; in other words, God was the divine concept
to which everything around us pointed.[2] The world, in this view, was
a text to be read like the Bible, and the things of this world were like
so many letters. In a sermon he exhorts Christians to read the "Book of
Nature" as well as the Holy Bible:

> Some people read books in order to find God. Yet there is a great book, the
> very appearance of created things. Look above you; look below you! Note
> it; read it! God, whom you wish to find never wrote that book with ink.
> Instead He set before your eyes the things that He had made.[3]

Augustine was also well aware that language and temporality were
deeply associated, since in Genesis both the world and time were created together. In a close analysis in his *Confessions*, Augustine makes
clear that man's existence is necessarily caught in temporality for which
the most ready example is language itself. God, he says, sees past, present, and future as one eternal moment, whereas human beings are
caught in a temporal scheme in which they remember the past, live in
the present moment, and anticipate the future as though all three were
different. Augustine considers how the declamation of a syllabic text,
during which one must anticipate (*expectatio*) the part still to come while
holding in memory as present the part already uttered, gives the Christian a glimpse of what God's perspective from outside of temporal time
would be like:

> I am about to recite a psalm that I know. Before I begin, my expectation
> (*expectatio*) extends over the entire psalm. Once I have begun, my memory
> extends over as much of it as I shall separate off and assign to the past.
> The life of this action of mine is distended into memory by reason of the
> part I have spoken and into forethought (*expectatio*) by reason of the part I
> am about to speak. But attention is actually present and that which was to
> be is borne along by it so as to become past ... When [the psalm] is done
> the whole action is completed and passes into memory. What takes place
> in the whole psalm takes place also in each of its parts and in each of its
> syllables ... The same thing holds for a man's entire life, the parts of which
> are all the man's actions. The same thing holds throughout the whole age
> of the sons of men, the part of which are the lives of all men. (*Confessions*
> 11:28. Trans. Ryan, 301–2)[4]

The extension of Augustine's analysis of the psalm to include whole lives and all of human time in the final two sentences is truly stunning and treats all of human existence as a great utterance.

Because of the analogy between the temporality of syllabic speech and all of human experience, Saint Augustine can, a little later in the *Confessions*, argue that human existence is like a written book for which the cover, which in his time would have been made of leather or parchment, is stretched over humanity "like a skin," such that we live, he says, according to the "syllables of time." Man, as a fallen book, lives in a world in which the temporality of our lives is analogous to the temporality of alphabetic scripts, the bridge between the two contained in the idea that as we live we are "writing" the books of our lives:

> You know, O Lord, you know, how you clothed men with skins, when by sin they became subject to death. Hence you have stretched out the firmament of your book like a skin, that is, your discourses, truly in harmony, which you have placed over us by the ministry of mortal men ... Let the supercelestial peoples, who are your angels, praise you, they who have no need to look up at this firmament or by reading to know your Word. They always behold your face and, without any *syllables of time*, they read upon it what your eternal will decrees. (Book 13: 15. Trans. Ryan, 345–6; my emphasis)[5]

This reworking of Platonic ideas that sees the things and events of this world as analogous to the letters of a book being written/read temporally is only part of the Christian view that conceives our cosmos in terms of alphabetic letters. Our lives are spelled out like the lettered words of a codex.[6]

Christianity also makes a distinction between New Testament law and Hebrew law. Exaggerating somewhat the Jewish view, Christianity has represented the Hebrew world as characterized by an overly strict observance of the letter of the law, while Christianity is said to emphasize the spirit of the law. Second Corinthians chapter 3 famously states that the new law is not written in stony tablets, as the Old Testament commandments were, but in the flesh tablets of the heart. In the Christian view, the unchangeable stone-inscribed "letter of the law" kills, whereas the spirit of the law vivifies. In the New Testament, Jesus redefines adultery and circumcision as well as all sins, as matters of one's inner intentions rather than external acts.[7] The moment of the commission of a sin takes place in one's heart – that is, in one's intentions – and it is only an accident of history if the intention is followed by an act.

Failure to read the letter, whether in the book of the Bible or in the Book of the World, for its divine meaning becomes, for Christianity, to read in an Old Testament fashion. In Christian thinking, the Old Testament privileges the signifier over the signified – that is, the outward forms of a covenant (e.g., physical circumcision) over the faith and love of God for which it stands (e.g., in Romans 2:25, even a physically uncircumcised man is "circumcised" if he is upright and obeys God's laws) – and for that reason the Hebrew law is seen by Christianity as leading to perdition, not salvation.[8] The new law, by contrast, proposes Christ as a living letter. Gregory the Great put it as follows: "For it is written: *The letter kills; the spirit gives life.* Every divine letter does this. For the letter is a body whose life is, in truth, the spirit."[9] Christ is thus the vivified letter that leads to eternal life. In the Christian view, the Old Testament letter never gets beyond its own obsession with the "letter of the law" to see the divine revelation letters signify, and hence it is moribund.

Clearly, Christian culture returns to and greatly reworks classical views regarding the alphabetic letter. We will remember that for the Greeks the alphabet reflected the order of the cosmos, and as a result the alphabetic order was the model of the ways in which other domains were ordered. Mathematics and music were reflections of (and were reflected in) the alphabet. Christianity adopts the view of the alphabet as almost a natural order. Collections of knowledge are often organized alphabetically, occasionally even when it is awkward to do so. A fifteenth-century medieval Spanish collection of exempla by Clemente Sanchez de Vercia, *Los Ejemplos por ABC*, arranges the exempla alphabetically not by subject matter, which would make sense for indexical reference, but by the titles, which, as it happens, are given in Latin despite the fact that the exempla are in Spanish.[10] Even more remarkable is the Greek medical text Περὶ ὕλης ἰατρικῆς (usually referred to by its Latin title, *De materia medica*) by Pedanius Dioscorides (mid-first century CE) in which the author specifically states his opposition to a purely alphabetical ordering of the material (since it makes no sense to separate items that may be related in terms of pathology and/or treatment just because they begin with very different letters). Authorial opposition, however, did not prevent later copyists from reordering the material and putting it in alphabetical order.[11]

The alphabetic ordering of texts in the Bible comes under special scrutiny, since it is felt that if divinely inspired writing is so ordered, there must be a special meaning for it.[12] Saint Jerome (ca. 347–420 CE) addressed this very question in an epistle to Saint Paula (ed. Labourt

2:31 ff.). From the fact that Jerome specifically states that his letter is designed as a kind of memory aid to what he had already explained orally and since he suggests that she allow another contemporary to copy his letter, it is evident that Jerome intended his exegesis to reach a wider audience. He notes the instances in which texts in the Old Testament have passages where the first letters of the lines are arranged alphabetically according to the Hebrew alphabet: Psalms 110, 111, 118, and 144, a passage in Lamentations (3:1–66), and the final proverb in the Book of Proverbs (31:10–31). The latter two texts are acrostics of which the Lamentations text is a triple acrostic; Psalms 110, 111, and 144 have a series of verses in which the alphabet is enumerated once by means of the first letter of the lines.

The text that retains Jerome's attention, however, is Psalm 118 in which blocks of eight verses in a row all begin with the same letter, and the successive blocks of eight are arranged in alphabetical order. The complexity and prominence of this example make of it a key example in Jerome's view, and as a result he chooses it for explication. Since Jerome is one of the Fathers of the Church, his views have great prominence in subsequent Christian thinking. Moreover, his analysis is based on the meaning of the words for which the Hebrew letters stand in their alphabetical order, and as such his argument would apply to any example of alphabetic ordering in Hebrew. As a result, Jerome's exegesis in fact details what he considers the divine message of the whole Hebrew alphabet to be, since the message would be the same for any instance of the Hebrew alphabet. He first gives the meaning for each letter (*aleph* = doctrine, *beth* = house, *gimel* = plenitude, *deleth* = tablets, *he* = that one, *vav* = and, *zai* = this, *heth* = life, etc.) and then he divides them into units of individual meaning. Here is Jerome's explication of the first part of the alphabet:

> The first group: "doctrine house plenitude of tablets that one" by which is meant that the doctrine of the church, which is the house of God, is found in the plenitude of the divine books.
>
> The second group is "and this life." For what other life could there be without the science of the scriptures through which indeed Christ himself is known who is the life of believers?[13]

So it goes through the whole alphabet.

From a modern, secular point of view one can certainly find fault with Jerome's interpretation. But that is not the point. The salient feature is that he finds that the Hebrew alphabet in the order in which the letters are presented speaks a divine text of Christ, both the Creator and the prime creation of the Christian universe. Moreover, as he comes to explain, he sees the alphabet as breaking into seven groups of discrete messages, the very seven-ness being significant to him for its analogical relationship to the seven days of Creation.

If, then, the Greeks saw the alphabet as comprehending, in every sense of the word, the cosmos, Christianity now sees the universe as created by God's speech with Christ as its central letter incarnate. The ABCs, beginning with the Hebrew alphabet, bind and express the Christian universe. God and his universe represent the infinite possible combinations of speech-sounds for which the alphabetic letters stand. Or perhaps it is better to turn this statement around: the infinite articulations made possible through combinations of the letters speak God and the cosmos.

Figure 12 is the illustration that accompanies the commentary on the Book of the Apocalypse in the Spanish Beatus of Fernando and Sancha manuscript (Madrid, BN 14–2, fol. 6).[14] The final book of the New Testament, the Book of the Apocalypse attempts to conceive of the end of the universe, which will also be the end of time. At the beginning of the book, Christ proclaims himself and his all-encompassing nature in specifically alphabetic terms. The passage is justly famous:

> I am Alpha and Omega, the beginning and the end, saith the Lord God,
> who is, and who was, and who is to come, the Almighty. (Apoc. 1:8)[15]

Alpha and omega are, of course, the first and last letters of the Greek alphabet, the beginning of the series and its end. Christ suggests here that he is the complete alphabet, from first letter to last. Christ expresses the all-encompassing nature of his Being as the complete compendium of the letters; as the Greeks had long done, he views the cosmos as an alphabet, and the complete alphabet (from alpha to omega) as analogous to the universe. But the cosmos is now a Christian one despite the fact that the alphabet is the same Greek one the pagans used. To enter the Christian universe is to enter the fold of Christian letters – of an alphabet that has written the two "books."

Indeed, if the Creator is also the complete alphabet, one does not need to represent both the letters and Jesus the man, as in figure 12.[16] Beginning with the eighth-century Beatus of Liébana (see note 14), the Beatus manuscripts often depict what is called the "Oviedo Cross," that is a more-or-less Greek Orthodox cross from which hang the letters alpha and omega.[17] This tradition has a long life. Figure 13 shows, for example, a leaf from a late Beatus manuscript, dated approximately to the 1180s but dissembled in the 1870s, now at the Cloisters Museum in New York City, in which the alpha and the omega simply hang from the cross.[18] The message is nevertheless the same: "I am the Alpha and the Omega." But the elision of the figural representation of Jesus suggests the degree to which the alphabet is seen as corresponding to the Creator and the universal Christian order. This view of the alphabetic compendium as not just corresponding to the Creator but as containing a more-than-totemic power may remind the modern reader of Levi-Strauss's famous "writing lesson" in *Tristes tropiques* in which a tribal chieftain intuits the power that inheres in Western writing and wishes to appropriate it; the chieftain understands writing as power, but he does not perceive the details of writing as a tool for communication, nor does he understand at all how alphabetic letters actually work. The power invested in the divinely appointed alphabetic order can be invoked, as for example it is in the mid-twelfth-century pontifical from Ely to which I have made brief reference in the introduction (p. 12).[19] The manuscript gives directions regarding how a bishop is to trace the Greek alphabet in the air with his crozier "from the left (i.e. north) eastern corner to the right western corner of the church" as he sings the antiphon *Fundamentum aliud* and then do the same with the Latin alphabet "from the right eastern to the left western corner of the church" as he sings the antiphon *Hec aula accipiat* (Hiley 425) in order to consecrate a church. In the manuscript, the two alphabets, Greek and Roman, are set out for the bishop on the manuscript page and a guide to the pronunciation of the Greek letters is given (Cambridge, University Library, Ll. 2.10. fol. 19r; reproduced in Hiley 424). The letters traced in the air are seen as an active principle that brings down God's power and effects consecration.

In Christianity, the alphabet, as an active agent, takes on a deeply moral cast: since God is the alphabet, mastery of his letters can become a means of approaching God. This is a view that will carry through the Middle Ages and beyond into the early modern period, after which it will be largely secularized in the eighteenth century. Figure 14 is taken from a Pericope manuscript composed in the twelfth century.[20] The term "pericope" comes from the Greek, meaning "cut out." It refers to a manuscript that reproduces the sections of the Gospels that are used in the Mass, those portions having been "cut out" of the complete evangelistic texts. In this image we see a nobleman climbing a large, foliated letter "I," the first letter of the Latin word "Igitur" (Therefore). This luxurious page opens the text for Easter Sunday.

In the liturgical calendar, Easter Sunday is a prime event because it represents the day of Christ's resurrection after the Crucifixion on Good Friday. It celebrates not just the spiritual ascension and reanimation of Jesus but also the potential for resurrection and salvation that is open to all Christian believers. In this image a young man literally ascends by means of climbing the letter "I," which has been turned into almost a kind of vegetative ladder. The representation suggests visually that one ascends towards salvation by means of the sacred texts – by "climbing" the letters of the Gospels. Given that one of the images for the Cross was a ladder (Christian congregations still sing "We are climbing Jacob's ladder, soldiers of the Cross"), this letter-ladder refers metonymically to the Christian letters that offer salvation. We can climb the Christian alphabet to heaven. At the same time, this foliated letter allows for a reference to yet another statement by Jesus: "I am the true vine" (John 15:1). In medieval manuscripts, the extraordinary number of illustrated letters cast as vegetative stalks or enlaced in vines and tendrils is yet another instance of the way letters are asked to bear the imprint of the divine.[21] Christ is the vegetative letter that is also a kind of ladder leading to salvation.

We can see that Christian alphabetic letters are imbued with a moral dimension and can become the means by which one seeks salvation. It is no surprise, then, that scribes and illuminators in the Middle Ages expended enormous energy and talent in order to decorate and emblematize letters. Many of the most luxurious liturgical manuscripts open with complex, stylized letters that do not lend themselves to the sort of easy reading we are familiar with in modern books. Many of the larger manuscripts were designed to be displayed at Mass to the faithful, whether the audience knew how to read or not. The display pages were not designed to be breezily "read through" as we do with modern letters; rather, the strange, even contorted forms given to the alphabetic letters were designed to impress upon the viewer the power of the sacred texts and the way in which the letters stood for a divine intervention in our world. Those who knew how to read could study the letters, puzzling them out and sounding out the text slowly in order to ruminate on it (medieval texts speak repeatedly of "masticating" divine texts, seeking the multiple meanings in them).[22] The rich, plastic letter forms convey the immanent presence of the divinity. Even the gold leaf that adorns some letters is intended to show how divine illumination "shines through" them.

Perhaps the most celebrated example of an opening passage that is transformed into pure visual magnificence is that of the famous chi rho

page in the Irish Book of Kells, the term "chi rho" referring to the letters "χ" (*chi*) and "ρ" (*rho*) that begin the word "Χριστο" or "Christ"
in Greek. The magnificence of Christ becomes the magnificence of the
opening three letters of his name ("Χρι") on a page in which the artistry
is so opulent and so commanding that it seems to surpass human talent.
There are other similar examples. In the Lindisfarne Gospels (ca. 700),
the Gospel of Matthew opens with a portrait of the saint writing his
Gospel, above which stylized letters proclaim "HAGIOS MATHEUS"
(fig. 15). The strangeness of the letter forms and the use of the Greek
"Hagios" (Saint) instead of the Latin term are intended to infuse the
text with a whiff of the divinity that is conveyed in the Gospel's content
(in the medieval imagination, the Greek language was "closer" to God
than Latin was, with Hebrew being the closest of all). The passage of
the Gospel on the next folio, taken from Matthew 1:8, similarly renders
the text as a geometric design, turning some letters sideways, collaps-
ing letters together, and occasionally placing one letter within another,
thus forcing the reader to pause and meditate on each individual letter
as he or she gradually teases out the text while being immersed in the
visual magnificence.

   Just as for the Greeks and the Romans, so also for medieval Christians
certain letters had special meanings, as though they contained a trace
of the external world – though no longer for their numerical or atomistic value, but for how they were seen as alluding to Christian events.
Of special value were the letters "t" and "x," both of which were seen
as figuring in their very form the Cross on which Jesus was crucified.
Isidore of Seville, for example, specifically sees the letter "T" as "figu-
ram demonstans Dominicae crucis" (showing an image of the Cross
of the Lord, I.iii.8). Moreover, the layers of significance were multiple
and mutually reinforcing. The "X" signified both the Cross and, as we
have already seen, the Greek "chi." The "t" was also doubly significant;
it stood not only for the Cross but it also appeared important that the
letter began the Mass, which opened with the words "Te igitur" (You,
therefore). A manuscript such as the Drago Sacramentary presents these
letters displayed around a capital "T" that is enlaced in vines.[23] Beyond
the simple meanings of the words, the letters convey the Christian view
of the world in which God's sacrifice of his son on the Cross (the "T")
is subsumed by the greater reality of eternal salvation and everlasting
life (Christ is the "living vine," hence the foliage that is wound around
the letter). In a later French ABC book from the twelfth century, known
as the "ABC par ekivoche," meanings are attached to each and every

letter (more on this in a subsequent chapter); the "t," this poetic work tells us, stands for "treason" (Old Fr. traison) because the Lord was betrayed and then sacrificed on the t-shaped Cross. In the Middle Ages, the universe is conceived in ways very different from those that animated pagan Greek and Roman thought, but for medieval Christians the alphabet still continues to speak the cosmos. Now, however, it is a Christian cosmos that one reads through alphabetical letters, and one in which Christ is the central Word.

Secular texts also modify the shape of their letters in an effort to make them "more than just letters" and imbue them with a power that goes beyond their mere content, and this is true not just in luxurious, illuminated tomes but also in more mundane manuscripts. Figures 16 and 17 (see Gray, *Lettering* 1:15) show a charter of Emperor Henry IV written by Sigehardus in 1067. Figure 16 gives the whole charter, while figure 17 shows a detail of the heading which gives the standard opening, "[in nomine] sanctae et individuae trinitatis Heinricus" (literally, Henry, [in the name] of the holy and individual trinity). Strange as these letter forms look, one can learn to make them out. Once one learns that the "s" is a straight line with a squiggle at the top or that the "t" is a straight line with a coil wrapped around its whole length, one can decipher the other letters and "see" the text.

For Carolingian charters, as for the Merovingian ones that preceded them, unusual and elongated letter forms were common. These were very different from the clear book hands in use by the Carolingians (see fig. 11 A and B). What is the purpose, one might ask, of such strange letters?

Charters are very different from other types of texts such as holy or literary works. They are designed to institute changes, proclaim and reaffirm rights, etc., and as a result their language needs to perform what linguists, following J.L. Austin, call a perlocutionary act – that is, it needs to have an effect on and in the real world. As a result, charters must be imbued with authority and must impress themselves on their readers. People need to feel that the texts carry the force of the people in the real world who have created the documents.

But how can one make the language of a document actually affect reality? How do you give a document authority over people?

Medieval charters impose authority in a number of ways. First, they invoke God and the king, as is indeed the case in figure 16. For the medieval world these are sobering injunctions. But the framers of the documents also need to make sure that the language is memorable – that the message "sticks" somehow in peoples' memories long after the exact text is forgotten. For this reason the writing is visually striking. Nicolette Gray has commented on this "peculiar ... writing" whose salient trait is elongation, remarking that "[t]he original idea of expressing the dignity and importance of the authority in whose name the document is issued is carried to a very remarkable and entirely successful conclusion" (*Lettering* 1:10). The strange letter forms impress themselves, due to their difference from the norm, on the peoples' consciousness and they thus endow the charter with a kind of aura that sets it apart. The witnesses to the charter need to see the document's letters as a departure from the normal run of texts – that is, as something remarkable and unique. As well, the signatures on medieval charters are often elaborate (the Carolingians favoured geometric monograms) so as to buttress the weightiness of the document. A trace of worldly power is carried over into the writing, the letter forms performing this transfer of the power from the people who created the charter into the document itself. In fact, it is less important that some of the people actually read the charter than that they witness it, or remember it, and have a sense of what it authorizes. Very few people would actually be able to read the text (one would have to be trained in Latin legalities); many more would have glimpsed the strange-looking document or would simply know about it, and that would be sufficient for the maintenance of rights, privileges, donations, etc.[24]

If the startling letter forms of a dry legal document could impress themselves on an audience, the richly illuminated letters of more luxurious medieval manuscripts had even greater power to do so. Many scholars have considered how in manuscripts oversize and ornate initials guided readers, marking the divisions of the texts, commenting at times on the content by means of illustrations, and providing aesthetic refreshment. But they also did far more than that.

As the title of Laura Kendrick's book *Animating the Letter* (1999) suggests, medieval manuscript scribes and illuminators often attempted to give a sense of a vivified letter, as was fitting for a religion in which the divine *logos* was made flesh. Indeed, a letter in a medieval manuscript (usually the first letter of a sentence or section, but not always) could become a person or an animal, or the body of the letter could house an entire scene. Economic, social, and political factors determined the nature of the illustrations and even the letter types and size in any particular manuscript; parchment was expensive, and to afford the luxury of illumination one had to be rich since the more illuminations there were (or the more expansive the calligraphy was), the more parchment one needed (student copies of works, for example, stood at the other extreme, their writing cramped and crowded and heavily abbreviated in order to take up the least amount of space possible). But for those who could afford luxuries – and we are speaking now of the elite nobles who ran the church, the government, and the teaching institutions – the alphabetic letter came to life, reproducing and reflecting the world that had created the book that housed the letters.

Medieval manuscripts literally re-viewed the world through their illuminated letters. Animal and human bodies were twisted and contorted into alphabetic letters (see fig. 18).[25] The medieval letter while it participated in constructing a word it also signified on its own because of its form, its pronunciation (the pronunciation of both the letter-name and of the letter in words), and the designs and scenes that it incorporated. For its form and phonetic aspects, it was viewed as containing something of the world: The "ABC par equivoche," already mentioned, finds meaning in the pronunciation of each letter: the pronunciation of "o," for example recalls the cry "haut" (halt) to end a battle.

In an illustrated manuscript, the letter could become a means not just to re-speak or reflect the world but also to meditate on the world. Its visual presentation made the reader stop and think. Letters that had large loops – for example, "B," "C," "D," "R," "S," etc. – offered spaces for depicting whole scenes. In sacred texts these might comprise biblical scenes. Figure 19 shows a large capital "D" in the Drogo Sacramentary in which a smaller "s" is enclosed, with a bar above the "s."[26] A bar above a letter in a medieval manuscript signaled an abbreviated word: any medieval reader would know that the abbreviated "D"s indicated the word "Deus" or "God." The "D" is wound about with foliage, referring back to Christ as the "living vine," which is entirely fitting for this most holy day in the liturgical calendar when Christians celebrate the Resurrection of Christ. At the same time, the "D" becomes a frame for a scene of one of the most important miracles of Christianity. We see depicted the arrival of the two Marys at Jesus's tomb and the moment when they discover that the stone has been rolled away and Jesus is gone. Within the space of the "D" itself we see two more scenes: one of Mary Magdalene washing Jesus's feet (Mark 16:9) and one of Christ worshipped by the two Marys (Matthew 28:9).[27]

Historiated initials could be far more elaborate. The "B" of "Beatus vir" ("Blessed is the man") that opens the book of Psalms in the Bible is often exploited in order to depict scenes from the life of King David who was supposed to have composed the psalms. The British Library Royal MS 2 B. ii, fol. 7 (mid-thirteenth century), is quite typical; in it, the upper circle of the "B" depicts King David playing the harp, while the lower enclosure depicts him fighting Goliath.[28] In figure 20 we find a more subtle treatment from the same century. In its upper register, the "B" represents the well-known biblical narrative of King David spying on Bathsheba in her bath. In the lower one, David repents and prays, and we see the miraculous and anachronistic appearance of Christ in Majesty in a mandorla. The scene is indeed a fitting one for the opening of the book of Psalms: "Blessed is the man who does not follow the counsel of the impious ... but his will is [placed] in the law of the Lord" (Psalms 1:1–2, my trans; along the side of the image one can see the opening words of the psalm in Latin). David sins, then submits to God's law and is rewarded with the apparition of the God of the new law. For our purposes, the interesting feature is the way the letter opens up to and contains a famous historical event. King David's moral fall and subsequent prayer (he is depicted, significantly, as kneeling at the edge of a precipice) are contained within and ordered by the large "B."[29]

We could multiply many times such use of manuscript initials in the Middle Ages. The point here is that the alphabetic letter is a key element of the Christian order: quite literally it is used as a lens through which to re-view the world. It is seen as both structuring the Christian order and structured by that order. Christ and his cosmos are the complete alphabet, and so the letters will "speak" his Creation in various ways. The alphabet itself is deeply moralizing and moralized as a result; we shall have occasion shortly to examine some further examples of this.

For the moment let me return to the analogy, already mentioned, between the Book of the World, in which everything in our world can be viewed as so many signs that signify God, and alphabetic letters. Medieval writers, renewing and Christianizing practices inherited from antiquity, cleverly call upon letters to reveal a second text that the initiated reader can perceive. Ancient Greek and Roman writers were fond of playing letter "games" in their poetry.[30] They made use of acrostics and anagrams. They composed pantograms (poems in which every word begins with the same letter), and lipograms (poems that deliberately do not use a particular letter), acrostiches and telestiches. Medieval writers adopted and adapted these literary games, and certainly there are many instances in which they are deployed purely for their ludic qualities. Many vernacular authors of the thirteenth to the fifteenth centuries reveal their names in elaborate anagrams. Similarly, one Carolingian writer of the ninth century, Hucbald, is famous for composing a "panto-grammatical" Latin poem, "Ecloga de calvis" (Praise of baldness), celebrating his ruler, Charles the Bald, with a poem in which every word of the 146-verse poem begins with a "c" ("bald" in both Latin and French begins with "c").[31] The opening runs as follows: "Carmina, clarisonae, calvis cantante, Camenae!" (Sing, clear-sounding muses, the songs of the bald!), and the rest of the poem follows in a similar mock-epic vein.

Christianity asked of its faithful that they become hermeneuticians. The innumerable things of this world were like so many signs or letters, which one could read for the Divinity they signified. For this reason Jesus spoke in parables – so that his hearers could learn to read divine meanings through his humble exempla. So, also, some writers deliberately encoded a second, spiritual message that could be teased out of the plethora of letters on the manuscript page. One of the most developed means of such writing was that of the *carmina figurata*, which medieval writers adopted from their classical predecessors. The most famous exemplars of this technique are the poems of Hrabanus Maurus (780–856) (Raban Maur in French), a Carolingian poet at the court of Charlemagne's son, Louis the Pious (figs. 21 and 22). As we have already noted, Carolingian court writers deliberately imitated the textual productions of antiquity while infusing Roman styles with Christian content. This is certainly true of Hrabanus Maurus's ingenius poetic constructs.

Hrabanus Maurus's collection of twenty-eight *carmina figurata* dates to around 840 CE and exists in several manuscript versions. The poems consist in each case of works in which each line of the poem has the same number of letters, allowing for their deployment across the page in a regular grid pattern such that the letters all line up horizontally and vertically. Portions of the uniform letters are coloured by painted images, and the letters defined by those images, while forming part of the grid-poem, can also be isolated and read on their own so that they contain a second message. In other words the letters in the painted images harmonize with the grid-poem that covers the whole page while also forming a second text. These messages are of a specifically Christian order. Figure 21, for example, contains a second message that is defined by both the cross Louis the Pious carries, his shield, and the crown he wears. For example, the letters of the crown read, "Tv, Hlvdovvicvm Criste corona" (You, Christ, crown Ludovic). His head and body, his cross, and his shield also bear separate messages (see Garipzanov 232, n. 108).[32]

One of the more remarkable of Maurus's *carmina figurata* is the final one of the volume (fig. 22) in which Hrabanus Maurus himself is represented on his knees, praying at the foot of a cross. The cross proves to be a double palindrome that crosses in the middle of the page so that the same message can be read from left to right, right to left, top to bottom, and bottom to top: "Oro te Ramus aram ara sumar et oro" (I, Ramus, pray to you at the altar so that at the altar I may be taken up, I also pray). This may not be the most elegant poetry, but it is certainly remarkable that the words can be read in any direction and that they also fit at the same time within the larger grid-poem that covers the page. In addition, the form of Hrabanus's own body also contains a second message: "Rabanum memet clemens rogo Christe tuere o pie judicio" (Christ, o pious and merciful in your judgment, keep me, Rabanus, I pray, safe). Both messages are thus pleas for salvation through God's mercy.

The literary game of the *carmina figurata* developed by pagan writers of antiquity here becomes an expression of the Christian order. If God is the alphabet that has written the whole cosmos, the alphabetic order is synonymous with the Christian order. Hrabanus Maurus places himself into the moral universe of the alphabetic letter in a text whose mechanics remind us – pleasantly and cleverly, but also quite seriously – that we need always to seek the second meanings in the signifiers all around us.

Hrabanus Maurus thus calls on the reader to read in a second fashion, seeking the divine signifieds behind alphabetical signifiers. Not only the writer but also the reader must set himself in the moral order of the Christian alphabet. Indeed, the medieval manuscript places considerable importance on the role of the reader, and medieval scribes knew how to exploit the hermeneutic demands placed on the reader. In the Spanish Beatus manuscripts from the tenth and eleventh centuries, scribal "signatures" exploited very cleverly the role of the reader in grappling with letters to ascertain meanings through the use of complex acrostics. In a Madrid Beatus containing Gregory of Great's *Moralia in Job* from 945 (Madrid, BN Cod. 80, fol. 3r), the scribe Florentius devotes a whole page to an alphabetic chessboard of sorts (fig. 23). The literary "game" consists of beginning with the "F" at the centre of the top line. One can then read down and out from the "F," going either left or right from the central axis, and "turning" vertically or horizontally whenever one chooses, and as long as a reader continues either down or out towards the side s/he will always come up with the same message: "Florentium indignum memorare" (Remember unworthy Florentius). In an act that paradoxically is one of both self-exaltation and self-humbling, Florentius counts on his Christian reader's ability to tease out meaning from the page's pattern. By calling himself "unworthy," Florentius is asking the reader to remember him in prayers above all, and thus the puzzle becomes a plea in which the reader's skill with letters is exploited to seek salvation for the "unworthy" scribe; at the same time, the pleasure of extracting Florentius's message (which is the same no matter which path one takes down and towards the manuscript edges) is a clever strategy to make sure that Florentius is not, in fact, forgotten. Alphabetic play becomes here a means to defeat temporality and open the doors to eternal life. Similar acrostic signatures are also found in the Beatus of Fernando and Sancha (Madrid, BN Ms. Vitrina 14–2, fol. 7), the Fanlo Beatus (Pierpont Morgan, M 1079, fol. 11), the Saint Sever Beatus (Paris, BnF Ms. Lat. 8878, fol. 1), Valladolid Beatus (Valladolid, Biblioteca de la Universidadad Ms. 433, fol. 2) as well as others.[33]

The strategy works because the reader and writer share a consensus regarding the alphabet, and they both partake of the same Christian community of letters that views the ABCs as part of the moral underpinning of their culture. Christianity is viewed as bearing forth its sacred letters, and those same letters are seen as the bearers of its moral order. In short, to possess the (Roman) alphabet is to be civilized – which, it is understood, means to be Christian – and to be civilized is to possess the alphabet. This view is inculcated in children as part of their Christian education. To recite one's ABCs is to enter the Christian moral order. In both Anglo-American and French culture until well into the seventeenth century at least, to say one's ABCs was called saying one's "God's cross" (in French: la croix de Dieu), and children were taught to make the sign of the cross before reciting the alphabet.[34] In a fifteenth-century book of hours that later belonged to King Henry IV of France (d. 1610 CE), the alphabet, preceded by a cross, quite literally forms a protective border around the religious prayers on the page (fig. 24 A and B). The ABCs form a fence around the devotional texts.[35]

Figure 25 shows Marguerite d'Orléans's book of hours (Paris, BnF Ms. Lat. 1156 B) from 1426. In the border around the prayers one finds a random diffusion of alphabetic letters. It has been suggested that a teacher or mother might have used the manuscript as a primer for teaching a young child his or her ABCs while also teaching the child to say prayers. As the anonymous author of the BnF *L'Aventure des écritures* article on this manuscript points out, the association of the prayers written out by the scribe with the letters set out by the illuminator in the margins suggests that the alphabetic letters are the raw material of the didactic texts a young Christian should learn and recite.

For Christian children, learning their ABCs is part and parcel of being educated to be a good Christian. A German woodcut from 1490 shows a benevolent teacher and his dutiful students (fig. 26). The teacher (who is also a preacher) is educating the students who sit up straight, paying attention, with their hands carefully folded. The "fruit" of the lessons is none other than the alphabet itself: letters are mixed with the catechism.[36]

Many are the texts and images that associate the learning of the alphabet with the learning of Christian doctrine and values. The shape of a letter, the letter name, and the way it was pronounced in words could all be harnessed for Christian edification. We have already glanced at the "ABC par ekivoche" and the ways in which the shape of the letter or a word beginning with it were used to reinforce Christian teaching. During the Middle Ages and beyond, children were taught to associate key terms of Christian culture with the initial letter of those same terms. For example, in German ABC books "G" inevitably stood for "Gott" (God). In French *abécédaries* the "D" for "Dieu" performed the same service. Figure 27 shows a typical moralizing alphabet from 1500. Each letter is given a word for which it stands: "A" for "Amitié" (friendship), "B" for "Benevolence," "C" for "Crainte," (fear), etc. The alphabet becomes a handy compendium of Christian values. Curiously, the names of the letters in French included one obscene one, since "Q," when named, was a homonym with "cul" (ass). Children reciting their "croix de Dieu" were taught to pause briefly in silence after "P" and then pick up again with "R" in order to avoid speaking the offending word. Moreover, the alphabet was often followed by key prayers such as the Pater noster and the Hail Mary, as is the case in this manuscript.[37] The phenomenon of moralizing alphabets characterized Protestant countries as well as Catholic ones. In England, Thomas Trevelyon created books in the early 1600s of moralizing alphabets in which each letter began a passage from the Old or New Testament.[38]

We could multiply almost infinitely the examples of how the alphabet is seen by the Christian Middle Ages as encompassing its world view: Christianity is expressed by the alphabet, and the alphabet is expressed by Christianity. The twenty-odd letters of the Roman alphabet speak

Christ and God's Creation, and the indoctrination into the world of letters becomes the entryway into the Christian order, and vice-versa. In a world in which the Divinity is cast as the complete alphabetic compendium ("I am the Alpha and the Omega"), learning the ABCs thus has meaning far beyond any practical applications. It becomes a badge of the allegiance to Christian civilization, and an analogy is set up between Christianity and alphabetic culture. It is but a short step to associating the alphabet with civilization itself, much as the ancient Greeks considered anyone who spoke Greek to be civilized and anyone who did not to be "barbarous" and without civilization.

This view had enormous sway and solidity as long as the underlying theological foundation was not challenged. But the developments of the late fifteenth century and then the sixteenth century were to undermine the Christian view of alphabetic letters. The advent of the Renaissance, the rise of humanism, the Reform and Protestant movements, and the printing press all contributed to a morphing of the rationale for the relationship between alphabetic letters and the world. The subtending notion of such a relationship would survive, but it would be mapped onto new elements of Western culture.

5

The Letters of Humanism

Escrire est faire un chemin, par & moyennant lequel voulons conduire & guider nous mesmes, & les autres aussi.

Honorat Rambaud

The Middle Ages lasted a thousand years. The Renaissance, by contrast, hardly lasted a century in Italy: it began in the mid-fifteenth century and by the 1550s had been destabilized by Mannerism, the transitional period between Renaissance and baroque styles. Even as the Renaissance moved north through Europe, it was largely spent when it finally reached England at the beginning of the seventeenth century. Still, it left a decisive imprint on the European mentality, and by the time Renaissance attitudes and styles morphed into the baroque, Europe was a very different place than it had been before.

The changes wrought by the Renaissance are too numerous to entertain in their entirety here. Fortunately, the most important ones are very well known. New standards of Greek and Latin scholarship led to the establishment of philology as a discipline; this new science combined with the newly invented printing press to make possible the diffusion of better editions of ancient texts. The increasing volume of books led to greater literacy, which in turn fostered an industry of vernacular translations and writings. Vernacular writing, read now by a wider public (including increasing numbers of women) led to the creation of new literary genres.[1] All of these developments had an influence on the alphabetic letter. While the letter was to continue to reflect the European world view, the secularization inherent in Renaissance approaches made significant modifications to how the alphabet was viewed. In preprint culture, alphabetic writing had been almost "naturally" in touch with the beyond, with the metaphysical. With the printing press it came to be viewed much less often as a set of signifiers for divine signifieds, although minority cabbalistic and mystical approaches continued unabated until the late nineteenth century.[2]

Moreover, if Europe embraced new horizons intellectually, it also did so geographically; the so-called Age of Exploration pushed both East and West – indeed, it pushed West even when trying to push East – and the most famous (or infamous) result was, of course, the "discovery" of the New World. Regardless of how people interpret the conquest of the New World – that is, whether we consider the views of sixteenth-century contemporaries or of twentieth and twenty-first-century peoples – the gradual awareness of the existence of the Americas changed forever the European view of its own culture. Europe was relativized within a new understanding of the planet's topography and systems of knowledge, and it had to recognize that for thousands of years it had lived with a false picture of the world. Even as Europeans scoured the texts of the Bible and of antiquity, they could not find any clear awareness of the continent to which the Spanish began to sail in 1492.

As the philosophers Paul Oskar Kristeller (1905–99) and Ernst Cassirer (1875–1945) have noted, what began as an educational revolt against the curricula and teaching methods of the Middle Ages evolved into a meditation on the nature of humanity (Cassirer, Kristeller, and Randall 2–3). Historians consider the Renaissance as marking the beginning of the modern world, and rightly so in many ways. That a new approach to studying Greek and Latin could lead to a revolution in how people lived and saw their world is due to the interrelations between many of the aspects mentioned above. The printing press, increased literacy, and the availability of the texts of antiquity weakened the hold of the Catholic Church and led to increasing secularization. Greater secularism made for the entertaining of new questions and speculations. The religious reform movements, which began within the Catholic Church, grew into the nascent Protestant churches in the first half of the sixteenth century. After so many changes, there was simply no turning back to the intellectual order of the previous thousand years.

The Renaissance brought with it considerable changes for the treatment of alphabetic letters, in part as a result of the printing press, in part because of humanistic trends, and in part as a result of exposure to foreign cultures. Indeed, the three features were intertwined. The printing of Greek, Latin, and vernacular texts by means of moveable type provoked much reflection on the letters that were to be cut, and at issue was not just what shapes the letters should have, though this was much discussed, but also what cultures had alphabetic letters and who controlled their forms and their dissemination. The concern to standardize letter forms (as well as orthography) was, of course, due to the fact that texts would no longer be subject to the idiosyncrasies of particular scribes. Letters became regularized as soon as type was cut, and this is true even in early incunabula such as the Gutenberg Bible that imitated Gothic letters. Nevertheless, the Gutenberg Bible cannot really be said to have entered the typographical era, because the letters were still being viewed through a medieval lens; the aim was merely to produce Gothic letters more efficiently.

Within a half century, however, Gothic scripts were being replaced by the "constructed alphabets" of Fra Luca Pacioli (1447–1517), Giovanni Battista Palatino (1515–75), and Geoffroy Tory (ca. 1480–1533 CE), all of whom used compasses and straight-edges to construct the letters, sometimes relying on mathematical ratios that descended from antiquity.[3] This approach was due to the humanists' misplaced belief that in antiquity Roman letters were constructed mathematically. The conscious attempt to renew antiquity is evident in the choice of Roman monumental capitals for upper case letters and the Caroline minuscule for lower case ones, the latter being chosen because it was mistakenly believed that they came from antiquity, not the Middle Ages. The early humanist Italian scholar Poggio Bracciolini (1380–1459) was instrumental in the diffusion of the Caroline minuscule, which, as Armando Petrucci has put it, he did not adapt so much as reproduce "photographically."[4]

Elizabeth Eisenstein (1923–2016) has pointed out that the invention of moveable type did not have the same galvanizing effect in non-Western cultures as it did in western Europe (*Printing Press* 1:31–2), although she does not offer an explanation for this. One must wonder, however, whether something in the very nature of the Roman alphabet, or the way it was perceived, played some motivating role in the rapid spread of printing presses?[5] Moreover, as Eisenstein also remarks, the standardization of letters brought about with it new modes of perception and reading: "The fact that letters, numbers and pictures were all alike subject to repeatability by the end of the fifteenth century … [meant that] … the printed book made possible new forms of interplay between these diverse elements [, and this interplay] is perhaps even more significant than the change undergone by picture, number or letter alone" (*Printing Press* 1:55).

People read differently as a result of a standardized text, and as spellings and layouts began to harden due to the repeated diffusion of printed texts, national languages began to gel and even certain letter types became associated with nationalistic tendencies. Indeed, moveable type, more than simply a new mode of treating alphabetic letters, revolutionized Western concepts of production and heralded the modern world since it introduced into Europe "the 'theory of interchangeable parts' which is the basis of all modern mass-manufacturing technique" (Eisenstein, *Printing Press* 1:32). The reverberations caused by the change in how alphabetic letters were deployed have thus proved more far-reaching than one could possibly have anticipated.

Sixteenth-century printers and artists also had strong views and widely divergent theories regarding what alphabetic letters stood for and what meanings the letters conveyed or should convey to readers. With increasing exploration, first in Africa and the East, and then to the West, there developed a new "global horizon" which was aware of the multiplicity of cultures, and in particular of alphabets, in the world. Giovanni Battista Palatino's tome presented to readers page after page of the world's alphabets: not just Roman and Greek, or Hebrew alphabets, but also Chaldean, Aramaic, Arabic, Egyptian, etc. Such a variety of alphabets was perhaps not superseded until the similar pages in the planches in the eighteenth-century *Encyclopédie* in France.

Concurrent with this nascent global view was a new understanding of the role of the European languages, including the role they could play in the expansion of European power. Europeans quickly realized that printed texts would play an important part in this expansion. In 1492, the humanist Antonio de Nebrija (1441–1522) published the first grammar of a vernacular Romance language, as we have already seen in chapter 3. I wish here to recapitulate Nebrija's arguments in order to examine sixteenth-century developments in more detail.

Published the same year Columbus reached America, the *Gramatica de la lengua castellana* was obviously written without specific knowledge of the New World. But, as Menéndez Pidal (1869–1968) put it some years ago, Nebrija's book "was written with the certain expectation of the New World, even though no one had yet sailed off to discover it."[6] Still, the initial effect of Nebrija's grammar was almost nil.

One passage of Nebrija's grammar is cited more than any other – namely the one we have already seen in which Nebrija makes the argument that for the Romans the Latin language always accompanied the empire, and the two waxed and waned together.[7] Nebrija proposes that for the Spanish Empire geographical and linguistic conquest will be twinned in a similar manner.

Nebrija's view was developed out of earlier Italian humanists, especially Lorenzo Valla (1407–57) who, in his *De linguae latinae elegantia*, had argued somewhat less militaristically that the Roman Empire surpassed other empires for having extended its language so far. The argument was also picked up by others, and in particular, as I noted in my chapter on Latin scripts, by the French humanist printer Geoffroy Tory who may have read Nebrija directly. In his 1529 treatise on alphabetic letters, the *Champ Fleury*, Tory nuances Nebrija's argument, claiming that the Romans prospered more and obtained more victories by means of their language than by means of arms. The French, Tory argues, need to order their language so as to have the same success.[8]

Tory's conception of the alphabetic letter is worth taking some time to investigate. A major printer in his time, Tory designs a new font for printers to use. The *Champ Fleury*, in which he develops his ideas regarding typefaces, is merely one of several treatises in the period to do so, though it goes into far more detail than do most others; Albrecht Dürer (1471–1528) and the Italian Fra Luca Pacioli (1445–1517) made similar proposals. What makes Tory's treatise unique is his long discussions of what he perceives in each letter and how he arrives at the forms he proposes. His theories are emblematic of the way in which alphabetic letters are seen as conveying a whole world view associated with Europe, going back to antiquity.

As is the case in the long tradition of writers before him, for Tory alphabetic letters are key to an understanding of the world, and his view of the world leads him to construct his letters in a certain way. What has changed with sixteenth-century humanism is the system of values with which one endows letters as well as the values that the letters are seen as conveying.

Like the alphabets of other theoreticians of his era, Tory's is a quintessentially Renaissance construction: it both arises from and articulates the Renaissance view of the world. The features we shall observe in Tory are also to be found, for example, in Palatino's treatise. Significant in Palatino is that when he comes to constructing his capital "O" he comments simply, "Questo O è perfectissimo" (This "O" is most perfect). In this brief sentence is summed up the Renaissance mentality that sees perfection in not only the simplicity of the letter "o" but also all the ideals the humanists hold dear: harmony, balance, symmetry, peace.

As Kristeller and Cassirer suggest, the Renaissance puts a meditation on humanity at the very centre of its thinking. This meditation is
much in evidence in Tory's treatise. The qualities of symmetry, balance,
harmony, and scale, so dear to the artists and architects of the Renaissance, inform Tory's alphabet. Tory maps the letters, one by one, onto
a 10x10 grid (fig. 28), and the inscription within this 100-square grid is
designed to construct an alphabet that is rational and harmonious – the
very antithesis of the animated, constantly morphing alphabets of medieval manuscripts. Even more significant, however, is that each letter is
also mapped onto the human body. In classic Renaissance fashion, Tory
chooses – like Michelangelo in his great sculpture of David or Da Vinci
in his drawing of a man in both a circle and a square – the image of the
male nude, an ideal inherited from antiquity. Each letter is thus inscribed
within the perfect geometric proportions of a square, and those proportions correspond to humanity itself. Tory also depicts in an engraving
how he sees each letter corresponding to a different part of the human
body (again, a male nude): "D" the right ear, "P" the mouth, "T" the
genitalia, etc. Nine of the letters also signify the muses of antiquity.

There is still more. Tory claims that the letters of the alphabet are all
derived from two proto-letters, the "I" and the "O." These two formative letters – one straight and one curved – that give rise to all the others
have special importance for Tory, and not just for the purity of their
forms (though it is certainly reasonable to consider that all letters are
some combination of straight and curved lines). More pertinent for our
purposes are Tory's humanist views that lead him to imbue the "I"
and the "O" with enormous cultural significance. Figure 29 reproduces
the page on which Tory articulates his ideas. The "I," he claims corresponds to Apollo and the nine Muses, comprising the ten items that fill
the ten horizontal lines of the grid in which he sets his letter. The "I"
is thus the letter that contains the arts of European culture. The shape
of the "O," by contrast, takes up two of the ten lines (the top and bottom ones), leaving only eight of them "free." Tory conceives of the "O"
as encapsulating Apollo and the seven liberal arts in those eight lines,
hence the sum total of Western learning "fills" the "O."

This view makes of the proto-letters "I" and "O" the bearers of the
whole Graeco-Latin intellectual tradition: antiquity's supreme, enlight-
ening god (Apollo), its arts, and its learning. Moreover, since all letters
are, according to Tory, combinations of the "I" and the "O," this means
that every time one forms any alphabetic letter, one is re-inscribing
the Western tradition on the surface of the page. Each and every act

of alphabetic writing carries in its ink the whole weight of European history, learning, and culture. The formative shapes of all letters thus express the *studia humanitatis*, and every instance of lettristic writing is a re-affirmation of one's deepest humanity and European identity. What is more, for Tory the letters are the means by which the people of antiquity bequeathed their learning to future centuries: "The Ancients," he says of the "I," "wished to signify secretly that the 9 Muses and Apollo ... are celebrated ... by good letters." The alphabet is thus both a code and a compendium that bears the European culture and heritage: those people capable of perceiving its meanings partake of European civilization, and those who do not have alphabetic letters are excluded. It is significant as well that Tory returns to and recounts the narrative of Io – that is, of the beautiful woman turned heifer who stamped out her name in letters in the sand because she had no voice with which to speak her identity. This ancient tale about the invention of alphabetic writing is, for Tory, a first instance of the proto-letters "I" and "O," which combine in this tale to reaffirm one's humanity, for indeed the secret that Io wishes to communicate in the tale is that inside her heifer's body she is still human.

In Tory, the Christian view has been supplanted by Renaissance humanism: if for the Middle Ages the alphabet expressed Christian civilization (a culture of the divine text) and Christ was seen as the complete alphabet ("I am the Alpha and the Omega"), for Tory the heritage from antiquity can be understood as the letters antiquity bequeathed to the future, and those letters are the bearers of the Graeco-Roman culture. The values have become more secularized than in the Middle Ages, but the logic is still the same. The Kristeller/Cassirer/Randall thesis is borne out in the most literal way. A program of letters – in this case a treatise for Tory's fellow printers on the letter forms that should be used for cutting moveable type – leads to a meditation on humanity and humanistic values. The printing press is but the most obvious emblem of a new approach to alphabetic letters, though it is doubly important because it underscores the deep bonds between the philological program that reformed the study of classical letters and a parallel reform of how antique literature ("letters") should be transmitted in printed editions. The antipathy shown by Renaissance humanists to medieval, specifically Gothic, letter forms is part and parcel of their rejection of medieval modes of instruction and thought.

The sixteenth century is also the period in which there is a profound realization that the Romance languages are not simply bastardized forms of Latin, but rather languages in their own right with their own grammars. The century abounds with treatises on grammar, syntax, and orthography, and it spawns the first serious historical linguists of whom Claude Duret (1570–1611) is one of the most important. Certainly, Duret's *Thresor de l'histoire des langues de cest univers* (1613) published two years after Duret's death marks in some ways the beginning of comparative historical linguistics; he is concerned with the origin of letters, which is to say with the Hebrew of the Book of Genesis above all. For Duret Hebrew letters are necessarily more than human ("lettres plus qu'humaine," 644) because they are derived from the position of the stars (643–4) and thus have "come from and proceeded from the celestial and divine nature" (provenues et procedees de la celeste et divine nature, 643). His universalism leads him to display the "original alphabets" of not only many Western tongues (including that of the Goths and the Francique dialect) but also the putative "alphabets" of the Chinese, Japanese, and Indian languages, and he credits Charlemagne with having first overseen the creation of letters for the German language and with having been the first to compose a grammar of German (826). Still, his main concern is with how letters, and Hebrew above all, reflect the divine order of the cosmos. Hebrew letters, for Duret, were originally "figured and engraved in the sky by the position of the stars" (figuree & engrauee au ciel par la position des etoilles, 142) and for that reason are "filled with celestial mysteries" (replis de mysteres celestes, 142). Hebrew letters thus have an organic relationship with an exterior, cosmic reality, a force they lose when translated into another language (143).

Duret and the sixteenth-century humanists, beginning with Geoffroy Tory, also occupy themselves with the etymology of the languages and they raise questions regarding what the most "pure" or most "correct" form of their language is. In France, Renaissance scholars disagree considerably regarding which dialect of a language is the purest, or even whether the so-called purity of the language should be defined as that which is closest to Latin. But as Charles de Bouvelles points out (*Liber*), the attempt to re-create a "pure" French by choosing either the dialect closest to Latin or by forming a *koine* that uses the most Latinate words from various dialects engages in a process that would logically result in the conclusion that the most "pure" French would, in fact, be Latin itself, effectively erasing French as a language (see Trudeau 35).

Moreover, there is competition between scholars of different countries regarding which language is oldest, and scholars of different nationalities occasionally put forth their national language as the *Ursprache*, often with fanciful pseudo-etymological arguments. Surely one of the most amusing theses is that of the Dutchman Johannes Goropius Becanus (1519–72) in his *Hermathena* who saw the Flemish of his native Brabant as the world's oldest language and the precursor even of Hebrew. Claude Duret in his *Thresor de l'histoire des langues de cest univers* took issue with Goropius, rejecting his arguments entirely (822 ff.).

From the middle of the sixteenth century onwards, there is a sustained (and very acrimonious) debate regarding the orthography of French, as we have seen in chapter 3.[9] French suffered vis-à-vis Italian and Spanish for a variety of reasons, and sixteenth-century grammarians sought to rectify its weaknesses. At the time, Italian was considered more prestigious for literature and for such serious subjects as philosophy and theology. The famous treatise in 1547 by Joachim Du Bellay (ca. 1522–60), *La Defense et illustration de la langue françoise* (*The Defence and Illustration of the French Language*), sought to raise the standing of French to that of Italian. As for Spanish, it was the dominant language from the 1520s onwards in Latin America, giving it enormous reach and prestige in the world. In their spellings, both Italian and Spanish had another advantage: they were written phonetically for the most part, hence pronounced as written; French, by contrast, had extraneous letters in many of its words.

The relationship between spelling and pronunciation in French is, as anyone who has studied French knows, hardly consistent. While the orthography of French is not quite as convoluted as that of English, it nevertheless presents many inconsistencies. Such was already the case in the sixteenth century, and the grammarians of the period were concerned to reform the spelling and make it more rational, as we have already seen. Some grammarians felt that if French wished to compete with Italian and Spanish as a language to be learned by foreigners, the orthography needed to be made more phonetic. These concerns had interesting implications for the form and deployment of alphabetic letters.

The most famous of the reformers was Louis Meigret. Declaring that "we write a language that is not used at all and use a language that is not at all used in writing" (Nous escriuons vng langage qui n'est point en vsage, & vsons d'une langue qui n'a point d'vsage d'escriture en France, Meigret, *Traité* 82), he proposed to eliminate redundant and unpronounced letters and to add accents and diacritical marks to distinguish between different sounds, with the result that one would be able to look at a word and know immediately how to pronounce it. Others proposed similar systems. But the resistance to any and all such changes was fierce. As we have already seen in chapter 3, the major charge against the "meigretistes," as they were called, was that the modified spellings denatured French, robbing the language of, as the critics said, its "naïve French grace." In other words, the traditional spellings were felt to capture something of the French identity (see de Looze, "Orthography"). Irrational though the spellings were (with letters that went unpronounced and numerous ways of expressing the same sound) the layout of the letters was nevertheless felt to capture somehow the speakers' world and world view, and the French felt stripped and lacking if the orthography was changed. Alphabetic letters, in other words, did not simply represent sounds or words: the ways they were put together were felt as conveying for the French who they were and what their culture was. Indeed, one glance at Meigret's reformed spellings and one can see that the words do not "look French." Nor were Meigret's changes the most radical.

We have already seen that one reformer, Honoré Rambaud, went so far as to create an entirely new alphabet (fig. 30) – an extreme project that was sure to fail. Moreover, printers were hesitant to go to the expense of cutting letters with new accents, etc., or to print books using a new orthography if they could not be sure the public would embrace the changes. But for Rambaud, the project of orthographical reform had moral value. He speaks of wanting to "repair the alphabet" (reparer l'alphabet, 16). For Rambaud, "the alphabet is the greatest possession that our ancestors have left us" (L'alphabet est la meilleur possession que nos ancestres nous ayent laissé, 16–18), but "the depravation of the alphabet is the cause of many ills, [just as] the reparation of it can be the cause of much good" (la deprauation dudit alphabet est cause de beaucoup de maux & que la reparation d'iceluy peut ester cause de plusieurs biens, 18). By "depravation," Rambaud means that the alphabet does not provide a perfect correspondence between each letter and a single pronounced sound – as he feels it should do since writing is supposed to be a representation of the spoken sounds (98); Rambaud thus proposes an alphabet of thirty-four letters ordered in this fashion. Moreover, this ordered alphabet will correspond to an ordered and virtuous way of living since, as he says several times, "writing is the path of virtues and knowledge" (l'escriture est le chemin des vertus & sciences, 54).

Against the reformers was another group called the "Latinizers" or the "etymologists" who not only favoured the traditional spellings but, in fact, insisted on adding more unpronounced letters that were designed to show the Latin words from which the French ones were derived. Though bitterly opposed to the reformers and meigretistes, the Latinizers also saw the spellings of French words as somehow containing a kernel of the French character and, like Tory, they conceived of alphabetic letters as bearers of the past. We have already seen that Jacob Dubois (Jacobus Sylvius) proposed a two-tiered system that would allow a reader to move back and forth between the French word and the Latin one from which it was derived. To read more than a sentence or two in such a manner was plainly impractical.

Regardless of errors and eccentricities, and regardless of which camp grammarians belonged to, they all believed, like Plato in the *Cratylus*, that the letters of words, though largely conventional, nevertheless should contain some trace of the real world when they were formed into words. There was for them a symbiotic relationship between aspects of French culture or identity and the letters that conveyed it. Much the same could be said for other European languages as well. The international horizon to which treatise authors, like Tory, addressed themselves viewed European letters as bearing the weight of their Graeco-Roman heritage. The jockeying between the different national groups and languages did not negate the common view that equated European lettered culture with civilization and thus also equated civilization with alphabetic letters, much as the ancient Greeks had considered that to be civilized was to speak Greek, and non-Greek speakers were by definition "barbarians."

At the same time, Europe was now aware of a wider, global culture. As Europe expanded into other areas of the world through imperial conquest – to Africa, the East, and the New World – their views regarding alphabetic letters as the bearers (or even as a defining characteristic) of civilization conditioned their reactions to other cultures. Europeans had been aware for centuries of the character writing employed in parts of Asia, particularly in China and Japan. In the sixteenth century, this was recognized as writing, though of an inferior sort. European thinkers meditated deeply on the hierarchy of different types of writing, and their thinking was nourished by a fascination with not only Asian character writing but also Egyptian hieroglyphics. One senses this new global horizon already in Giovanni Battista Palatino's 1509 book (see note 3) in which he reproduces not only the many scripts of European cultures since antiquity, but also those of Arabic, Chaldean, Syrian, Egyptian, etc. Inevitably European writers placed alphabetic letters, which represented sounds through convention, at the top of the hierarchy. At the bottom were hieroglyphics, seen as an imagistic writing in which the image represented an object. In between stood character writing which, like alphabetic letters themselves, had begun as a recording of images but which, over time, had become conventional signs whose visual relationship to the object had been largely lost. Still, European writers consistently maintained that Chinese characters represented things, not sounds, and for that reason they were considered inferior to alphabetic letters.

European convictions regarding the relationship between alphabetic letters and the level of a civilization are well evinced by Thomas More's (1478–1535) famous book, *Utopia*, published in Latin in 1516. Figure 31 shows the opening page of the first edition, published in Louvain, Belgium. Published twenty-four years after Columbus's first voyage to the New World and three years before Hernán Cortés's arrival at the Meso-American empire in Mexico, More's *Utopia* (the title, of course, means "no place") was written with a conscious awareness of the discovery of cultures hitherto unknown to Europeans though More was not yet aware of any imperial New World empires. The island of Utopia is indeed a strange land and culture, which is how Europeans saw the recently discovered island cultures of the Caribbean. The difference, however, is that Utopia is a society based on rationality (almost terrifyingly so at times), whereas the societies Columbus happened upon were seen as primitive and, often enough, savage.[10]

Figure 31 shows the beginning of the text of *Utopia*. It is interesting that the very first thing More presents to the reader is a "Utopian alphabet" (Vtopiensivm alphabetvm). The introduction to the work consists of More's invented "utopian alphabet" followed by a poem, supposedly written in Utopian and "translated" into Latin. For More, a rational society necessarily will have an alphabet because, for him as for most educated Europeans, the alphabet and civilization go hand in hand.

Let us look at this alphabet more closely. First of all, there is a one-to-one correspondence between the twenty-two Utopian "letters" and the European alphabet. Both are advanced civilizations, and both have reason as hallmarks of their culture, hence the one-to-one correspondence establishes what we might call a mutual "cultural intelligibility." The actual letter forms differ, however: the Utopian letters, in particular, are based on fundamental geometric forms: the circle, the square, the triangle. In fact, the alphabet is perfectly balanced on the pyramidal triangle at the twelfth position, the most central one in an alphabet of twenty-two letters. The left wing consists of letters all based on circular forms, while the letters to the right of the triangle are all characterized by right angles.[11] The European alphabet, by contrast, is filled with many asymmetric and idiosyncratic forms. For More, a more rational (and perhaps superior) society must have a more rational alphabet. Moreover, the equation can be turned around: a more rational alphabet will be the sign of a more rational society. Before we begin reading, then, we already know that this "New World" must be highly rational – hence, anything but "savage" – because of the geometric perfection of its alphabetic letters.

The fictional world of Utopia was of course influenced in part by the discovery of the New World. It deliberately inverts the strangeness Europeans felt they had found when they sailed to the West: the strangest aspect of Utopia is, in fact, its consistent rationality. Thomas More creates this fictional "other world" in order to comment on sixteenth-century European society and its ills.

Three years after More wrote *Utopia*, Hernán Cortés began the two-year conquest of Mexico. The campaign has been well documented, in part through letters Cortés himself wrote to Emperor Charles V back in Spain and in part because several participants in the conquest later wrote chronicles detailing their experiences. We must, of course, bear in mind that all the accounts that we have were written by the victors. But even after one accounts for the propagandistic elements in the documents and the simple fact that each author has an argument to make – an argument that of course colours the narration of events – certain features emerge. One such aspect, surprisingly perhaps, is the extraordinary admiration Cortés and his men had upon seeing the imperial capital city of Tenochtitlan, the "floating city" that occupied the site of modern-day Mexico City. Each Spanish author comments on the beauty, organization, and sophistication of the city and the society they found there. One of their rhetorical conundrums is finding a known city with which to compare Tenochtitlan. They describe the city variously as being as impressive as Seville, and even Jerusalem. One writer, Díaz del Castillo (1492–1585), famously insists that the only suitable comparison would be to the fabulous cities of the knightly romances, such as those of the popular *Amadis of Gaul*, in which the knight travels to all sorts of miraculous "other worlds": "we stood there amazed, and said that it looked like the kind of enchantments that are told about in the book of Amadis [of Gaul]" (nos quedamos admirados, y decíamos que parecía a las cosas de encantamiento que cuenta en el libro de Amadís [de Gaula], Díaz del Castillo 176).

Now, Meso-American culture did not have alphabetic writing (it also had not invented the wheel). What the people had instead was a complex and sophisticated system of pictogrammic texts in which interpreter-priests could read the accounts of their origins, history, legends, geography, and tribute agreements. Scholars to this day debate whether such pictogrammic texts constitute "writing," with a gathering consensus for a positive decision (see Boone). For sixteenth-century Europeans, the situation was quite different. They comment often on the fact that, as they say, the peoples of Mexico have no writing – by which they mean alphabetic writing – and they marvel at this. The term they generally use for indigenous pictogrammic texts, beginning with Hernán Cortés himself, is an equivocal one: the Spanish call them "painted books" (*libros pintados*). They see the indigenous folded screens (*lienzos*) on which the accounts were spread as books somehow, but they can only conceive of the colourful pictograms as painting, not writing.

To the European mind, the lack of what they would consider "writing" was an almost inexplicable state of affairs: how could a grand and majestic imperial culture capable of constructing a large, beautiful, and well-organized capital with lovely temples also be a culture that lacked written texts ("writing" understood as "alphabetic writing")? On the one hand the Meso-American civilization was unquestionably impressive, but on the other hand it did not have letters – Christian letters – and was thus inferior and uncivilized by definition. (Where this pagan society fit into the Christian cosmology was also troubling to Europeans, since the Bible showed no awareness of it. Why was there a lacuna? After all, according to the Bible, all humans had to be descended from Adam and Eve.) For the Franciscan missionary Pedro de Gante (1480–1572), the Meso-Americans were a "people without writing, without letters, without written characters and without any kind of enlightenment" (see Mignolo 312–13). The Franciscan Juan de Torquemada (1562–1624) and José de Acosta (1539–1600) also commented on the lack of alphabetic writing (Torquemada, *Monarquía Indiana* 2:314, co. 2; José de Acosta, *Historia natural et moral de las Indias*, Book 6 chs. 4–7).[12] According to Diego de Valadés (*Rhetorica* 93–4), as both Anthony Pagden (*Fall* 92–3) and Francisco Rico have noted (906–7), Juan Maldonado maintained at Burgos in 1545 that the peoples of the New World constituted a demonstration that to not have letters was to be devoid of humanity (*huminitatem penitus exuerant*).[13] As Rico argues, for the European mentality the use of letters was an important part of the *dignitas hominum* (906–7).

The Spanish response to this strange culture was one of awe and admiration twinned with a desire to destroy it. The New World culture was clearly advanced and sophisticated, but the lack of alphabetic letters meant it was also barbarian and dangerous. The Dominican Diego Duran (1537–88) and Diego de Landa (1524–79) admire the beauty of the indigenous pictogrammic texts, but, as Diego de Landa says, "because there was no one thing that did not contain superstitions and lies of the Demon, we put fire to all of them."[14] Even Bartolomé de las Casas (1484–1566), the great defender of indigenous rights in Mexico after the conquest, considers that people who "lack the use and study of letters" are barbarians.[15] What was done to pre-Columbian texts was done to the culture more generally: an alphabetic conquest accompanied the geographic conquest.

The result in "New Spain" was a strict application of Antonio de Nebrija's 1492 argument. The sons of prominent indigenous chieftains were schooled in alphabetic letters and Christianity to make them "civilized." A branch of the Cromberger family, the most important book printers in Seville in the period, set up the first printing press in Mexico in 1549. In 1609 Mateo Alemán (1547–1615) chose to publish his *Ortografía Castellana* (*Spanish Orthography*) in Mexico City rather than in Spain. In his book Alemán proposed modifications to the Spanish alphabet: a reversed "c" was to stand for the Spanish "ch," and the "R fuerte" of Spanish, for which the usual graphie was either a double "r" ("rr") or a capital "R," would now be designated by a new letter. More important than the details of Spanish spellings is the fact that New Spain (Mexico) not only participated henceforth in the alphabetic world of Spanish letters, but it was also now put forward as a centre for diffusion of a corrected alphabet. Alemán specifically boasts that "from the newly conquered land comes a new and true mode of writing for all nations." With these words he proclaims the full entry of New Spain into the Western alphabetic order.[16] One of the proofs for Europeans that Mexico has joined the world culture of "civilized" nations is that it is now a cultural and political centre capable of ruling on the nature of alphabetic letters. The letter is seen as a civilizing influence – that is, as the hallmark of civilization itself.

With Mateo Alemán we cross over, if only just barely, into the seventeenth century. As we have seen in this chapter, the humanist world reinterprets the medieval view of the alphabetic letters as key to the European world view and as a compendium of civilizing virtues, displacing the emphasis from specifically Christian virtues to ones conditioned by humanism. The alphabet is no longer considered "God's cross" so much as an expression of humanity and the heights to which man aspires not through faith but through the exercise of his intellectual faculties, particularly his reason. Letters carry the weight of the Graeco-Roman past, they express the human form and human aspirations, and they are a key element in what Europeans of the period viewed as a process of exporting "civilization" to other parts of the world. The subsequent movements of the early modern period tell a tale of new metamorphoses of the views and values regarding alphabetic letters.

6

Baroque Variations and the Search for a Universal Language

The weight of primary noon,
The ABC of being.

– Wallace Stevens

Another name for the historical period covered by the Renaissance is mutatis mutandis the "Age of Exploration." The term implies a view of the period from the mid-fifteenth century to the mid-seventeenth century as one of travel to distant lands and thus it puts an emphasis on the contact Europeans had with foreign cultures. This contact inevitably led to a realization on the part of Europeans of the relativity of their place in the world. The encounters with the civilizations in Africa, in the East (Asia) and in the West (the New World) posed many questions that European civilization was at a loss to answer. One of the most disturbing aspects, for Europeans, of the "discovery" of the Americas was the fact that, although there had been a limited knowledge of Africa and Asia prior to the travels of fifteenth- and sixteenth-century explorers, neither classical writers nor the Bible displayed any awareness of the New World. These lacunae demonstrated that antiquity had bequeathed a mistaken view of the world to subsequent centuries (see Grafton). As Michel de Montaigne and others pointed out, if previous centuries had not known about the Americas, might there not still be other "new worlds" on the globe that were waiting to be discovered? In the late sixteenth century Lancelot Voisin de La Popelinière (1541–1608) suggested to the French crown that, having missed out on some of the major discoveries in the Americas, the French should turn their attention to the austral area in which there was perhaps an as-yet-undiscovered continent (Australia would not be discovered by Europeans until 1606).[1]

The silence of the Bible was even more troubling than that of pagan antiquity. The Book was authored by God, after all, and it was inconceivable that God would not know of peoples and places in his own Creation. Were the indigenous peoples of the New World descended from a lost tribe of Israel? After all, according to Christian beliefs the Meso-Americans, like all other humans, had to be descended from Adam and Eve. Where did they fit into the Christian universe, and why was the Bible silent about them? Might it be that some tribe in the New World or in some as-yet-undiscovered place still spoke the language in which God first created the world as a speech act? Christopher Columbus, after all, became convinced that his explorations might lead to a recovery of the lost Garden of Eden (see Watts and Eco).

The question of what might be the human *Ur-Sprache* was, as most intellectuals of the Renaissance and baroque period knew well, as old as Herodotus's *Histories*. Herodotus tells (2.2) of how the Egyptian King Psammeticos wanted to discover who the original peoples of the earth were, so he had two newborn children raised with no exposure to human language whatsoever on the assumption that what they uttered would necessarily be the original human speech. At age two, the children both uttered "bekos," which meant "bread" in the Phrygian language, for which reason Psammeticos concluded that the Phrygian people were the oldest ethnic group. What is curious is that during the Renaissance, this anecdote, repeated by Claude Duret, Becanus, Guillaume Postel (1510–81), and others, has its focus shifted slightly to become an attempt to discover "le plus ancien et naturel langage de tous ceux qu'on parle au monde," as Laurent Joubert (1529–82) puts it (cited in Dubois, 23: the oldest and most natural language of all those that are spoken in the world). Herodotus's tale of a search for the oldest ethnic group has become rather a search for the oldest language.

The contacts with foreign cultures resulted in a spurring of intense interest in cultures that were distant in time and/or space and thus in other modes of writing and communication. But these interests also threw European society back on itself in an interrogation of its own origins (a process which often led, interestingly enough, to repeated proclamations of European superiority). These two movements may seem contradictory at first, but in fact they were deeply associated with each other. Aware of non-alphabetical writing systems, European thinkers became fascinated, as we shall see, with the search for the world's originary language and also with the possibilities offered by invented writing systems that did not note down spoken sounds, as alphabets usually did, but represented concepts and the concrete world directly (what came to be called a "real character language"). Many scholars were intensely interested in Egyptian hieroglyphics, which were believed, mistakenly, to reflect the world directly and not as a matter of convention.

As Europeans surveyed the writing systems of the wider world, they tended to conclude that alphabetic writing was superior to other systems, whether Chinese characters, Egyptian hieroglyphics, or Meso-American pictograms (the last, as we have seen, was generally not even considered "writing"). Michele Mercati's *Gli Obelischi di Roma* (1589) is quite typical for the way it evidences these multiple tendencies (the interest in obelisks, indeed, was part of the fascination with all things Egyptian – to this day Rome is a city of obelisks as a result). For Mercati, there were three types of writing: simple pictures, hieroglyphs, and letters. Mexican pictogrammic texts, of which Mercati had seen two examples in the Vatican Library, ranked lowest:

e ai tempi nostri si è veduto il medesimo nel mondo nuovo tra gli abitatori del Mexico, città principale della nuova Spagna, ai quali parendo troppa fatica il dipingere tutte le figure intere, o vero perché occupassero troppo spazio, messero in uso di figurare di molti animali solamente i capi ... Era perciò questa manera di scrivere molto imperfetta, sì per la moltitudine delle figure come ancora per la difficultà di formarle, et perché con esse non si poteva interamente esplicare tutto quello che sovienne al concetto, non potendosi rappresentare altro agli occhi che, tra le cose corporee, la specie e l'individuo con alcuni accidenti. Il che era pur assai a quei popoli, i quali non avrebbono avuto (come altri sopranominati) alcuna maniera di scrivere, non potendo eglino per instinto naturale venire alla divina invenzione delle lettere nostre, con le quali si compongono le parole. (Mercati 111)

(and in our times the same thing has been seen in the New World among the inhabitants of Mexico, the capital city of New Spain, for whom since it seemed too exhausting to paint all the whole figures, or indeed because they would take up too much space, they [the Mexicans] put in use the representation only of the heads of many animals ... It was thus a very imperfect manner of writing, as much for the multitude of figures as for the difficulty in forming them, and because one could not entirely explain everything that was included in the concept since one was unable to repre-. sent to the eyes anything other than, among the corporeal things, the species and the individual with a few details. This however was a lot to these people who would not have had (like others mentioned before) any other means of writing, unable through natural instinct to arrive at the divine invention of our letters with which words are composed.

In Mercati's writings we can see the fascination with foreign modes of writing as well as what he views as the superiority of alphabetic letters, and in his arguments and conclusions we see the double movement that both looks outward and yet also turns back onto the past. For Mercati, alphabetic writing is superior because created by God ("divine intervention") and not the result of "natural instinct." What is his justification for this divine origin? Mercati is perfectly aware of the various classical myths that derive writing from pagan deities and he is also aware of the historical transmission of letters from the Phoenicians to the Greeks. However, he chooses to trace alphabetical writing back instead to the Garden of Eden. His argument parallels the much-discussed question of which language was nearest to God, for which the answer was generally given throughout the Middle Ages and the early modern period as Hebrew, since it was assumed that God spoke in some version of Hebrew to the Jews of the Old Testament. Mercati raises the related question of when the Hebrew alphabet was first invented. Clearly, he says, it had to exist when God gave Moses the Ten Commandments. Mercati then notes that writing was already in use among the Jews earlier in Exodus when Moses wrote down Joshua's deeds (Ex. 17:14). It therefore seems reasonable to him that God created alphabetic writing at the same time that he gave language to Adam (Mercati 109). Adam then passed on the knowledge of writing to Noah, who gave it to Abraham, and so on. According to Mercati's view, alphabetical writing was therefore not only divinely instituted but it was also older than all other writing and it was a quintessential sign, along with speech, of humanity itself. For Mercati, these features gave alphabetic letters unchallenged superiority. Nor is Mercati's backdating of Hebrew writing the most extreme. Alexander Top in his little 1603 book *The Olive Leaf* considers that God's mark on Cain's forehead in Genesis 5 could only have been the Hebrew letter *Tau*, meaning "sign" or "mark," and could only have had meaning if people already knew how to read: "Here had the Lords writing been vaine, if men could not read the Mark" (quire B 1 recto).

The sixteenth century, as we have seen, was a time of great creative energy that expanded the possibilities for vernacular language and sought to incorporate elements of many cultures. However, these tendencies did not result in the seventeenth century being more open and tolerant of foreignness and difference. On the contrary, the seventeenth century sought to impose orthodoxy, conformity, and purity through the establishment of authoritarian structures. Two centuries later, the American writer Nathaniel Hawthorne (1804–64) quite rightly saw the relationship between seventeenth-century politico-religious authority and the alphabet in his great novel *The Scarlet Letter* in which his seventeenth-century protagonist Hester Prynne is made subject to a capital, crimson "A" as a symbol of her adultery.[2]

What is usually referred to as the baroque period (roughly 1600–1700) was characterized by resplendent artistic creations on the one hand and the scourge of repressive institutions such as the Inquisition on the other: both sides of baroque culture were in fact designed to maintain religious or political orthodoxy, at least in Catholic countries. There were similar developments regarding language and secular culture, particularly in France, Italy, and Spain, which had already developed strong grammatical traditions. Academies that would have the power to rule on language and the arts were established in numerous countries, beginning in France with the Académie française, set up in 1635 by the powerful Cardinal Richelieu (1585–1642) precisely so that the French crown could maintain control over the language and what was written in it. In France, a pared down, "pure" French diction became the norm – the very antithesis of the sixteenth-century French of Rabelais and Pierre de Ronsard (1524–85) who imported words from all quarters and believed that, as Ronsard put it, "Plus nous aurons de mots en nostre langue, plus elle sera parfaitte" (6:460: The more words we have in our language, the more perfect it will be. See also Brunot 2:167–71). The search for purity, whether linguistic, political, theological, or even in terms of one's bloodline (an especially important phenomenon in Spain where it became crucial to prove that one's family had not been "tainted" by intermarriage with Jews or Muslims), could only lead back to the past.

If the French crown was greatly concerned with "letters" in the sense of literary production, it was also equally concerned with the form and presentation of the alphabetic letters themselves. The promulgation and control of typography was an expression of the absolutist vision of the Sun King, Louis XIV (1638–1715). The power and order of the realm was expressed through the regularity and elegance of the official printed works. Louis XIV was able to build on the extraordinary advances in typography of the humanist era when France had some of Europe's finest printers. In the sixteenth century, François I (1494–1547) had been actively interested in promoting humanist values and had appointed two of the greatest printers of his age to the position of "imprimeur du roi" (king's printer): Geoffroy Tory and then Robert Estienne (1503–59). These interests had led to the creation of "les grecs du roi" (the king's Greeks) by another celebrated printer, Claude Garamond (1490–1561); these letter forms constituted an official typeface for the publication of ancient Greek texts. Unsurpassed to this day, the "grecs du roi" were made up of over 500 different pieces of type, including all manner of ligatures in addition to the letters and diacritics.

As part of the movement towards absolutism under Louis XIII (1601–43), the royal printing house ("Imprimerie Royale") was established by Cardinal Richelieu (1585–1642). The Sun King, Louis XIV (1638–1715), subsequently made the printing house, and in particular its typeface, an expression of his absolute power. In 1692 the king ordered a committee at his Academy of Sciences to develop a set of Roman letters that would be the official typeface of his empire. They were to be used only by the Imprimerie Royale, and it was, as Meggs and Purvis have noted, a "capital offence" (122) for anyone else to use the font. For our purposes, the most interesting aspect is that the manner of creating the typeface heralded the attitudes of the Enlightenment period. The approach was to be rational and scientific above all, and, rather significantly, the project was directed by a mathematician, Nicolas Jaugeon. Letters were now mapped on a grid far more detailed than those of Albrecht Dürer or Geoffroy Tory. The letters were constructed on an initial grid of 8x8 units of which each unit was then subdivided into thirty-six smaller ones, giving a total of 2304 units for the construction of each letter (Meggs and Purvis 122). Known as the "Romains du Roi" (the king's Roman letters), these letter forms were the epitome of control and order. The alphabet reflected the political order of the absolute ruler as well as the nascent Enlightenment championing of logic and scientific reasoning as the dominant means for approaching the affairs of men.

The explorations of the sixteenth century, as we have seen, also gave rise to the unexpected pairing of a fascination with foreign writing systems and an interest in the origins of European languages and writing. In chapter 5 we observed that the desire to find the "purest" French led, for at least one scholar, back to Latin itself. The search for the origins of linguistic diversity also led Christians back to the Bible and to the period before mankind was scattered linguistically. Numerous scholars devoted time to studying and comparing the languages of the Bible: Hebrew, Chaldean, Aramaic, etc. Some proposed elaborate theories and tables comparing the respective alphabets in an effort to recover man's original language. Franciscus Mercurius Van Helmont (1618–95) concentrated primarily on the articulation of words in Hebrew and Chaldean, coming to the conclusion that Hebrew offered the most "natural" alphabetic system. John Dee (1527–1608) in England returned to one of the biblical Apocrypha, the Book of Enoch, according to which the angel Metatron revealed to Moses the angelic alphabet of creation and "the letters by which Heaven and Earth were created, the letters by which were created rivers and seas, the letters by which were created the trees and herbs" (quoted in Drucker, *Alphabetic* 195). In other words, letters made up the world, and the natural phenomena of the world gave back nothing so much as alphabetical letters. Dee, along with Edward Kelley (1555–97), conducted séances in which they supposedly had direct communication with the angels, who gave them the Enochian alphabet. Both of them wrote out versions of the alphabet (fig. 32) (see Dee, unpaginated pages before p. 1; also Harkness 42). Their ideas, and those of some of their contemporaries represent a return to the long-standing Christian notion of the world as a readable book – the Book of Nature.[3] In fact, for Dee God's language in speaking to Adam was the same speech with which he had created the world, so that world and language were one. In Dee's opinion this was why Hebrew and Chaldean (as well as Greek and Latin) were alphanumeric (i.e., the letters were also numbers), since God's speech joined language and mathematics.[4]

Similarly, John Webster (1610–82) in his *Academiarum examen* (1654) sought to return to the original Adamic language, one which would "speak the world" in a way similar to how he thought Egyptian hieroglyphics functioned. Webster considered (from a Neoplatonic standpoint) that it was a waste of time for people to learn different languages: "[Even] if a man had the perfect knowledge of many, nay all languages [...] yet knows he no more thereby, than that he can onely name them in his mother tongue, for the intellect receives no other nor further notion thereby, for the senses receive but one numerical species or *Ideal*-shape from every individual thing" (Webster 21). Far more useful, Webster says, would be a universal language that could "lay down a platform and seminary of all learning and knowable things" (22). Thus the only

solution, Webster believes – and this is a view that characterizes the
whole of the seventeenth century – is to create a universal "real character" language. Referencing Asian languages, which, Webster states,
good authorities insist can be read by different nations even though
they speak different languages, he proposes to replace conventional letters with new signs on the model of mathematical or mineral symbols.
After all we cannot get back to the language of Adam in which language and substance or world were one. He writes:

> Adam, made in this image of God which is his eternal word, was made in
> the out-spoken word, and so lived in, understood, and spoke the language
> of the father. For the divine essence living in its own infinit, glorious, and
> central being, having this eternal word, or character of his substance, in
> and with himself, and was himself, did by the motion of its own incom-
> prehensible love, expand and breath forth this characteristical word, in
> which man stood. (26–7)

The closest one can come to the Adamic correspondence between
essence and language/writing is an artificial real character language.
As his model, Webster proposes to "let a character denoting man be
appointed, as suppose this *, and though to persons of divers languages, it would receive various denominations according to their several vocal prolations, yet would they all but understand one and the
same thing by it" (26). The real character language would be an entirely
textualized reversal of the linguistic scattering after the Tower of Babel.
The asterisk would signify "man" universally.

Now, for Webster as for others, the key biblical narrative expressing
man's lack of linguistic unity was (and is) the story of the Tower of
Babel in Genesis 11 in which man's desire to get closer to God by building a tower to the heavens is seen as a sin of pride by God who then
demolishes the tower. To make sure that man never tries to overreach
his natural limits again, God scatters the people across the face of the
earth and gives them many different and mutually unintelligible languages. Man's attempt to get closer to God results, paradoxically, in his
being made more distant.

There are many ways of approaching the tale of Babel, and one of
them is that it is designed to explain linguistic diversity. Part of a series
of "troubled relations" between God and his Creation that begins with
the expulsion from Eden and stretches through to the haunting and disturbing narrative of the Book of Job, the Babel episode articulates man's

distance from God as a specifically linguistic one. Before the building of the tower, we are told, "the whole earth had one language and few words." Not only is there no linguistic diversity, but there seems to be no need for an extensive vocabulary. Communication between God and man, as between man and man, is still easy and direct. Rather than the arbitrary, conventional relationship between words and their meanings that exists after the scattering (which is why, after Babel, different words mean the same thing in different languages: "horse," "Pferd," or "caballo" all stand for a four-legged creature), there appears to be something more like an organic bond before the building of the tower. As Webster says, Adam speaks God's language, which is still a language of essences; for this reason, when Adam was given the power to name the animals, they became in a certain sense what he named them to be. If, as Mercati wished to argue, the Hebrew language and Hebrew writing were born together, that would suggest that the written language, even though it was alphabetical, carried or contained directly something of the real world in its letters. The alphabet would have consisted of "natural characters" that did not so much signify the world by convention as actually model it.

To seventeenth-century thinkers, this was food for serious thought. The period was one of consolidation and orthodoxy while also being one of great scientific advances, though even the scientific discoveries of Newton and others were designed to help uncover the divine laws ruling the universe. Grammarians wondered whether universal rules could be established for written languages as well. Was it possible to create a language in which the letters would not signify arbitrarily, but rather would speak the world and a universal order directly to all readers? This would be a secular recovery from the disaster at Babel (a theological resolution already existed in the miracle of Pentecost in Acts 2:4 in which each follower of Christ heard God's voice miraculously in his own particular language).

One direction was in a turn towards mysticism. Might certain combinations of letters and words contain secret meanings, and if so could they be used to influence the world or to cast spells? Conversely, might the configurations in our universe be spelling out messages for us? In the sixteenth century Guillaume Postel (1510–81) had already proposed that the astrological constellations were in fact letters, which was simply a new way of seeing alphabetical letters as elemental in our cosmos. Closely associated with mystical approaches to writing were treatises on cryptography since they also were concerned with secret

meanings "behind" the letters. It may seem surprising that cryptography and mysticism were twinned, but both were predicated on the
idea that each letter of a text in fact stood for something occulted. As
a result the systems for coded invocations that would bring forth spirits, as in Johannes Trithemius's (1462–1516) *Steganographia* (1499) and
Polygraphia (1506), were not so different from cryptography that used
elaborate systems of letter-substitution in order to disguise messages.
Indeed, cryptography based on a systematic substitution of one letter
for another continued from the Middle Ages right into the twentieth
century; the famous Enigma machines of the Nazis were simply an
elaborate version of this system. (In the case of the Enigma machines the
substitutions were various and passed through three alphabetic disks
that were recalibrated every day.) The weakness of all such approaches
to cryptography was that one had to have the key that revealed the
substitutions in operation at any particular time, and if the key fell into
enemy hands, as was in fact the case of the Enigma manuals early in the
Second World War, the messages could be deciphered. Only with the
digital encryption that we all now use in our computers was this weakness overcome (Simon Singh 124–42).

There was not a sharp distinction between the alphabet's role in
mystical invocations and in cryptography, nor was there a clear line
between these two fields and the nascent linguistics or even the mathematical sciences. Since alphabetical letters were arbitrary signifiers,
one could potentially substitute other symbols for letters. Numbers
could represent letters, and so could points on a grid; in the case of
John Wilkins's (1614–72) *Mercury, or The Secret and Swift Messenger*
(1641), geometrical shapes, points, and lines were used systematically
to stand for letters. Francis Lodwick (1619–94) in his *A Common Writing:
Whereby Two, Although Not Understanding One the Others Language, yet
by the Helpe thereof, May Communicate Their Minds One to Another* (1647)
proposed, like John Webster, to replace letters with universal symbols.
In particular, he suggested giving numbers to many common words,
which would facilitate written communication across languages since
the same number would stand for an object, regardless of the particular
word a language had. He also invented many new letters. Cave Beck's
(1623–1706) *Universal Character, by which all the nations in the world may
understand one anothers conceptions, reading out of one common writing in
their own mother tongues* (1657) devised a system as well in which numbers represented whole words, to which were added alphabetical letters for inflections: tense, number, gender, case, etc. For example, "S"

universally represented the plural, as in English. The letters "p, q, r, and x" before a number marked a noun. "Honour thy Father and thy Mother" came out as "leb2314 p2477 and pf2477" (Knowlson 63).

It may seem strange that some of the same thinkers who meditated on cryptography and the means for occulting messages in a written system also turned their attention to the possibility of the creation of a written language that all peoples could read, regardless of the particular language they spoke. But what might appear to be three strands of thinking were in fact deeply linked: the nostalgia for an originary language in which *nomen* and *res* were linked, the realization that signification in the languages (and alphabets) of the day was entirely arbitrary, and the dream of constructing a universal language (by which was meant a universal alphabet) that would again link word and thing in a way that reflected the reality of man's existence. The bond between these three aspects was what Claude-Gilbert Dubois has called "the mystique of oneness" (la mystique de l'unité, 36) of monotheistic Christian culture in which a single god spoke a language that became reality such that the only true language that could express the world properly had to be a single, universal language (whether pre-Babelian or post-Babelian through a triumph of human reasoning). As Dubois points out, the line between the meaningful and the meaningless is finely drawn since "the proliferation of meanings ends up as nonsense" (La prolifération des sens aboutit au non-sens (42; see 36–42). When Hamlet answers the question "What do you read, my lord" with "Words, words, words" (II. ii) he could just have easily said "Letters, letters, letters."

As we have seen, one model for a universal language or alphabet was mathematics, a science in which the seventeenth century excelled. Numbers were intelligible to everyone, regardless of a person's pronunciation, and as a result even very complex algebraic constructions were not subject to linguistic barriers. Was it possible, scholars wondered, to create a written language that would be universal as well? Rather than trying to reconstruct an original, pre-Babelian language, could not a new universal writing be constructed "scientifically," as it were? In the early fourteenth century the Catalan philosopher Raymon Llull (1232–1315), as seventeenth-century thinkers knew, had already attempted to create a universal language of sorts – or at least a calculus of propositions – through his *ars combinatoria* which would be intelligible to all people, regardless of the language one spoke. But the limitations of Llull's system were many and the reasoning was ultimately tautological (see Eco 56–64).

Still, the idea of a universal language seized the imagination in the seventeenth and eighteenth centuries, particularly in France and England. Just as scientists had discovered the fundamental laws of physics that ruled the universe, might one also discover the universal properties that gave rise to languages and thus design a language accordingly? One must caution that many of the assumptions regarding "universality" were in fact based in the features of Western, alphabetic languages, even though a key impetus for the invention of a universal language was the fascination with non-Western character languages that were seen as representing not pronunciations but rather objects and concepts. For all their misapprehension of Egyptian hieroglyphics, New World pictograms, and Chinese characters, Europeans were nevertheless impressed by the fact that people whose oral languages were very different could nevertheless read and understand the same characters.

European thinkers were thus inspired to search for a language that people of different nations could use to communicate with each other. Among scholars, Latin had been the *lingua franca* for a thousand years, but in the aftermath of the Reformation, it no longer had the universality that it had had formerly. The corrupt church Latin had been banished by the humanists, and now only a select erudite group learned a pure, classical Latin, but classical Latin was not suited to modern topics and was no longer used as a living language. With the elimination of the bastardized Latin that had been the means of communication for educated people of different vernaculars, there was a lacuna that needed to be plugged. What is more, people did not regularly study foreign vernacular languages (we have already seen Webster's arguments regarding the utility, or lack thereof, of foreign language study). In the eighteenth century, French would of course become if not a universal language at least a widely spoken, pan-European one, especially among the aristocracy, but that was a gradual development that accompanied the rise of French political power politically. In the seventeenth century vernacular language study was not yet seen as a serious intellectual activity and some languages, like English, had not yet been fully codified as grammars. Because of geographic location or the experience of living in a foreign country, one might learn another language, but it was a haphazard and piecemeal process. Moreover, most foreign language acquisition took place between languages that were similar: an Italian learning French or Spanish, for example. Few Romance-language speakers could read or understand English, and very few Englishmen ever learned another vernacular language.

So in the seventeenth century the first linguists began to consider seriously the invention of an alphabetical language that could be learned easily, that did not depend on pronunciation, and that would be intelligible to all who submitted to the system. Some writers still attempted to find the original substratum beneath the known languages and thereby to reinvent something close to what was believed to have been the original Adamic language. Alexander Top, for example, attempted to (re)create a "universal alphabet" in his 1603 book, *The Olive Leaf or Universall Alphabet*. But important thinkers such as John Dee and Seth Ward (1617–89) in England were becoming convinced that the original language of Genesis was beyond recovery (Knowlson 14). At the same time, important works on cryptography by such writers as Giambattista della Porta (1535–1615) (*De furtis litterarum notis*, 1563) and Gustavus Selenus (1579–1666) (*Cryptomenytices et cryptographiae*, 1624) had shown that signs or letters could be made to stand for whole words or even entire sentences. More and more, thinkers considered the possibility that people could create a "real character" written language, which would reflect the world directly. In some ways this constituted a return to the idea set forth in Plato's *Cratylus* that the letters could actually contain some kernel of the world. For example, René Descartes's friend Marin Mersenne (1588–1648), in his *Harmonie universelle* (1636), suggested that the alphabetic letters actually contained meanings about the real world: the fiftieth proposition in his "Book of the Voice" proposed "to determine if the sounds of the voice – that is, the vowels, consonants, the syllables and the pronunciations – can have an analogy and a relationship with the things signified, such that one can form a natural language" (1963 [1626], 2:75). Mersenne, taking his examples from Latin, argued that "i" stood for thin and tiny things, "o" for "great passions," "m" for great things, "n" for negative and occulted things, etc.

Some of the finest minds of the period were bent towards projects to create a real character language. Francis Bacon (1561–1626), like others, pointed out that in Asia character writing already constituted a kind of real character language. Marin Mersenne corresponded extensively with René Descartes (1596–1650) on the topic. The German philosopher Gottfried Leibniz (1646–1716) read some of the most important English treatises before publishing his own views on the subject. Influenced early in his career by the writings of another German Athanasius Kircher (1602–80) who, in his 1663 *Polygraphia nova* and his 1679 *Turris Babel*, attempted to construct a universal language (seeking in the latter work to discover Adamic language by interpreting Hebrew

words as so many rebus), Leibniz sought to create a propositional language in which signs, which could be letters, numbers, or of some other
sort, would represent simple concepts, and more complex ones would
be able to be constructed logically from the combination of the simple ones. Seen often as the father of modern symbolical logic, Leibniz
saw mathematics as the model for such a system of logical propositions
(Knowlson 106–11; Madeline David 61–71).

Leibniz's system, however, fell short of having the range and nuance
of a complete alphabet – which is to say, of a complete language. In
fact, as Michèle Jalley has pointed out, Leibniz's program was designed
simply to create a writing ("écriture") rather than an actual language
(70) – that is, a set of conventional signs that would represent concepts
according to the operations of human understanding and not actual
words. As such, it fell prey to the same problems as those that Descartes
identified for Marin Mersenne.

In England many of the figures in and around the new Royal Society were involved in discussions and writings regarding a universal
real character language. George Dalgarno (1626?–87) published his *Ars
signorum* (*Art of Signs*) in 1661 in which he produced the first chapter
of Genesis in his new language (fig. 33). Dalgarno and others sought to
create a language that aped the order of reality, and one of the questions
that arose was whether the project should seek to reconstruct the pre-
Babelian universal language or create a new, artificial one (Dalgarno).
Dalgarno favoured the latter option, but then, as David Cram has
noted, he believed that the Adamic language "was a perfect but human
creation" (Cram, "Language" 193, n. 3). Another question that had to
be resolved was the relationship between alphabetic letters and spoken
words: did written words stand for things in the world or only for the
sounds of spoken words that in turn stood for the things of the world?
In other words, were letters simply the signs of signs?

Perhaps the most important treatise of the period was John Wilkins's
Essay towards a Real Character and a Philosophical Language (1688) (fig. 34).
On the analogy with contemporary biological and botanical studies
that ordered things according to *genera*, species, etc., Wilkins, like some
others, used the letters of the alphabet in an attempt to reflect that universal order. Letters no longer represented sounds: instead, they were
designed to show the structure of the real world. In a sense, the alphabetic letters were merely place-holders for constituent parts of reality,
and in fact one could use any system of notation: lines, dots, numbers, etc. Wilkins devised both a system of lines and slashes as well as

an alphabetic representation. Wilkins's system moved taxonomically: for example, for the word "diba" "di" was the generic sign for stones; the "b" introduced a differentiated subgrouping, in this case a "vulgar stone." Diphthongs and vowels were then used to add further distinctions in terms of species. As a result, "diba" signified a rough, vulgar stone.

The hopes for a real character language were very high in the seventeenth century. Not only would such a language provide the means for all peoples to communicate with each other easily, but it could make for religious harmony. Europe had been rocked by a period of religious strife in the sixteenth century, which pitted Protestant reformers against Catholics, and in France in particular this had resulted in a murderous civil war from 1562 to 1593, known as the Wars of Religion. Many controversies and misunderstandings were based on differing translations of biblical passages. With a real character language translation into individual tongues would not be needed. The same Bible could be read by everyone in the real character language.

The great hope was that written letters (or some combination of letters and numbers/ciphers) would be able to express the world directly. The seventeenth-century thinkers were looking once more for a language whose alphabet would allow readers to move between world and text with no gap of arbitrary signification. The new language would reveal the world – reveal, in fact, the order that existed in the world. As John Wilkins put it:

> But now if these inarticulate sounds be contrived for the expression not of *words* and *letters*, but of *things* and *notions* … then might there bee such a generall Language, as should be equally speakable, by all people and Nations; and so we might be restored from the second generall curse, which is yet manifested, not only in the confusion of *writing*, but also of *speech*. (*Mercury* 43)

As this quotation shows, the project was utopian in scope. Similarly, the displaced Moldavian writer, John Amos Comenius (1592–1670), claimed in his own book, *Via lucis* (*The Way of Light*) (1668) that the project would arrive at the "discovery not only of a language, but of thought, and, what is more, of the truth of things themselves at the same time" (187). Comenius was convinced that the language would provide the foundation for a new science, *pansophia*, that would draw together all knowledge.

Because the awareness of different and exotic writing systems and the dream of a universal language seized hold of the imagination in the seventeenth century, fictional languages also appeared with some frequency, a bit the way they have in twentieth-century science fiction. We have already seen that Thomas More created fictional alphabetical letters at the beginning of his *Utopia*. The forms of More's letters comprised a geometrized version of Greek capitals (More did not create any lower case letters), while his alphabet as a whole was clearly modelled on Latin since it had the same alphabetical order and comprised the same number of letters in a one-to-one correspondence. Also in the sixteenth century François Rabelais, in a celebrated scene of *Pantagruel* (1532), depicted Panurge as replying to the titular character's questions in thirteen different languages, three of which were made up. The French critic Emile Pons has worked to decipher two of Rabelais's invented languages and, if Pons's theories are correct, Rabelais added or changed letters or deformed the expressions of both French and other languages: for example, for Pons *delmeupplistrincq* is in fact "donne-moi please to drink" (Pons 193). Since there does not seem to be a clear system in operation in Rabelais, one has to wonder to what extent Rabelais simply encourages the reader to "see" an answer – that is, to (re)write one – in what are, in fact, nonsense syllables. Rabelais is reworking an older tradition of nonsense "baragouin" that one finds, for example, in the fifteenth-century play, *La Farce de Maître Pathelin*, as well as perhaps glancing back at the long tradition of anagrammic puzzles found in late medieval narratives (see de Looze, "Mon nom"). The line between sense and non-sense in lettristic play is very thin indeed.

Subsequent fiction writers attempted to provide the rudiments of a grammar with their invented languages, though no one invented anything like a complete grammar for a fictional tongue. In the wake of More's *Utopia*, fictional utopian societies necessarily were said to have more perfect languages than known societies did. The example best known to English readers is of course the language of the Lilliputians in the eighteenth-century *Gulliver's Travels* (1726). But Jonathan Swift (1667–1745) was not alone in this endeavour. The contact with Asian cultures and the nascent linguistic studies of New World languages, which Europeans were quick to write down using alphabetic letters, fuelled a fascination with novel languages and writing systems. To conceive of a new culture, even a fictional one, was to conceive of a new language and a new way of alphabetic writing; this equation reiterated the long-standing view that there was a deep relationship between how one conceived the world and the letters one used to write about it. These imaginary languages sometimes used European letters and sometimes invented ones, and at times used a combination of the two.

Gabriel de Foigny (1630–92) imagined a "langue australienne" in *La Terre australe connue* (1676); the book was translated into English in 1693 (quotations here are from the English translation). Foigny's imaginary language had many of the qualities of the real character languages proposed by his contemporaries. In Foigny's ninth chapter, dedicated to a discussion of the putative Australian language, he claimed that one became a philosopher as a process of learning the language since the words reflected the world directly: "as soon as a Man hears [words] pronounced, he presently conceives the nature of things they signify" (Fr. ed. 170; Eng. trans. 115). All words were monosyllables, and the language had thirty-six consonants and five vowels. The vowels, however, each stood for one of what Foigny saw as the five (not four) elements of the world: A fire, E air, G salt, I water, U earth. The slight variation in the vowel letters (G for O) suggested the putative otherness of the Australian conception of the world.

More important, each letter contained some quality of the concrete world and communicated it directly:

> The more we consider that way of writing, the more secrets we shall find in it to admire. B signifies clear, or bright, C hot, X cold, L moist, F dry, S white, N black, T green, D disagreeable, P sweet, Q pleasant, R bitter, M desirable, G evil, Z high, H low, J consonant red, A join'd with 2 peaceable. Thus as soon as they hear or pronounce a word, they apprehend at the same time the nature of the thing signified by it. (Fr. ed. 172; Eng. trans. 117)

The letters therefore taught speakers the world, such that to understand the words was to understand reality and vice-versa. By age twenty, Foigny says, the speakers were all philosophers and could begin to contemplate the stars, that is the cosmos.

Denis de Vairasse (1630–72) (the name sometimes appears as Denis Vairasse d'Allais) was a seventeenth-century French grammarian who published his *Grammaire méthodique* of French in 1681 and, prior to that (1677–9) the account of a fictional English captain named Siden who had supposedly spent many years among the Sevarambes/Sevarambians/Sevarites (the name gets written variously). Vairasse lived for a number of years in England where he almost surely came into contact with projects for a universal language, including Wilkens's most probably, and in fact his fictional account was written first in English and then in a longer form in French, which was subsequently translated into English in 1738 (it is this longer version that will interest us here). Vairasse's *Grammaire* is concerned in part with the orthographical reform of French and to that extent it returns to the questions that obsessed some sixteenth-century grammarians, especially in the way his "methodological alphabet" attempts to attach a single sound to each letter. To achieve his orthographical goals he invented some new letters or modified existing ones in his 1681 grammar (see Cornelius 131, n. 65).

Vairasse's interest in orthography and the relationship between letters and their sounds led him to create a fictional language that had as the fulcrum, on which the natural character language rested, the sound attached to each alphabetical letter. In the sounds, gentle or harsh, of the letters the language sought to reproduce the qualities of the world. In the Sevarites language the "[s]ounds are, as far as is possible, accommodated to the Nature of the things expres'd by them" (1738, 378). Having "studied the Nature of things" (379) they employ soft sounds for gentle or delicate matters and harsh ones for fierce or hard things, unlike "almost all other Nations, who have no regard for these [natural] rules" (379). The natural universal order in the world is thus that of the language as well, and vice-versa: "whenever one finds a harsh Termination, it is always used to express something of a like nature in the thing signified" (379). The difference between Foigny's system and Vairasse's is that "whereas the spelling of the word implied a knowledge of the Nature of the object with Foigny, the Sevarites [according to Vairasse] tried to make the *sounds* of their words conform to the nature of the thing expressed" (Atkinson 132, my emphasis).

It is possible that Vairasse knew something of Mersenne's *Harmonie naturelle* or perhaps the *Linguarum methodus novissima* by the Czech John Amos Comenius (Knowlson 135). Whether Vairasse was familiar with these works or not, however, he continues the notion, dating back to Thomas More, that a superior society is reflected in a superior alphabetical system, and vice-versa. Vairasse concludes his chapter on the Sevarites' language as follows: "we may conclude, that they [the Sevarites] surpass us as much in the Beauty of their Language, as in the Innocence and Politeness of their Manners, and that they are, excepting only the Article of Religion, the happiest People on Earth" (388). The felicity of a language that reproduces the natural order is the cause and also the result of the felicity of the people themselves. The more perfect the society, the more the alphabetical system does not rely on convention but echoes the real world directly.

Paul Cornelius has remarked that the fictional language of this "grammarian philosophe" (philosopher-grammarian) was "a kind of 'logical language'" (140), and in this sense Vairasse anticipated the eighteenth century that would demand of language that it be increasingly logical in order to mirror a world the century saw as ruled by logic. So, while projects for a universal language and alphabet continued into the following century, they took on a slightly different colouring in the eighteenth century.

To readers of the twenty-first century it is evident that the European thinkers of the seventeenth century, despite increasing contacts with foreign cultures, were not fully cognizant of the degree to which their idea of the natural order of the cosmos was infused with their own ideologies and could never really be universal. Their projects were also doomed for other reasons. The great French philosopher René Descartes realized this early on and pointed it out in a letter of 20 November 1629, to Marin Mersenne. For a language to signify the world directly without recourse to convention, he noted, it would not only have to describe the order of the world but it would also have to establish a "true philosophy" that defined the very order of existence, including the concepts and thoughts of all mankind. In other words, the definition of the natural order of all things in the cosmos was a prerequisite to the invention of a language based on such an order. Quite clearly, such a program was utopian and unattainable. There was no way to know the complete universal order from the vastest aspects down to the tiniest detail. As a result, no program of a real character universal language could possibly achieve its goals, although the ultimate futility of the project did not dissuade some of the finest minds of the period from trying all the same.

7

Logical Letters: The Alphabet in the Age of Reason

Tout homme qui possède son alphabet est un écrivain qu'il ne faut pas méconnaitre.

Louis-Ferdinand Céline

Beginning in the sixteenth century, the book trade in Europe and beyond flourished as a result of the printing press that democratized book acquisition. Literacy came to be not just a luxury of the noble classes and the church but part and parcel of a typical bourgeois education, including for women. The seventeenth century is often considered a century in which the paramount literary form was theatre – witness Lope de Vega (1562–1635) and Pedro Calderón de la Barca (1600–81) in Spain, Pierre Corneille (1606–84) and Jean Racine (1639–99) in France, and William Shakespeare (1564–1616) and Christopher Marlowe (1564?–93) in England. But we should remember that successful plays were also published soon after they were performed, and many were written purely to be read in printed form, as in the case of much of Lope de Vega's enormous output. A new genre also came to the fore: the novel. Cervantes' *Don Quixote* (1605) is often considered the first modern novel, though it was in fact preceded by such picaresque novels as *Lazarillo de Tormes* (1554) and *Guzmán de Alfarache* (Part 1, 1599; Part 2, 1604) by Mateo Alemán, as well as the almost unclassifiable (and more revolutionary) works of François Rabelais (*Pantagruel*). *Don Quixote* was certainly an extraordinary bestseller throughout Europe and the New World. By the eighteenth century, the novel genre was a dominant one in many European countries, including England where the seventeenth century had still been heavily under the influence of the epic genre, as evidenced in particular by John Milton's *Paradise Lost* and *Paradise Regained*.

"Letters," in every sense of the word, clearly played an important role in the culture, and by the eighteenth century this role was increasingly secular. The alphabet continued to have moral weight and it was still seen as playing a crucial role as a "civilizing" agent, quite apart from Christian teaching. In the eighteenth century – that is, in the Age of Reason or Enlightenment, as the period is often called – writing came to be seen as emblematic of one's participation in civilized, even elegant society. To write clearly and form one's letters with grace, both in terms of content and penmanship, was key to one's socialization, and it was a major concern of the educational system. One's letters, in all the various meanings of the word "letters," were the badge of one's participation in the cultural values of the "civilized" world, defined as western European. This is also true for the European-ized culture of North America from the eighteenth century onwards, as Patricia Crain has shown. She writes that "[b]y the early nineteenth century [...] alphabetization becomes more than a rite of initiation. It is now the primary means of socialization, the lack of which renders one not just déclassé [...] but subhuman" (103). The final word of Crain's sentence is telling: alphabetization is seen as a defining criterion for being civilized.

Although it may seem paradoxical at first glance, one of the results of the rise of the printing press was a change in handwriting – that is, in people's penmanship. Book printing gradually put the medieval scribe out of business. The medieval *pecia* system in which one could borrow an unbound portion of a book from a bookshop for a fee (rather like the way one checks out a book from a library), copy it by hand, and then return it for the following section, died out. But for personal correspondence, accounts, etc., handwriting was still not only useful but necessary. As a consequence, penmanship took on new importance, and the graceful formation of one's alphabetic letters was a prime concern. Hitherto, the development of letter forms had been guided by a desire for clarity as well as the ease and speed of writing. Preprint "hands," whether Gothic, Carolingian, or Roman, had been developed for practical purposes, taking into account the type of document to be copied (and hence the reading audience), the available supports (type of writing tool, writing surface, etc.), and economic factors (how luxurious the document was to be).

In the eighteenth century, however, handwriting was no longer simply a practical tool for copying books and documents but rather one that was important for expressing one's *maîtrise* of the social grace and elegance needed to succeed in personal and business matters. Clarity of presentation still mattered, but elegance was also a prime consideration: one's writing expressed one's social standing and gave to the reader a visual demonstration of the way a person wished to represent him- or herself. The aesthetics involved in writing a comely script became the proof of one's adherence to a particular echelon of society and a ratification of that society's world view. Order and grace in writing were attributes that were transferred from the letters on paper to the person who had formed the letters. From the sixteenth century onwards educated people wrote their own personal letters, and mastery of the complex web of the epistolary system, from the shape of one's alphabetical letters to the rhetoric that was de rigueur, was a way of declaring one's adherence to a particular world and its values.

The first treatises on penmanship had already appeared by the mid-sixteenth century, and whole books were printed that presented the alphabet in different letter styles. The first was that of Lodovico degli Arrighi (d. ca. 1527) who published his *La operina da imparare de scrivere littera cancellaresca* (*The Manual to Teach the Writing of the Chancery Hand*) in 1522 and then followed it up with a second volume in 1523.[1] More were written during the seventeenth and eighteenth centuries. As Philip Meggs and Alston Purvis comment, such manuals "sounded the death knell for the scriptorium" (105) because it opened up writing to a larger group. To pen well-formed alphabetic letters became a necessary social skill for those who wished to distinguish themselves from the ignorant lower classes, quite apart from any moral qualities or a concern for the transmission of an antiquarian past. Both men and women of the upper classes engaged in handwritten, private correspondences (Gray, *History* 137). The seventeenth century, which reacted against the intellectual free-for-all of the Renaissance and clamped down on many aspects of thought, culture, and languages, became obsessed with notions of linguistic purity, yet when it came to people's handwritten documents, the culture was more concerned with form than with re-form: the baroque mentality regulated content through the organs of the state and the church, but left spellings largely untouched except for the reformers who wished to create, as we have seen, a universal language. Ideology mattered, and penmanship mattered, but the combinations of letters that formed words – that is, orthography – were left largely unregulated. People still spelled words however they thought best.

There was not the same freedom in letter forms, however.

To express oneself smoothly was of key importance, and in hand-written correspondence it was equally important that the writing be visually elegant on the page. Public texts were the province of print, while beautifully penned letters occupied the private or semi-private sphere. By the seventeenth century there were manuals giving models of written texts for educated people to imitate. The grammar school exercises in penmanship that most readers who have been educated in the twentieth century will remember from their childhood have their roots in the manuals of the seventeenth- and eighteenth-century writing masters. German handwriting revived pointed Gothic letters in a style called "Fraktur," shunning the loops and swirls of the Italianate penmanship that took hold in most other parts of western Europe, especially in the Catholic countries of Italy, France, and Spain (Gray, *History* 139–47). Although Roman capitals, with slight variations, were embraced all across Europe, the divergences for lower case letters could be great. Fraktur undoubtedly took on nationalistic and even religious (Protestant) overtones as an expression of identification with things Germanic, even though the letter forms did not extend to all countries that had rejected Catholicism. Certainly the dominant culture in the eighteenth century, namely that of France, favoured not only flowing, rounded letter forms, but also extensive calligraphic flourishes at the end of texts that signified nothing more than elegance, leisure, and luxury. These graceful swirls were, in essence, the rococo style made penmanship.

The Enlightenment thinkers searched for universal laws that governed the universe in a rational manner. This emphasis on reason and rationality was a shift from the views of seventeenth-century scholars who were still seeking God's divine laws behind the phenomena of this world. For the eighteenth century, logic and reason reigned supreme, and these were secular phenomena over which the human mind, not a divine force, ruled. Language was not exempt from this quest for the rational. Grammarians did not so much look to invent a universal language as to discover the universal laws that already subtended all languages, and in the process they collected alphabets and writing systems from around the world.

By the Enlightenment, European society was fully aware of the range and diversity of languages and writing systems across the globe. Scholars were interested in these phenomena for their own sake, not because they were looking to establish when, after Creation, the alphabet was invented or to determine which was the primordial language in which God spoke to man. Indeed, the treatises on the origins of language, whether by Étienne Condillac (1714–80) or Jean-Jacques Rousseau (1712–78), were concerned more with how man first began to communicate than with reconciling linguistic phenomena with biblical history. Did gestures, for example, gradually lead to speech? Were the first utterances literal or metaphorical? (Rousseau supported both views in different works.) The key relations for these thinkers were between individuals and their nascent societies.

The fascination with exotic writing systems allowed for some excesses and even the occasional charlatan. In England, George Psalmanazar (1679–1763) claimed, falsely, to speak "Formosan" fluently, and he invented an alphabet, wrote a book that included material on the supposed language (*An Historical and Geographical Description of Formosa* [London, 1704]), and even "taught" the language to some "gentlemen of Oxford." All was fanciful invention, however, beginning with his name (Psalmanazar was in fact a Frenchman). What is more, the language and its alphabet were as fictitious as the author's identity (fig. 35). In his book Psalmanazar carefully avoided giving a complete grammar of Formosan, covering himself by claiming, "I do not intend to write a Grammar of the Language but only to give some Idea of it" (Knowlson 126) and providing merely a list of words, some general remarks on the supposed morphology of the language, and an alphabet of largely geometric letters that – in somewhat of a giveaway as to their invention – corresponded to European ones in a one-to-one manner. Psalmanazar's letter forms reveal, yet again, the attitude, going back at least to Thomas More's *Utopia*, not only that a rational, highly evolved society should have an alphabet that parallels the Roman one, but that the letters should be composed of simple geometric forms.

That Psalmanazar could hoodwink many nobles in England is testament to the contemporary appetite for exotic languages and scripts. People wanted to understand how other cultures might have conceived the world through their own written letters, and in this case the duped Englishmen were convinced that they were getting a glimpse of a different world view by means of what they thought was a unique language that bore resemblance only to Japanese, or so Psalmanazar claimed.

Serious attempts were also still made to formulate a universal language. The nascent symbolic logic theorized by Leibniz in the seventeenth century was very palatable to the Enlightenment taste for the logical. The idea was that concepts represented by letters could be

combined in ways similar to how numbers and symbols were combined in mathematics, making for communication that was transparent
to the people who learned the system and that was clear and logical in
its assertions. At the end of the eighteenth century, Joseph de Maimieux's (1753–1820) *Pasigraphie* (1797), designed to replace alphabetical
letters with new signifiers, would be published in both French and German. It received a warm welcome, was presented to Napoleon, and was
even taught in some institutions of higher learning (Knowlson 155).
Indicative of the period's predilection for orderly classification and
logical construction, the *Pasigraphie* proposed to order the world by
moving "from genre to species and from species to the individual"[2] for
which it then gave long taxonomic lists – what it called the *Petit nomenclateur* and the *Grand nomenclateur*. A series of strange visual symbols
were then used to modify words. In the end, the whole system proved
ungainly, since it would take years to master the long taxonomical lists.

But the underlying notion of ordering an alphabet in such way that
it would allow for a logical ordering of the world remained current. To
the extent that Enlightenment scholars were interested in a universal
language, however, their goal was often not an invented "real character" language such as that proposed by John Wilkins and others in the
seventeenth century. Wilkins and others, we should remember, wished
to create an alphabet that would mirror the structure of all of creation.
Theirs was a philosophical endeavour: to determine the taxonomies of
reality and then create an alphabet that would mime those categories.
Their interest was thus not in what humans would naturally speak but
rather in creating an artificial language that all peoples could learn. By
contrast, eighteenth-century thinkers tilted towards what we might call
nascent anthropological or ethnographic approaches, and they were
more interested, like Heroditus's Egyptian king Psammeticos so many
centuries before, in what humans "naturally" expressed. Rather than
classifying the philosophical order of reality, they sought to classify the
worlds' languages and investigate whence language arose. It is no surprise that the beginnings of comparative linguistics and comparative
literature are to be found in the Enlightenment era. And both Condillac and Rousseau constructed theories regarding how language first
arose – theories that took no account of biblical accounts. The scholars and speculators of the period were keen to discover the universal
characteristics that underpinned all of the world's languages and then
to create an alphabet that would systematize the graphic representation of that *Ur-sprache*. If the seventeenth century wanted to construct a

universal language, the eighteenth century wanted to discover a natural, universal language.

Two elements must be underscored here. First is the adoption of an international horizon. The desire was to determine the language that expressed universal mankind or that, at some level, all of humanity expressed. Second was a strong Rousseau-ian aspect in the desire to discover what was the most natural state of an originary language and then represent that speech in a new, universal alphabet. The alphabetical projects thus partook of the larger cultural discussions regarding the true nature of man and the role society had played in modifying that nature – discussions that influenced much thinking of the period, from the "self-evident" truths regarding all mankind in the first sentence of the American Declaration of Independence to the many copies of Rousseau's *Social Contract* that people were reading clandestinely under the Ancien Régime. The phenomenon of the so-called "wild child" in the eighteenth century – that is, children who had been raised by animals or otherwise deprived of human contact – also aroused great interest, giving rise to the hope of learning what first utterances would issue forth from a human being who had not been exposed to any particular language. Was this a way of rediscovering man's natural language?

But there were problems inherent in many of these materials. It will come as no surprise that there was a persistent strain of Eurocentrism in virtually every study designed to elicit the underlying "natural" language of humankind. Despite a long-standing fascination with Asian character writing and Egyptian hieroglyphics, most European writers seeking to find the hidden structure of the world's languages took their examples from their own language plus a few neighbouring European ones and sometimes Latin. In a similar manner, the evidence of "wild" children was tainted, since in most such cases, the individuals had had some contact, however limited, with human civilization or a particular language.

Nevertheless, as an endeavour, the investigations and proposals tell us much about the relationship the various authors saw between their world and their alphabet. One major contributor was Charles de Brosses (1709–77), the author of a *Traité de la formation mécanique des langues* (*Treatise on the Mechanical Formation of Languages*), published in 1765. In many respects De Brosses is emblematic of the period. De Brosses proposed a comparison of all known natural languages in order to boil them down to "une langue primitive organique, physique et nécessaire, commune à tout le genre humain, qu'aucun peuple ne connoît ni ne pratique dans sa premiere simplicité; que tous les homes parlent néanmoins, & qui fait le premier fond du langage de tous les pays" (De Brosses xv–xvi: a primitive, organic, physical and necessary language common to the whole human race, which no people knows or practises in its original simplicity; which all men speak nevertheless and which forms the primary basis of language in all countries.)

It is easy to dismiss De Brosses's "findings," based as they are almost entirely on French. Reviving and expanding the argument set forth by Cratylus in Plato's dialogue, De Brosses decided that certain consonants (universally) mirrored certain features of the world. Like Socrates in Plato's dialogue, De Brosses found that "r" stood for movement, though also for things that were harsh (as in *rude*, *roc* [rock], *racler* [to scrape]). "L," "n," and some combinations that contained them ("ln," "gl") were, by contrast, "liquid" and stood for fluids, whereas "t" or "st" connoted fixity, firmness, and immobility. And so forth.

There is no need to give De Brosses's entire list of correspondences (Genette [*Mimologiques*] gives more of them). What is of interest here is that in De Brosses there is a direct relationship between consonants – and consonants above all – and the extra-linguistic world. Not that De Brosses maintains à la Cratylus that these letters or letter clusters actually contain a kernel of the extra-linguistic world in them. That is to say, for De Brosses letters are not *stoicheia* (elements) as such. Rather they mirror or mime the world and provide a linguistic gloss that follows the contours of reality. However, De Brosses insists that language "n'est donc pas arbitraire & conventionel, comme on a coutume de se le figurer; mais un vrai systême de nécessité" (De Brosses xiii–xiv: is thus not arbitrary and conventional, as people have the habit of imagining, but a true system of necessity, my trans.). If De Brosses concentrates on consonants, it is because he views all vowels as basically the same – simply the passage of air and thus not really articulations. For De Brosses, "a" ["ah"] is the base vowel, and other vowel sounds are due to the obstructions produced by the consonants, which change the shape of the articulating organs and thus affect the vowel sounds.

Alphabetic writing, or at least the meaningful quality of alphabetic letters, thus comes down to the consonants. For De Brosses, part of the proof of this is the fact that Semitic languages are written entirely in consonants. Furthermore, it also follows for him that minimal pairs that differ only in terms of vowels are, in fact, related. This idea also goes back to Plato who argued in *Cratylus* for an "etymological" relationship between "sema" and "soma" on much the same basis.

De Brosses approaches the question of the alphabet by means of the physiology of human language articulation. It is of course entirely in keeping with his age that meditations on the alphabet should take a (pseudo)scientific turn. Since letters stand for sounds, De Brosses considers first the sounds of each letter as they are formed by the speech organs, in particular the consonants, for reasons we have already seen. Claiming that "[l]'organe prend, autant qu'il peut, la figure qu'a l'objet même qu'il veut dépeindre avec la voix" (De Brosses 9: the [vocal] organ takes on, to the extent that it can, the shape [*figure*] of the very object it wishes to depict with the voice), it creates sounds that "signify ideas representing real objects" (signifient des idées représentatives des objets réels, De Brosses 10). De Brosses sees, in other words, a twofold correspondence: between sounds and the things they represent and between the articulatory organs and the objects for which they utter sounds. This theory, centred in the body, is, despite a partial affinity with Plato's *Cratylus*, decidedly un-Platonic in its refusal to transcend the physical in favour of some divine concept. Rather, De Brosses proposes to attach letter forms to that very physicality. The alphabet he creates is designed to represent through its marks the physiological articulation of each sound. He begins with five basic shapes that identify – indeed, that represent iconically – the sites of consonantal articulation: the lips, throat, teeth, palate, tongue, and nose. The letter shapes for each of these recall the physiology of the organ in question: the throat becomes a circle, the lip a wavy line, the tooth a kind of crenelation, the tongue a line that curves up at the tip, and finally the nose a line giving the nasal profile (see fig. 36). De Brosses then adds a series of secondary signs that nuance the nature of the articulation: voiced, unvoiced, fricative, affricative, etc.

As with so many other proposed alphabets, De Brosse's letter forms bear no relationship to the traditional letters of any known script. Their universality – they are designed, after all, to express any and all utterances – is inversely proportional to the ease with which they might be adopted. Because this new alphabet is designed to express any and all languages, since it is a map of sounds only, it in no way represents grammar or morphology (Drucker, *Alphabetic* 213). The script would express all the languages of the world and, what is more, according to De Brosses, both the letters and the vocal organs would also mime the character of the things in this world. One could not wish for a more complete universality that, at least in theory, would hold for all human speech (though we must remember that the basis for the relationship between sounds and objects was largely due to French). What we have, in essence, is an eighteenth-century scholar's dream of mapping the alphabet onto universal humanity, entirely free from theology and social history. The result, of course, is in fact an alphabet deeply marked by the historicity of its time, its creator, and the creator's intellectual orientations.

De Brosses' theories constitute a new way of mapping the alphabet onto the body and creating a new alphabet that is designed to express universal humanity. This project is very different from the humanist proposals of Geoffroy Tory who created letters of the traditional alphabet that expressed the human body. De Brosses creates a script – one is hard pressed actually to call it an alphabet – or rather he creates two scripts: one for vowels in which a straight vertical line is crossed by a short dash, depending on "the length to which the vocal cord or windpipe is drawn" and another for consonants which combines the six schematized representations of the place of articulation discussed above with an array of dots or wavy lines that indicate specifics of the physiology of articulation. The result is a representation of spoken sounds partly made up of representational signs (the six consonantal "letters") and partly of arbitrary signs (the dots and wavy lines that stand for, but do not mime, the physiology of articulation). Despite all of its problems, De Brosses's system is laudable for how it addressed an international horizon and sought (or at least claimed) to represent all of humankind in a new script.

To use French as a basis for an international language (or script) made a certain sense to many Europeans of the Enlightenment period. By the eighteenth century, France had succeeded in its goal of making the French language pre-eminent in Europe. This was due to a number of factors. In England, the French language got a boost from the many Huguenots who fled there. Perhaps more important, France was the richest, the most populous, and the most powerful country in Europe, especially militarily, and under Louis XIV (1638–1715), the "Sun King" who built Versailles, it was also the most prestigious in terms of cultural productions. French became *the* language of diplomacy and culture, for which reason it is still, alongside English, a language of treaties and international relations. Already in the eighteenth century, French was used as the language of treaties, even when neither of the countries involved was French speaking (Knowlson 140; Brunot 5:135–45; 423–31). Modifying somewhat the Nebrija-Tory argument from around 1500, we might say that the French language had achieved supremacy without recourse to arms, as one Frenchman pointed out: "La langue française s'est emparée, non par la violence des armes, ni par autorité, comme celle des Romains, mais par sa politesse et ses charmes, de presque toutes les cours de l'Europe" (Brunot 5:138: The French language has taken over in almost all the courts of Europe, not by means of the violence of arms nor by means of authority, as the Romans did, but because of its politeness and its charms.).

In the eighteenth century, the French language was seen as the most rational, even the most "logical," of all the European languages, and for that reason it was deemed that it should become the universal one. The Academy of Berlin had French as its official language from the date of its founding in 1700. In 1782 it held an international essay contest for which the topic took for granted the supremacy of the French language. The question posed was, "What has made the French language universal?" The winner was one Antoine de Rivarol (1753–1801) whose essay, "Discourse on the Universality of the French Language," was published in 1784. In it, Rivarol famously remarked that "what is not clear is not French" (ce qui n'est pas clair n'est pas français) and he argued that the usual word order of subject-verb-object (so unlike German which often put the verb at the end) conformed to universal laws and "the natural logic of all men."

To write clearly in French – that is, to express oneself well in this language of man's "natural logic" and to form one's letters with grace and clarity – therefore became throughout Europe the mark of the civilized honnête homme. One crucial articulation of this participation in the civilized order was the writing, already mentioned, of epistolary letters. The seventeenth century, and even more particularly the eighteenth, raised letter writing to the level of an art, particularly in France, and elegant epistolary letters at times bridged the personal-public divide. Madame de Sevigné, Countess of Grignon, whose life straddled both centuries (1646–1705), is one of the most famous writers of the period even though she published no novels or books of poetry; her entire oeuvre consists of more than 1000 long letters that she wrote to her distant daughter after the latter's marriage. To this day the letters are studied in school throughout France as models of French prose. Similarly, what is perhaps the greatest novel of the eighteenth century in France, and certainly one of the most audacious, is Les Liaisons dangereuses (Dangerous Liaisons), published by Pierre Choderlos de Laclos (1741–1803) in 1782, and which consists entirely of letters passed back and forth between the principal characters.

The writing of clear, well-formed alphabetic letters, like the writing of graceful epistles, was, as I have already remarked, taken as a sign of one's socialization. The Christianization of the alphabet was less important than the deployment in society of good penmanship and good prosody as proof of one's full participation in what was seen as the most civilized culture on earth. When Denis Diderot (1713–84) and Jean le Rond d'Alembert (1717–83) published the vast *Encyclopédie* between 1751 and 1772, that huge compendium of secular knowledge that sought to resume all practical knowledge in the European culture of the period, they included among its many items entries on the proper way to write and to form alphabetical letters. How one approached the act of alphabetic writing was crucial, from knowing what tools were needed to maintaining the required posture at the writing table. There were separate entries for males and females, illustrated in both cases by engravings that modelled the proper position for writing as well as the necessary tools one needed to have at one's disposal (fig. 37 A and B). Even the non-epistolary elements in the engraved scenes reinforce the association of writing with a certain world-view. The writers are elegantly dressed in the latest fashions and the room is spacious and orderly – of the sort one found in the finest Parisian "hôtels" (mansions) of the period. How different from medieval and sixteenth-century images of writers, often religious monks, scribbling away in their dark, narrow cells. The *Encyclopédie* also included other articles, with engraved illustrations, detailing how to make ink, how to sharpen a quill, etc., as well as many pages of the extant alphabets of the world in the first volume of *planches*.

Clarity and rectitude, with all of their attendant moral values, were now the watchwords of alphabetical writing, whether the letters were formed by hand with a pen or printed by a professional printer. The grace of an individual (or the lack thereof) was seen as reflected in the order and beauty of that person's penmanship. As for the printed word, if one takes a book printed in the late eighteenth century and glances at the title page, the most stunning feature is that there is absolutely nothing unusual about it. That is to say, the page largely has the look of a book that could have been printed at the end of the twentieth century. The eighteenth century sees the disappearance of the sort of title pages so common in the seventeenth century in which scenes are etched in perspective on title pages, coats of arms are engraved, and book titles constitute whole paragraphs.

The sobriety of eighteenth-century printing styles reflects a new approach to the alphabetic letter, the result of a process that had been prepared for by the gradual evolution of the printed letter since the late fifteenth century. The incunabula of the fifteenth century imitated the look of medieval manuscripts in their letter forms and layouts, for which the Gutenberg Bible (1454–5) and the Nuremburg Chronicles (1493) are among the most celebrated examples. With the sixteenth century we can speak of the development of typography as such, and Renaissance printers, as we have seen, cut new letter forms that corresponded to the humanist view of the world, prying the letter loose from Christian associations and Gothic scripts. Still, as in the letters proposed by Geoffroy Tory, they were "motivated" – that is, the letters were seen as having a metaphysical dimension beyond their role as signifiers in the construction of meaningful words.

Such attitudes would disappear in the eighteenth century.

The watershed events are the publication of the Englishman John Baskerville's (1706–75) edition of Virgil's *Aeneid* in 1757 (fig. 38) and the Frenchman Firmin Didot's (1764–1836) edition of the same that appeared in 1798. Baskerville's edition of Virgil inaugurates a sober, elegant style that would be picked up by continental printers such as Didot after him. Baskerville, who had been a penmanship master, was meticulous in his approach to printing: he created new serif letter types that graced an uncluttered page, and he also developed his own process for making paper and his own inks. The result is a printed page whose beauty has perhaps never been surpassed. For his part, Didot was the son of a well-known printer in Paris and he belonged to a genealogy of printers that would continue with Firmin's son and grandson. Like Baskerville, Didot was part of a wave of typographers in the second half of the century looking to modernize alphabetical letter styles. His letters and his *mise en page* were quite similar to Baskerville's, though he did not use paper and ink that was as elegant as Baskerville did. Yet still more austere were the typefaces of the Italian Giambattista Bodoni (1740–1813), Didot's Italian contemporary and rival. Significant technological advances were brought about by Baskerville's experimentation with ink, his meticulousness regarding his metal type, and his development of "hot-pressed" paper (Meggs and Purvis 128–9), though subsequent printers found it too expensive to imitate Baskerville in all his particulars.

Baskerville's and Didot's editions of the *Aeneid* are thus justly famous for being the first examples of "modern" typography and printing. The plain white paper with sober script centred in capital letters sets the standard for how books are to be printed in subsequent centuries. In his edition of Virgil, Didot created his typeface specifically for the *Aeneid* although he then used it for many subsequent books. The Didot letters are significant for how they make use of the contrast between very slender vertical lines and thicker curves, and to this day they are considered a highly readable font.

The Baskerville and Didot *Aeneid*s thus owe their fame to the departure from earlier letter styles, and they set the tone for publishing down to our day. Indeed, in Didot's concern for readability the edition represents a new approach to the alphabetic letter and the whole readerly process. The letter is treated as a neutral sign that, as Laura Kendricks has put it, we are encouraged simply to "read through" for the content of the text. In other words, the letter's existence as letter is minimized, all but wished away. The letter is not motivated, and it is seen neither as containing some kernel of the real world nor as participating in some metaphysical "beyond." If earlier periods called attention in different ways to the "letter-ness" of the letter such that the presence of the letter itself was foregrounded, the late eighteenth century reverses matters. The reader is encouraged to treat the alphabetic letter as simply a means of accessing the "content" of a text, and an effort is made to make the letter as unobtrusive as possible. Obviously, a reader cannot retrieve the content without passing by way of the letters, but the desire is for the letters to act as a window through which the content simply flows, providing the illusion that the reader is in direct contact with the content. As Johanna Drucker, who calls such letters "unmarked" (as opposed to "marked" letter forms that call attention to themselves), puts it, such a text presents

> words on the page [which] "appear to speak themselves" without the visible intervention of author or printer. Such a text appears to possess an authority which transcends the mere material presence of words on a page [... It] wants no visual interference or manipulation to disturb the linguistic enunciation of the verbal matter [...] The aspirations [...] are to make the text as uniform, as neutral, as accessible and seamless as possible. (Drucker, *Visible* 93)[3]

The letter's importance as a sign is downplayed, even though it clearly continues to function as a signifier with a signified; but there is no moral quality attached to the letter forms here, and no analogy between the alphabetical signs in a text and the nature of our world as containing similar signs that we can "read" like so many letters.

The Didot Virgil is thus the very antithesis of a text such as the Book of Kells with its spectacular Chi Rho page. Instead, we are pushed to forget that we are reading signs and are encouraged to delve into the illusion that we are absolutely present to the content of the work. The alphabetic letter will henceforth be as unobtrusive as possible except as needed to startle the reader and attract the reader's attention, as will be the case, for example, with advertising in the nineteenth and twentieth centuries.

This new treatment of the alphabetical letter quickly becomes the dominant mode for printed texts from the eighteenth through the twentieth centuries, and from all evidence it looks to continue on through the twenty-first. Some scholars, such as Kendricks, have reacted to how modern editors of earlier works, and in particular those of the Middle Ages, have altered the texts by printing them in the manner of modern works with clear, standardized blocks of black Baskerville/Didot-like letters on white paper, thus removing any qualities that point to the tangible quality of the letters. Kendricks is undoubtedly correct that many modern editions lose a great deal of the meaning of earlier manuscript texts by metamorphosing the insistent medieval letters that proclaimed themselves as such into neutral, passive signs through which the "content" is to pass untrammeled. One can also speculate on the aptness (and even the influence) of the modern printed letter for post-eighteenth-century literary developments, in particular the rise of realism in literature in the mid-nineteenth century. A literature whose rhetoric encouraged the reader to forget that s/he was reading a book filled with alphabetic letters and to simply receive the narrative as though it were reality was aided by the advent of printed letters that one hardly realized were there; the omniscient third-person narrator of the traditional novel could thus appear to be speaking directly to the reader.

The eighteenth century can thus be seen as a movement that secularized the alphabet to a great extent. One's relationship to alphabetic letters reflected one's social position and image, but the letters did not in and of themselves continue to have moral (or Christian) values. How one approached letters had moral value to be sure: a proper person wrote proper letters. But the letters were not metaphorized: "t" was no longer singled out as standing for the cross or the "treason" in the betrayal of Christ. Nor were letters seen in terms of human forms or as the carriers of the liberal arts, the nine muses, and Apollo, which of course was the case for Geoffroy Tory. The grace of calligraphy was a social grace, not a theological one. And the printed word was simply a vehicle through which the content of a text was to pass untouched.

By the end of the eighteenth century, the industrial revolution had already taken hold in England. It was to have an enormous effect on European society, and not surprisingly industrialism would have an equally great effect on how the alphabetic letter was treated. Mass production would lead to new modes for the dissemination of the alphabet as well as to reactions to – even the rejection of – the changes industrialism brought to the letter.

8

The Alphabets of the Industrialized World

L'alphabet magique, l'hiéroglyphe mystérieux ne nous arrivent qu'incomplets et faussés ... retrouvons la lettre perdue ou le signe effacé, recomposons la gamme dissonante et nous prendrons force dans le monde des esprits.

Gérard de Nerval

In France the Ancien Régime was swept away by the Revolution of 1789, or so manuals of history would have it. For better or worse, the French Revolution provides a convenient, symbolic marker of a shift in French culture and one that had repercussions for European culture more generally. The turn of centuries from eighteenth to nineteenth can, at the risk of oversimplification, be seen as a shift from a society dominated by aristocrats whose power was based in land, titles, and traditions to one ruled by an urban bourgeoisie whose power derived from industrialism and money. The alphabetic letter not only participated in these changes, it was also uniquely expressive of this new approach to society and the world. The letter was, not surprisingly, at the centre of educational reforms, as the system of ad hoc tutors and church-run schools that had prevailed in many parts of Europe gradually gave way to programs of national education. Germany was one of the most precocious of the national entities, setting up free and compulsory education in the eighteenth century. In France, a system of nationalized lay education was instituted in the 1830s, but only in the 1880s was public school also made free and obligatory for all French children. The timeline in England and Scotland was similar to France's, although Scotland had had a national network of religious schools in operation since 1561; both, however, moved towards state-sponsored schools around the 1830s and then towards compulsory attendance and an abolishment of fees in the 1880s or 1890s. Italy and Spain lagged behind, due to a lack of national unity in the former and both political upheavals and the overweening power of the Catholic Church in the latter. But with the coming national unification of Italy in 1861, a system of public education was instituted in 1859. In Spain, political turmoil greatly slowed developments. Less urbanized and less industrialized than its neighbours, Spain was also dominated to a much greater extent by the Catholic Church. With the Revolution of 1868, attempts were made to wrest the educational system from the claws of the church, but this was reversed by the Restoration of the monarchy in 1874. It was not until 1931 that the newly elected government of the Second Republic made education free and compulsory. Even so, national education came to be dominated by the Catholic Church after the triumph of the Fascist forces under Generalísimo Franco at the end of the Spanish Civil War (1936–9).

The sort of letters Didot had designed for his edition of Virgil, or that John Baskerville had introduced in England and Bottoni in Italy, were going to be put to great use in the nineteenth century. But the vast majority of nineteenth-century readers were not going to be reading Latin texts. The democratization of education led to a democratization of reading, and the genre that would reach an enormous reading public was the novel. Novelistic production may be best summed up in *La Comédie humaine* (*The Human Comedy*), that massive collection of novels and short stories by Honoré de Balzac (1799–1850) in which he tried to give a detailed portrait in literature of contemporary France in its many regions and social spheres. These books were read by the burgeoning middle class, including female readers who now made up an important sector of the reading public (one of the prosecutor's charges against Gustave Flaubert's *Madame Bovary* in 1857 was that "the light pages of *Madame Bovary* will fall into even lighter hands – into the hands of young women, sometimes of married women" [LaCapra 728]). Women now constituted a major portion of the reading public, and thus of the marketplace for literature. Balzac, in particular, was a writer with a huge following among female readers, and he, like Henry James (1843–1916) in America, was seen as uniquely gifted among writers in expressing women's sentiments.

Balzac's mode of production was influenced by the printing press. Whereas in the seventeenth or eighteenth century, writers would read drafts of their works in aristocratic settings in which their friends and rivals would offer comments and criticisms, Balzac now had his draft printed as printer's proofs, which he then revised and corrected, often rewriting whole paragraphs and pages. He would sometimes go through five or six sets of galley proofs before finalizing the text for public consumption. At each stage, the matter of seeing the text neatly ordered in clear type allowed for a new, individual reception to which only Balzac and the content were present, the seamlessness of the communication between the two nuanced only by the unobtrusive printer's typeface. It was as though Balzac could not fully "hear" the narrative he wrote until it was cast in self-effacing Didot-like type.

The nineteenth century, then, is characterized by an approach to the alphabetic letter that, on the one hand, empties it of any metaphysical dimension, treating it in an entirely utilitarian manner. In fact, the full picture is more complex. First of all, the nineteenth century also turns out to be a period in which alphabetic letters often *do* call attention to themselves, and often in the most insistent ways. But the letters are unmotivated and do not suggest anything beyond their value as signifiers, even when their shapes are unusual or they are deployed in innovative ways. It is not as though the alphabet is devoid of ideology, however. One playful (or seemingly playful) example can illustrate this: a poem much circulated in the nineteenth century and which continues to appear in twentieth-century ruminations on alphabetic play.[1] The anonymous poem exists in a number of variations, and it was often published and republished in newspapers, not just in France but in other countries as well. It begins as follows:[2]

Le jour où l'on nous mari	A
Je m'en souviens, monsieur l'a	B
Nous dit d'un air fort compa	C
Enfants, il faudra vous ai	D
Madame, vous obéir	E
A votre époux, à votre ch	F....

(The day they married us [maria]
I remember that the abbot [l'abbé]
Told us in a stuffy tone [compassé]
Children, I need to help you [aider]
Madame, you will obey [obéirez]
Your husband, your boss [chef] ...)

And so it goes through the alphabet, enumerating the place and the duties of a good wife. The alphabet and alphabetic "play" are used to inculcate the ideology of marriage and gender relations according to nineteenth-century thinking, and it is precisely the seemingly ludic quality that makes for international diffusion of this "innocent" poem.

The nineteenth century knows a bifurcation in the treatment of the alphabet, one which is quite different from the unmotivated norm. The second stream treats letters as mystical and motivated, though not necessarily as the result of a social consensus or shared ideology. As we shall see, this second "branch" associates mystical readings of the alphabet (readings that veer towards solipsism) with the most scientific approaches of the age.

The urban world of the nineteenth century is a world of letters. Newspapers, which go back to the seventeenth century for their origins, are cheap and they are everywhere. Ubiquitous as well are the advertisements that cover the billboards and buildings of the cities in Europe and North America. Mass advertising, as we know it today, is born in the nineteenth century. But if the advertising in our current world is heavily based on the visual image, whether shocking, poignant, romantic, etc., in the nineteenth century it was based much more on the lettered texts. The challenge for both newspapers and billboards was to grab the attention of viewers and readers in a world of competing rivals. As a result, printers in both realms resorted to the use of many decorative typefaces, mixing them on a single page or ad in an effort to provide visual stimulation and hold a viewer's attention, if only momentarily. As Philip Meggs and Alston Purvis have put it, "It was no longer enough for the twenty-six letters to function only as phonetic symbols" (145). And they continue: "It seems that English typefounders were trying to invent every possible design permutation by modifying forms or proportions and applying all manner of decoration to their alphabets" (149), including extremes of shading, perspective, white letters on black background ("reversing"), etc. As the Victorian age took shape, sentimental views of childhood led to the growth of children's ABC books.[3] "Ornate elaboration" and "fanciful distortion" characterized much Victorian typography.

The overriding concern was thus for letter types to stand out, to be noticed. Not that this means that they were designed to be beautiful. Just as modern advertisements do not need to be pleasant but only memorable – one need only think of some of the irritating advertisements for household products – so, too, nineteenth-century ads and posters and billboards participated in an aesthetics that was designed simply to arrest attention, however briefly. If the letters could stand out or surprise, they accomplished their purpose. New typographical forms, as a result, were designed as an aid to a capitalist, market economy, and slowly but surely cityscapes became textual wonderlands. If previous centuries had seen the world as a text to be read in theological terms, nineteenth-century urban centres were now turned, quite literally, into worldly texts, though entirely of a secular nature and devoid of any metaphysical qualities.

The nineteenth century also moved in the direction of the science of the letter. Scientific methods were trained on a number of the aspects of writing that the preceding centuries had already begun to investigate. The understanding of Egyptian hieroglyphics, for example, which had obsessed thinkers since the early Renaissance, was revolutionized by the discovery and decipherment of the Rosetta Stone. Discovered during the Napoleonic invasion of Egypt in 1799, the Rosetta Stone (now in the British Museum) dates from the second century BCE and gives the same text three times, once in Egyptian hieroglyphics, once in ancient Greek letters, and once in demotic Greek script. The stone provided scholars with the possibility of cracking the "code" of the ancient hieroglyphics, and when Jean-François Champollion (1790–1832) succeeded in doing so in 1820, this news was received as a major intellectual breakthrough. One of the major findings, however, was that Egyptian hieroglyphics were not a "real character language" in which the glyphs represented concrete objects in the world, as had always been supposed, but were, in fact, phonetic signifiers. Long-held beliefs that viewed the hieroglyphics as mystical and mysterious signs had to be abandoned. Strange though they might look, the hieroglyphics were closer to a proto-alphabetic script than to some mysterious encryption.

What was a loss for cabbalistic, alchemical, and other fantastical approaches to letters was a gain for rational science. The investigation of languages and writing could now be carried out from a secular, scientific standpoint. Theories of the origin of the languages no longer had to kowtow to the Bible. Hebrew did not have to be the oldest language just because God might have spoken it in Genesis; Egyptian did not have to derive somehow from Hebrew; and an account of language development did not have to maintain that there was a single world language that was spoken by Adam and Eve and everyone else up until the Babelian scattering in Genesis 11. Already in the eighteenth century,

De Brosses rejected the idea of Hebrew as the original language, arguing that there was no hard evidence for such a theory. In the nineteenth century, the issue will be debated less and less.

This new outlook did not mean that attempts to find a universal language or at least a universal script disappeared. Rather, they took on a scientific (or, at times, pseudo-scientific) cast, and one that is more familiar to us today. Wilkins and his lot had attempted to invent a universal script in the seventeenth century, but their writing had to represent what they believed to be the theological and philosophical structure of the universe. The nineteenth century, building on eighteenth-century secularism, felt free to abandon that approach. Indeed, nineteenth-century scholars created the new, more scientific discipline of "philology" and through linguistic comparison they attempted to climb back up the genealogy of many known languages. Comparative linguistics led to many advances, more of them, certainly, than can be mentioned here. In short, the new discipline of philology changed the nature of the search for origins as well as for a language or notational system that would be international. The extrapolation of the entwined relations among different languages or even different language groups could proceed on the basis of scientific observation, and a resolution of linguistic diversity did not have to consider the nature of reality or what the Bible claimed. While some nineteenth-century attempts at philological reconstruction may seem somewhat naive to modern observers (and they were occasionally tainted by nationalistic prejudices), the nineteenth-century proposals to create an alphabetic notational system that could be used for all languages were the precursors to our current International Phonetic Alphabet. Superficial and even fanciful similarities between languages and letters were pressed into service to further narrow nationalistic agendas. Nevertheless, a growing interest in linguistic history began to sketch not only the common derivation of the Romance or Germanic languages, but the ways in which both groups, along with Slavic and Sanskrit tongues, went back to an originary Indo-European language.

The shift to science made the alphabet into a new kind of lens for viewing the world. The alphabet no longer referred to concrete reality nor was it seen as motivated morally. Alphabets, and writing more generally, could provide a kind of web or ladder which researchers could climb back up towards the past, linking linguistic features and reconstructing Ur-words, lost to us, that had existed thousands of years before. Moreover, these reconstructed terms could be written alphabetically with nothing more than an asterisk before them to indicate that they were nowhere attested in historical documents.

Without specifying the past tradition of viewing letters as representing sounds not things (as, for example, in the sixth-century CE *Etymologies* of Isidore of Seville), some nineteenth-century scholars sought to use or invent an alphabet that would be entirely indexical of human sounds. Phonetics was coming into its own as a field of study, in part to understand the physiology of articulation and in part to improve the teaching of languages, English in particular. In the new industrial world, the ability to take down dictation at high speed led to the development of various methods of shorthand that would replace letters with marks designed to abbreviate words through the notation of key sounds, often consonants or letter clusters. Sir Isaac Pitman (1813–97) is perhaps best known for his system of shorthand that went through several incarnations, though his and others' methods were influenced by, and owed a debt to, John Wilkins's efforts in the seventeenth century. Closely associated with shorthand were proposals that retained the alphabetic letters, sometimes with slight modifications or the accretion of diacritics, in order to reform the orthography – again, particularly of English – or to permit the accurate transcription of the sounds of other languages. To the extent that authors proposed reforming everyday orthography, they, like reformers in earlier centuries, almost universally failed.

Still, phonetics and phonology became of increasing interest. What is somewhat astonishing, however, is the way in which modern science harnessed the alphabet in order to express these new "scientific" approaches to language while at the same time the alphabet was called upon to express fantastical or even solipsistic theories of a universal language – and often enough both in the same treatise. In other words, the nineteenth-century phonological and philological approaches became wed to the desire, inherited from the seventeenth and eighteenth centuries, for a universal language.

So, for example, the phoneticist Charles Kraitsir's (1804–60) *The Significance of the Alphabet* (Boston, 1846) combines cogent phonetic analysis with a personal theory about the traces of a real character language in English and the relationship between English and a universal language. Declaring that "natural language, which lies at the basis of all languages [...] is the object of philology, the foundation of which is a knowledge of the elementary sounds," Kraitsir seeks to cover the full inventory of these sounds "which are expressed to the eye in the writing of different nations" (9). First, however, Kraitsir sets aside vowels

because, he says (like De Brosses), they are created simply by air passing through the vocal chords. After all, he argues, the wind passing
through the trees is capable of producing the sounds of the vowels.
Consonants, on the other hand, are the products of deliberate articulation that modify or even cut off the vowel sounds. Consonants, for
Kraitsir, therefore express the human: "An inarticulate sound is not
worthy to signify a human thought; for thought is produced by the
exertion of the brain, and must consequently be followed by an exertion of the organs of speech" (14).

Here is where Kraitsir's personal mythology takes over. Like Hermogenes (and even Socrates) in Plato's *Cratylus*, Kraitsir finds that a trace
of the world carries over into the consonants because of the sounds
they represent. All consonants, he argues, are made up of "gutturals,"
"palatals," and "labials." The gutturals (g/h/hard c/k/) name, first
of all, the *guttur* in various languages (*gosier, collum, gorge, kehle, gula*,
etc.) and what resembles it physically, hence *height* (also depth), *hiding*,
covering. But the gutturals are also "symbolical of the *internal, essential,
central, causal* [...] *connecting* [...] the *cutting into anything*" etc. (15). The
liquids (*l/m/n/r*) all "express movement" (15). "M expresses meeting"
through such words as "*middle, means, measure, amity*," etc. (14) while
"L expresses soft and secondary movement" (150) as well as *linear* and
lengthened. As for the labials, they name the lips in many languages
"and express all that the lips signify" (15) as well as "the *fleeting phenomena of life*: and metaphorically, *love, life, liberty*" (15).

What began as philology and phonetics has bridged in Kraitsir to the
age-old view that a trace of the world is somehow present in the alphabetic letters and their pronunciations in an elemental way. The physiology involved in the articulation of the consonants becomes a pathway
into the depths of human consciousness. The book concludes with a
theologizing of articulated, "organic" sounds: "In short, a treatment of
languages with reference to organic sounds, sharpens the senses, and
reveals the original poetry of the unworn human mind [...] For the languages of men are the images of man, as man is the image of God" (33).
As if this is not enough, Kraitsir then closes with the "ancient verdict"
from the beginning of the biblical Book of John, set in italics, slightly
modified and truncated, and with an exclamation mark at the end:

*In the beginning was the word, and the word was with God, and the word was
God; without which nothing was made that is made, and in which is the Life that
is the Light of men!* (33)

Alexander John Ellis's (1814–90) *The Alphabet of Nature* (London, 1845) is also a serious treatise on phonetics and one that well represents the state of scientific study of phonology in the mid-nineteenth century. Combining phonetics with an almost phenomenological approach, Ellis searches for a way to tweak the alphabet, without inventing many new letters, so that it would represent all the sounds made in the languages of the world. He wishes the alphabet to comprise all of the languages, and hence all verbal communication, and in this he asks the alphabet to be universalizing, drawing into its symbols all the sounds of human language. Hence the notion of an "alphabet of nature" – really an alphabet of the human sounds that vowels and consonants can create. Like Kraitsir, he divides consonants *grosso modo* into gutturals, labials, and palatals, though without impressionistically seeking to find in each a trace of the real world. Ellis is more rigorous, and his treatment of vowels, nasals, dipthongs, and tripthongs is solid indeed.

Before discussing human articulation, Ellis addresses the nature of sound in general. Here, phenomenology enters. In his first sentence he declares that "sound is sensation, and is, therefore, like all other sensations indefinable" (1). The implications for a natural alphabet or an "alphabet of nature" are that one can never know if the exact sensation of another hearer matches one's own. How can we be sure that we have captured and represented precisely the sounds of another, since each person's perception of a sound will be different? Two sounds that are alike to one person may be subject to a subtle distinction in the ears of another. And two sounds that one person hears as different may seem the same to another hearer. In short, there is no Archimedes point outside our world from which to observe the sounds of language and record them with complete objectivity.

The almost utopian, and certainly unrealizable, nature of Ellis's project now becomes apparent. Even if he could construct a perfect "alphabet of nature" in which each person's articulation of the represented sounds would be consistent with itself (even if it did not match another speaker's), the project would be daunting. Ellis explains as follows:

> The term "Alphabet of Nature," we should apply to a *series of symbols representing certain Mechanical Conditions requisite for the production of the sensations termed spoken sounds*, so that those conditions being fulfilled, the same set of sensations in the same order may be produced in any individual. The sensations will, indeed, differ in different individuals, but it is

absolutely necessary to the idea of perfection in an alphabet that the sensations should be precisely similar every time that they are experienced
by the same individual. (145; italics in the original text)

No sooner does Ellis suggest this project than he concedes its impossi-
bility in the very next sentence, writing: "Such an alphabet is at present
impossible to construct" (145).

What Ellis actually sets out, therefore, is thus what he calls a "transition alphabet" or an alphabet of approximations. He confesses his dis-
appointment at his inability to achieve a true "alphabet of nature" and,
somewhat dejectedly, proposes the mere use of diacritics and modified
letter forms to represent the sounds of the language more accurately.
Like sixteenth-century orthographical reformers, he seeks to come as
close as possible to a purely phonetic rendering of speech – Ellis is
somewhat oriented towards English, but not entirely – and he suggests
that his "alphabet" may need further modification. Before ending his
book, Ellis reviews earlier alphabetical proposals, beginning with John
Wilkins to whom he acknowledges a deep debt.

Ellis then concludes his book by printing the last seven pages (183–
90) in his approximate "alphabet of nature" (fig. 39). One habituates
quickly to the letter forms, and the text is easily deciphered. In traditional orthography the first sentences of figure 39 read: "The third
question that we had to consider was: is it possible or expedient to
bring such an alphabet as this into common use? Alphabetical writing
was certainly originally intended to be a guide to the sound of words,
and that only" (183). This assertion regarding the origins of alphabetical writing is highly debatable and perhaps betrays the "*déformation
professionelle*" of a phoneticist. Earlier thinkers often stressed that letters were designed to keep things in memory, and that one of their
virtues was the ability to transfer knowledge and information across
time and space.

As was the case with earlier orthographical reforms, particularly
those that changed the actual letters, Ellis's new orthography stood little chance of being adopted on a wide scale, despite the fact that, as he
noted, he confined himself in many instances simply to altering letters
with diacritical additions so as not to oblige printers to cast new type.
His linguist's orientation and his concern for the economics of book
production frame alphabetic production within the scientific and market forces of nineteenth-century culture. He also offers another reason
for adopting his alphabet of nature. Even though we can never be sure

that the sensation produced by one sound or letter will produce the same effect on one person as on another (147), we can, Ellis argues, be reasonably confident that the "sensation" elicited by "rait, dzhɐstis, tshɐrtsh" would be more "uniform" than that provoked by "right, justice, church." Ellis seems to be suggesting that his phonetic orthography would also be a means of freeing readers from cultural contexts and connotations. While he does not consider that many associations with words would creep back in as the spellings became habitual, his view nevertheless associates phonetically sponsored alphabetic reform with a way of transcending the habits of culture and creating a more just (Ellis would say "dzhɐst") world. Ellis believes that his "alphabet of nature" would in fact free letters from implying a particular world view, a theory supremely indicative of a nineteenth-century faith in objective science. The utopian drive of universal communication peeks through the modern, scientific program.

If scholarly writing on the alphabet embraced scientific approaches in the nineteenth century, the same cannot be said for artists and writers. The Romantics and the symbolists, for example, favoured the mysterious, the mystical, and even, in the case of the writers of "gothic" fiction, the macabre. They privileged the irrational over the rational, and sought transcendence in personal mythologies of the letter.

A division thus operates between the scientific and pseudo-scientific community on the one hand and artists or writers on the other, many of whom resist modern, industrial society. Far from considering rational approaches to letters a virtue, many nineteenth-century poets feel that the modern world risks reducing the alphabet to a mere utilitarian tool and nothing more, robbed of its mythic and mysterious qualities. However, a return to past, shared mythologies of the letter is no longer possible in the mechanistic world of the nineteenth century. As a result, the alphabet is made expressive of personal rather than cultural mythologies as writers seek to retrieve letters from becoming simply the servants of advertising and empire.

One of the most famous instances of a writer who attempts to recover the mythic qualities of letters is undoubtedly Arthur Rimbaud's (1854–91) celebrated symbolist poem "Vowels":

A noir, E blanc, I rouge, U vert, O bleu: voyelles,
Je dirai quelque jour vos naissances latentes:
A, noir corset velu des mouches éclatantes
Qui bombinent autour des puanteurs cruelles,

Golfes d'ombre; E, candeur des vapeurs et des tentes,
Lances des glaciers fiers, rois blancs, frissons d'ombelles;
I, pourpres, sang craché, rire des lèvres belles
Dans la colère ou les ivresses pénitentes;

U, cycles, vibrements divins des mers virides,
Paix des pâtis semés d'animaux, paix des rides
Que l'alchimie imprime aux grands fronts studieux;

O, suprême Clairon plein des strideurs étranges,
Silence traversés des Mondes et des Anges:
– O l'Oméga, rayon violet de Ses Yeux ! –

A black, E white, U green, O blue: vowels,
Someday I will tell your latent births;
A, black corset furred with exploding flies,
That bulge around cruel stenches,

Gulfs of shadow; E, candors of vapours and tents,
Lances of proud glaciers, white kings, shivers of flower crowns;
I, purple, spit blood, laugh of beautiful lips
In anger or penitent drunkennesses;

U, cycles, divine vibrations of green seas,
Peace of grazing lands sown with animals, peace of wrinkles
That alchemy prints on great studious foreheads;

O, supreme clarion full of strange harshnesses,
Silences crisscrossed by the Worlds and by the Angels:
– O, the Omega, violet ray of His/Her Eyes!

Quite obviously, Rimbaud's poem seeks to reinfuse the alphabetic letter with a metaphysical dimension. Rejecting the reified, utilitarian, and ubiquitous letter that, in Rimbaud's world, has become nothing more than a sign that one "reads through" in a practical manner to arrive at a content, Rimbaud discovers, or rather, as he says, "speaks," the vowels' mysterious and even mystical qualities – what he calls their "latent births." The synaesthesia of this celebrated poem is possible only because, for Rimbaud, the letters of the vowels express the hidden correspondences of the cosmos.

The symbolists championed a rejection of positivistic nineteenth-century attitudes. Rimbaud's poem of course builds on Baudelaire's even more famous symbolist sonnet-manifesto "Correspondances" that sees mystical correspondences between the senses and the elements of our world. The symbolists seek to rediscover the mysterious dimensions that are occulted by the daily, rational world in which they live.

The symbolists, however, were building on the sentiments already expressed by the Romantic writers and artists who, seeing their positivistic and industrialized society as increasingly mechanistic, attempted to recover the mystery of earlier times (in particular, the medieval period), exotic places, and extreme experiences (the sublime). These attitudes extended to their approaches to alphabetic letters. As a result, alongside the modern Didot-inspired printed texts in which the letter was drained of all but its value as a signifier of a pronounced sound, many nineteenth-century Romantics sought to reinvigorate the alphabet with a sense of magic and power.

Telling, for example, are the ruminations on letters by the greatest French writer of the Romantic era, Victor Hugo (1802–85). The man who in his century dominated every literary genre, excelled as a painter, and even made his own furniture, meditates numerous times on the nature of letters. Like so many thinkers in the past, he sees a whole world in the alphabetical letters, but the mystery and the messages he discerns in letters and their shapes is not one that is given by the church or by a Graeco-Roman past. Rather, his mythology of alphabetic letters is personal and thus entirely in keeping with romantic views of the artist and artistic genius. Something as simple as the single word "nuit" (night) becomes a whole landscape for Hugo:

> NUIT, quel mot! Tout y est. Ce n'est pas un mot, c'est un paysage. N, c'est la montagne. V, c'est la vallée, I c'est le clocher, T, c'est le gibet.
> – Et le point ?
> – C'est la lune.   (*Portefeuille* 1046)

> (Night, what a word! Everything is found there. It isn't a word, it's a landscape. N is the mountain, V is the valley, I is the bell tower, T is the gallows.
> – And the dot?
> – It's the moon.)

Hugo envisions a universe in which the things of this world appear to him as letters and the letters as things in this world. There is no scientific justification for this, nor does Hugo refer back to any myth of origins or a longstanding tradition. Like Rimbaud, who comes a few decades later, Hugo here becomes a seer, a visionary.

Like many other writers, Hugo comments on the letter Y, and in fact he does so more than once. In the concluding chapter of this book, I will consider why the Y has elicited the attention of so many people throughout the centuries and I will return to Hugo's musings. For the moment, I wish simply to cite a single instance in which Hugo makes the Y into a sinister, dangerous force that can bring death rather than life:

Y. Défiez-vous de cette lettre-là. Regardez ! Qu'est-ce qu'un Y ? Deux courants qui se réunissent. Un Y de plus, NOÉ était NOYÉ. (*Portefeuille* 601)

(Y. Don't trust that letter. Look! What is a Y? Two currents that unite. With the addition of a Y Noah [NOÉ] would have been DROWNED [NOYÉ]).

Hugo's word play here is of course both ludic and deeply serious. Noah, who saved all the living species, most definitely did not drown, and of course he also kept others from drowning. As Hugo points out, however, the addition of a single Y, that he considers a dangerous letter, to Noah's name (in French) would have turned him into a drowned man. Hugo is implying, in a fashion that is both playful and poetic, that the imposition of the Y could have changed the whole course of the planetary development, wiping out all living things. This view is a lot to load onto a single letter, to be sure, and the potential "overkill" is saved precisely by the ludic quality of a poet who loves words. But the mysterious power of the alphabetic letter is reaffirmed, and letters are made a force that can make and unmake the world, which has, in fact, created them. In another context Hugo again discusses the letter Y, finding in it tree branches, a fork in a river, a glass with a stem, etc., before going on to see objects in the shapes of all the letters of the alphabet. He then pronounces in more general and abstract terms on the alphabet:

La société humaine, le monde, l'homme tout entier est dans l'alphabet. La maçonnerie, l'astronomie, la philosophie, toutes les sciences ont là leur point de départ, imperceptible mais réel; et cela doit être. L'alphabet est une source. (*Alpes et Pyrénées* 50–1)

(Human society, the world, man in his entirety is in the alphabet. Masonry, astronomy, philosophy, and all the sciences have their point of departure there, imperceptible but real. And that is as it must be. The alphabet is an origin.)

Despite his very personal mythology of the letter, Hugo is here restating the millennia-old view of an analogy between the alphabet and the world. Remarkably, this sense of the long-standing analogy, refracted of course through a deeply personal experience, also surfaces in Hugo's visual art in which, instead of describing a word as a visual image, the picture occasionally depicts written letters. Furthermore, the letters depicted are at times those of Victor Hugo's own name. The personal investment in the letters could not be stronger – but then, what could be more fitting for a man whose whole life and career was bound up with letters? Hugo is the poet who declared when he was twelve that he wanted either to be as great as the famous Romantic poet Chateaubriand or nothing else ("Chateaubriand ou rien!").

Almost as talented an artist as a writer, Hugo also did numerous drawings and paintings of his name and initials, sometimes superimposing them on a landscape (he occasionally did this with other words as well). For example, in one instance Hugo's own name is spread across the skies and disappears behind the hills like a sun setting (or rising). The equation between self and world, letter and cosmos, is conveyed by Hugo's self-depiction as not just the sun but also the letters that spell his name in the place where we would expect the sun to be. Perhaps the best known instance of his initials is a depiction of them as the tentacles of an octopus (many images of this are available online); easily accessible as well are monograms he drew as designs for a fireplace in Hauteville House. Perhaps the most striking example of Hugo's self-representation as initials is an interlocking VH, drawn as three-dimensional blocks. In this version of the initials the "H" is broken, truncated.[4] In other words, Hugo represents himself as mutilated initials – and by extension as a broken man. I would wager that this image was made after the death, by drowning, of Hugo's favourite child, his daughter Léopoldine. The sense of loss, the self-depiction as incomplete, even mutilated, is very much how Hugo felt after the death of his daughter. We should remember that this is the same man who saw a single letter, the Y, as transforming the survivor Noah into a drowned man. Is the drowning of Léopoldine behind Hugo's self-depiction as an amputated letter?

The desire to reanimate the alphabetic letter neutralized by the Baskerville/Didot approach in which letters are "unmarked" and one simply "reads through" them leads to a kind of backlash in some printing circles towards the end of the nineteenth century. Bifurcating away from mass printing, specialty presses create type that conveys through its forms more than simply the content of the text. The most famous figure in this reaction is undoubtedly the Englishman William Morris (1834–96), the great printer, artist, poet, and thinker who championed the preservation of the medieval past and was a driving force behind the "Arts and Crafts" movement. Like the Romantics, Morris (and the Arts and Crafts movement more generally) felt that the depth and mystery of medieval culture was being destroyed by nineteenth-century industrialism. He advocated the preservation and restoration of medieval architecture and he wrote poems and created paintings that reprised the great love stories of the Middle Ages (Tristan and Isolde, Lancelot and Guinevere, etc.). Against the depersonalized industrial worker he championed the artisan craftsman. Morris's contribution to typography consists in having published books for which he created three different typefaces ("Golden," "Troy," and "Chaucer") that recalled the forms and interlacing ligatures of medieval manuscripts. More than a simple product of nostalgia, Morris's books comprised a return to a view of letters as pregnant with meanings that went beyond the mere literal content of the words they formed. Morris decried the "grey" look of books from the Didot-Baskerville era onwards, and he sought to get back to the blocks of deep black letters that one found in the columns of medieval manuscripts and early incunabula. If nineteenth-century advertising used novel typefaces simply to attract attention, Morris, on the contrary, created medieval-esque letter forms in order to convey dimensions of the mysteriousness that he also attributed to medieval stone buildings. His letter forms were the alphabetic equivalent of the Romanesque and Gothic churches that were key to the European identity and heritage and which stood in silent contestation to a shallow, mechanistic modern society. Indeed, the re-creation of medieval scripts is thus used as part of a political and sociological statement regarding the modern world view and man's place in it. The beauty of Morris's books derives from a reverence for a past in which alphabetic letters were infused with secular or divine power and in which comely books were homologous with the divine "Book of the World" written by god.

If Morris is the best known of such printers, he was not the only one. One finds examples of similar archaizing small-press editions in other languages, even ancient Greek. The rejection of practicality, and the sense that a different approach to the alphabetic letter could signal a different social path in the modern world are hallmarks of these limited book productions. Moreover, many of these qualities will be passed on to twentieth-century artists and writers who also will try to re-animate the dead letters of the modern world in which they live. The key difference in the twentieth century will be that, rather than a return the past, the lettristic experiments of twentieth-century figures will be seen as avant-garde – that is, as pushing ahead beyond modernity and tending towards the future. Twentieth-century lettristic creations will see themselves as outstripping the practical, day-to-day world in which they live. Though there is continuity in the view that letter forms must be reanimated, the rejection of modernity will move in a different temporal direction, pushing ahead rather than turning back.

9

From Modern Experiments to Post-Modern Experiences

Il peut y avoir des instants où des alphabets et des livres de comptes nous paraissent poétiques ... Une véritable lettre est poétique d'elle-même.

Novalis

The twentieth century is one of mass culture. Literacy, which increased steadily during the nineteenth century as more and more Western countries instituted national programs of education, made for a more extensive reading public, which in turn led to an increase in terms of authors and books published. Didot and Baskerville-type letter forms were almost universally adopted for printed books aimed at a broad reading public. Unmotivated, unmarked letters became the standard, allowing readers a sense of untrammelled access to pure content, unimpeded by having to contend with letters that asserted themselves obtrusively. Modifications to letter styles were intended almost exclusively to enhance readability.

Narrative literature, as one moved from the nineteenth to the twentieth century, consisted mainly of the realistic novel, which sought to give the reader a vision of daily reality around him or her, handing back the world supposedly just as it was, with no interference from the letters on the page. The seeming lack of rhetorical manipulation in which one could almost forget that everything was being filtered through letters was, in fact, a very successful way of manipulating the reader to believe that a text was simply presenting the truth of the external world. Such letters that wished away their own presence were perfectly suited for a culture – namely that of western Europe and North America – that dominated the world and presented its vision of the planetary culture not as a "vision" but simply as an unchallengeable record of reality. Alphabetic letters, by seeming not to present a "take" on the world, in fact, imposed, almost insidiously, a "take" on readers. The realist novel, which began in France in the nineteenth century, became a worldwide phenomenon, and in fact it is still the dominant fictive genre in our world today.

At the same time, among writers and artists there was a growing resistance in the first decades of the twentieth century to the bland acceptance of the ubiquitous textuality that permeated modern, developed nations. The worldview of the industrialized world, carried as it was by letters that almost went unnoticed, met with a reaction in the form of creative challenges. If William Morris represented in the late nineteenth century an archaizing return to the letter that demonstrably set itself before the reader *as a letter*, more radical artists and writers, inspired by the reflections of the symbolists and early modernist thinking, championed self-conscious lettered texts that would also be resolutely modern in the way they stretched and deformed letter shapes, rejecting the uniformity and mechanization of industrial society. Charles Baudelaire (1821–67), Arthur Rimbaud (1854–91), and Stéphane Mallarmé (1842–98) suggested towards the end of the nineteenth century that letters were imbued with dimensions far greater than the simple utility of advertisements, newspapers, or as a vehicle for a realistic narrative. The twentieth century would carry these tendencies much further, taking full advantage of the alphabetic letters' forms, of typographical variation, and, most important, of the disposition of letters on the page (or on a canvas). No text speaks the modern world so much as the many poems, paintings, lithographs, and novels that play with the typography and disposition of their letters. A new relationship to the world is expressed as a new relationship to letters, and vice versa, and this is the case whether we are speaking of a calligramme by Guillaume Apollinaire (1880–1916), a synthetic cubist work by Pablo Picasso (1881–1973) or Georges Braque (1882–1963), a Futurist poster by Filippo Tommaso Marinetti (1876–1944), or – in the second half of the century – a canvas by the Uruguayan painter Joaquín Torres-García (1874–1949) or a novel by Georges Perec (1936–82). In all of these instances writers, artists, and typographers sought to revitalize the alphabetic letter: to rescue it from a purely utilitarian status. In a world that now denied the letter the transcendent values that religion and myth had formerly given it, an attempt was made to infuse it, nevertheless, with an essence of the modern that would make of the letter more than simply a visual signifier of a spoken sound.

Scholars have often seen the typographical experimental poem by Stéphane Mallarmé "Un Coup de dés" (A Roll of the Dice) as a watershed moment in the path towards a new way of understanding the relationship between word and world. In his twenty-page 1897 poem (first published in book form in 1914) Mallarmé radically modified the traditional disposition of letters on the page – that is, words neatly arranged in stanzas – and spaced his letters and words as he pleased, creating new relationships between the portions of the text and producing a poem that was similar in some ways to a musical score (Meggs and Purvis 261). He also had some variations in the size of the letters and he italicized certain passages, which made for a system of echoes between passages from one page to another (fig. 40). As Johanna Drucker has noted, Mallarmé was clearly influenced by the aesthetics of visual advertisements and treatises on advertising that emphasized how, in advertising, one could arrange text loosely around an axis or axes (*Visible* 55). In this redistribution of letters on the page, Mallarmé sought to shake up centuries of reading habits in which the succession of linearity had numbed or lulled readers as they read "through" letters and unthinkingly absorbed content. Mallarmé's typographical experiment must be seen as a call for greater self-consciousness and self-awareness, and what may seem simply an aesthetic choice is, in fact, political in its resistance to a long tradition. As Mallarmé himself put it, "Let us have no more of those successive, incessant, back and forth motions of our eyes ..." (Drucker, *Visible* 54).

A new approach to the alphabetic letter is thus used to telegraph a shift in how the world is to be viewed. The insistence that letters must be arranged differently on the page and read differently carries the message that the world, as a text, must also now be viewed or "read" differently. Not that Mallarmé was putting forth any sort of social program. Like other symbolists, Mallarmé was more wont to retreat into a reticulated world of art and aesthetics. The implication that the old attitudes towards reading, like the old attitudes towards many things in society, could not continue was, in the case of the symbolists, more of a turning one's back on the social world and adopting a solipsistic approach to reality. Baudelaire, in a prose poem in which he described what he saw through a window across Parisian rooftops, asserted that he would see even more if he closed his eyes and simply let his imagination run.

If nineteenth-century advertising opened up new graphic possibilities, Mallarmé's "roll of the dice" was timid in comparison to the aesthetics of commercial graphics. Advertising made use of eye-catching letter styles and sizes, often jumbling them together on a single page or poster/billboard. It also favoured collages in which different planes of letters crossed and covered one another, often at various angles. Advertisements screamed at the viewer from billboards and magazine pages. Mallarmé's poem stated something new, but it certainly did not scream. It may have broken apart the staid stanza of traditional poetry, but it was still rigorously disposed along strict vertical and horizontal axes. Its lines did not run at angles nor did its letters turn any which way. Moreover, the typography used was still of the Didot-Baskerville sort first introduced with the eighteenth-century editions of Virgil's *Aeneid*. Advertising, meanwhile, was using letters that had patterns, that imitated earlier writing or cursive scripts, and that were decorated with all sorts of flourishes and shadings. Finally, Mallarmé's poem was for a tiny, elite audience, while advertising, by contrast, was for the masses. Within a generation his experiments would seem staid in comparison with the wild graphic scripts of the Futurists or some of the daring alphabetical graphic work of the Germanic world.[1]

Early in the century writers and artists began to make use of new technologies for printing and writing (or often typing), and the ubiquitous lettered world began to invade artists' and writers' creations in ways unknown hitherto. The *Calligrammes* of Guillaume Apollinaire (1880–1918) was written between 1913 and 1918 and then published in 1918. It is often seen as marking a pivotal moment in the transformation of belles lettres. It is no surprise that the poems grow out of the First World War. The horror of the Great War swept away the ideological certainties and aesthetics of the nineteenth century, and, as Walter Gropius (1883–1969) put it, "[e]very thinking man felt the necessity for an intellectual change of front" (*New Architecture* 48). The *calligrammes* are celebrated for the ways in which the disposition of the letters on the page is as much a part of the meaning as is the pure "content" of the words. Many of the poems are clever, even whimsical, such as streams of letters cascading down the page in "il pleut" (it's raining). A series of rebus that may or may not constitute a profound reflection on time in the modern world marks the hours of a pocket watch ("La Cravate et la montre" [The Tie and the Watch]) (fig. 41); Certainly in the case of the poem-watch there is great fun in teasing out the hours ("my heart," marks one o'clock; "the eyes" marks two ... "a week" stands for seven; eight o'clock is "the infinity sign laid down by a philosophical fool"; and so forth). Moreover, the tie ludically refers to the modern workaday world for which the pocket watch marked a new approach to time, satirized by such figures as Charlie Chaplin and Kafka, in which a stern boss noted if an employee was even a couple of minutes late to work. Hence a radical new take on letters is made the means to express anxiety about a society whose temporal flow has changed significantly. Some of Apollinaire's *calligrammes* were published exactly as he wrote them in his own handwriting, the letters forming the shape of an object, and such publication made use of the technologies now in place to create facsimile copies. Others, although originally done in handwriting were published as printed letters using the fonts of the modern typewriter so that they looked as though they were typed.

Coming together, then, are new technologies for lettered compositions (facsimile, typewriter), new alliances between the form and disposition of letters and their "content," and a sense that the modern world cannot be expressed by asking letters merely to do the work they did in preceding centuries. Apollinaire's *Calligrammes* occasionally makes specific reference to the First World War and uses the new alphabetic approach to make a political statement about the contemporary world. In his *calligramme* shaped like the Eiffel Tower – Eiffel's steel construction being the very image of the modern, industrial world – Apollinaire makes the letters of his poem (letters that increase in size as one descends to the base of the Eiffel Tower) into a kind of broadcast that "shoots" (tire) its French letters at the Germans (the real Eiffel Tower broadcast radio signals beginning in the early twentieth century). In another poem, Apollinaire has some of his letters speak and also represent the explosions of military ordonnances, turning his letters into, as the poem puts it, "the points of impact of my soul which is still at war."

That letters can have an explosive force that both speaks and represents the speed of the modern technological world is perhaps best emblematized by the visual poems of the Italian *futuristi*. The Futurists were an eclectic group in the first decades of the century, and *futurismo* or Futurism as a movement had several branches of thought as it formulated and reformulated itself several times. A complex movement, Futurism had both left-wing and right-wing adherents, and it proved influential in both France and Russia. Certainly the most famous representative of the movement was F.T. Marinetti whose *Parole in libertà* or *Words in Freedom* sought, almost literally, to explode words onto the page (fig. 42). Marinetti's reputation in history has been tainted by his enthusiasm for violence, war, and Mussolini, but his importance for European letters, in every sense of the world "letter," cannot be overstated. The Futurists embraced with great enthusiasm the new technologies, of which there were so many in the early twentieth century, and they felt that the arts needed to match the energy and sped-up motion that the increasing mechanization of modes of production (the assembly line) and of travel (trains, cars, etc.) had wrought. Marinetti declared in his *Manifesto del futurismo*, that

> Noi affermiamo che la magnificenza del mondo si è arricchita di una bellezza nuova: la bellezza della velocità. Un automobile da corsa ... un automobile ruggente, che sembra correre sulla mitraglia, è più bello della *Vittoria di Samotracia*. (6)

> (We affirm that the magnificence of the world has been enriched by a new beauty: the beauty of speed. A race car ... a roaring car, which seems to run on a machine-gun, is more beautiful than the *Victory of Samothrace*.)

For Marinetti, the old forms of writing no longer sufficed, and a new approach to the letter was needed. Influential on Apollinaire, Marinetti in fact went much further in his poetic experiments, and indeed in comparison to Marinetti's "words in freedom," the typographical innovations of Mallarmé and Apollinaire look quite staid. Marinetti championed what he called *simultaneità* or "simultaneity" in which syntax, punctuation, and even grammar were blown apart. Often instead of the normal lexicon of the Italian language, Marinetti created onomatopoeic neologisms that he felt were better to express the signs and sounds of the new technological age. In his "Typographic Revolution" (1913) he articulated his stance rather vociferously:

> Io inizio una rivoluzione tipografica diretta contro la bestiale e nauseante concezione del libro di versi passatista e dannunziana, la carta a mano seicentesca, fregiata di galee, minerve e apolli, di iniziali rosse a ghirigori, ortaggi, mitologici nastri da messale, epigrafi e numeri romani. Il libro deve essere l'espressione futurista del nostro pensiero futurista. Non solo. La mia rivoluzione è diritta contro la così detta armonia tipografica della pagina, che è contraria al flusso e riflusso, ai sobbalzi e agli scoppi dello stile che scorre nella pagina. Noi useremo perciò in una medesima pagina, *tre o quattro colori diversi d'inchiostro*, e anche 20 caratteri tipografici diversi, se occorra. ("Rivoluzione tipografica" in *I Manifesti del futurismo* [143])

(I initiate a typographic revolution directed against the bestial and nause-ating concept of the outdated and traditional [literally, "D'Annunzio-like"] book of verses, with its seventeenth-century handmade paper, ornamen-tal gods and goddesses, large red initials with curlicues and vegetation, mythological missal ribbons, epigraphs, and roman numerals. The book must be the futurist expression of our Futurist thinking. Not only that. My revolution is directed against the so-called typographic harmony of the page, which is contrary to the flux and motion, and to the undulations and surges of the style that flows in the page. We will therefore use, in one and the same page, three or four colours of ink and also twenty different typefaces, if necessary.)

The desire for letters to somehow directly express the real world is, of course, as old as Plato, but the manifestation in Marinetti is novel. Traditional typography has been abandoned as letters of all shapes and sizes are jumbled together on the page, designed to convey both through sonority and through the visual arrangement the essence, the speed, and the noise of the modern world. "SCRABrrRrraNNG" and the other neologisms and truncated words of figure 42 attempt to give us a sense of the experience of a soldier on the front in the First World War. So, too, Marinetti's long book-poem "Zang TUMB TUMB" (pub-lished as a book in 1914) seeks to reproduce the sense of the Battle of Adrianople (1912).

As is clear from Marinetti's "Typographic Revolution," he was seek-ing to revitalize the alphabetic letter and to infuse it with the energy and power of modern technology. The questions of how the alphabet can be rejigged to express the modern age occupy the thinking of not only poets and writers in the early twentieth century but visual artists as well. We have seen that in literature the strong realist mode gives way to new experiments in form and content; so also in visual art the high mimetic grip is pried loose in the first decades of the twentieth century. The Fauvists, other post-Impressionists, and above all the cub-ists break with how the world has been represented hitherto in art. The clear frame that has separated the painting from the real world becomes porous as objects from the external world begin to make their way into the canvases: Pablo Picasso and his fellow cubists paste down bits of paper and other objects in their paintings. As the real world invades the painterly one, so also do letters. As metafictive movements will come to realize later in the twentieth century, visual artists call attention to the fact that letters are part of the real world, and thus to represent or reproduce letters and lettered elements in a work of art is to include a portion of the real world that has hitherto not been reflected in artistic works. Picasso and his friends are particularly fond of pasting down pages from newspapers, often cutting them into the shapes of different objects – say, a goblet or a musical instrument. They also paint letters on their canvases along with other objects, and in particular the paint-ers in Paris such as Georges Braque, Juan Gris (1887–1927), and Pablo Picasso favour the first letters of the French word for "newspaper," that is, *journal*. Rarely does the whole word figure in the paintings, however. Most commonly the first three letters appear, the "jou" alluding to the timeliness of the quotidian that is expressed by the word *journal*, itself derived from the French word for day, *jour*. But, as critics have long recognized, the truncated form "jou" is also the first three letters of the verb "to play" (*jouer*), and in this respect the painters allude to an artis-tic vision of the world in which art is both serious and ludic. The letters in these paintings participate in a conscious and even self-conscious breakdown of the barriers between high and low art, between high-brow and lowbrow culture. The cheap daily newspaper of the masses is made part of a unique work of art, and attention is deliberately drawn to the role of the alphabetic letter in bridging between mass culture and elite art.

The presence of letters in works of art will characterize the art of the twentieth century from its first decades to its last. This consistency attests to the role the alphabetic letter has come to play in modern West-ern societies. With high rates of literacy, Western countries now see the letter as one of the elements that cut across social boundaries and strata, and hence it is a unifying force that expresses the culture as a whole. The alphabetic letter, once largely the province of a wealthy minority, now forms the basis of mass communication every day. Nothing is more emblematic of the twentieth century than the newspaper vendor dishing out the latest edition to an eager public.

But then the twentieth century has proven to be a century absolutely devoted to questions of letters, language, and how language functions within a larger system of signs or semiotics. It is not by chance that we now speak of a "language" or a "grammar" in diverse contexts in which discrete elements function as part of an organized system to cre-ate meaning. We can speak of the "grammar" of, for example, a city layout or the "language" of fashion. The whole consciousness of semi-otics as such is due to the revolutions in linguistics at the beginning of the twentieth century, and in particular to the teachings of the Swiss linguist, Ferdinand de Saussure (1857–1913). In the first decade of the twentieth century, Saussure introduced the notion that linguistic meaning is predicated on minimal differences within a system of arbitrary signifiers. The word "cat," for example, has no intrinsic relationship to the world; Saussure, in other words, completely negates Cratylus's old argument that letters and/or words can somehow carry a trace of the external world. For Saussure, the English "cat" and the French *chat* and Polish *kot* and Spanish *gato* only mean a particular four-legged, furry animal because of social convention, and unlike Plato's Socrates Saussure admits of almost no exceptions. Moreover, the word "cat" can have meaning only because it differs from "bat" and from "sat" and from "mat," etc., by a single letter, making all of these other words "minimal pairs" for "cat" because they have a minimal difference of a single differentiated sound (in practice the alteration of a single letter often creates a minimal difference, though not always since a cluster of two or three letters can sometimes stand for a single sound: "that" is also a minimal pair with "cat" because "th" is the orthography for the [ð] sound). Saussure's famous dictum that in languages there are only differences ("il n'y a que des differences" 166) means that meaning is always predicated on difference – an observation that will give rise to enormous developments in French philosophy towards the end of the twentieth century. Of course minimal difference could be created by any one of the three sounds making up "cat," not just the initial letter: "cut" is a minimal pair with "cat," and so are "cad" and "calf" (the "l" is of course silent). Saussure's *Course in General Linguistics*, authored not by Saussure himself but by his students who had extensive notes from Saussure's courses, has cast a huge shadow over the twentieth century and has permeated popular discourses as well as esoteric philosophical writings. The view that language is a signifying system made up of linguistic signs in a system of differences and the sketch of a larger field of semiotics that could interpret all features of a society as a signifying system have proven very powerful.

Saussure's "minimal differences" refer primarily to aural differences but they also characterize those differences as represented in scribal terms, though they do not always refer to the change of just a single letter, as we have already seen. In practice, however, many if not most minimal differences will also be signaled by the simple change of a letter. What is more, meaning for Saussure defers along a chain of linguistic signifiers, strung along as in the following example: get/bet/bat/cat/cut/gut/nut/not ... etc. Although not intended to draw attention to written alphabetic letters per se, Saussurean linguistics often does so anyway since one conceptualizes the word "cat" as differing minimally from "bat" or "gut" through the change of a letter, even though "that" or "kit" are also equally minimal pairs with "cat." As the Czech structuralist Jan Mukařovský (1891–1975) put it:

> Saussure's discovery of the foundations of the internal structure of the linguistic sign differentiated the sign from mere acoustic "things" (such as natural sounds) and from mental processes […] As a result, the claim that a work lives its real life only in an oral recitation was refuted, a fallacious claim, for there are poets (not only readers) in whose minds a written, not spoken, work has its existence. (18)

The upshot of this view is that alphabetic letters become key players in a quintessentially modern view of how meaning is created and organized. Linguistics becomes the model for how meaning arises in all fields, and the arbitrariness of the signifier as well as the idea that meaning arises from a system of trace differences characterizes much subsequent thinking in the century.

The letter is thus a great equalizer in twentieth-century culture and it is seen as one of the building blocks of meaning in its largest sense. It is also, as we have seen, a powerful tool for creative processes. After the calligraphic experiments of the First World War period and its aftermath, surrealism picked up the baton of alphabetic experimentation. The surrealists were fond of playing language games, as when different people wrote part of a sentence without knowing what the others had written (giving, of course, strange results), and the surrealists were also engaged in automatic writing – that is, writing that "free associates" in an attempt to bypass any conscious control of the words produced.

More focused on the alphabetic letter per se are the writers associated with what is called the OuLiPo movement. The name stands for *Ouvroir de littérature potentielle*, which we can translate as "Workshop for potential literature," and in its selection of the first two letters of each key term – ou-li-po – it announces its self-conscious interest in the alphabetic letter. This post-surrealist movement arose in France in about 1960 and brought together a number of writers and mathematicians. In its favouring of mathematical and systematic models for the generation of literature, Oulipo can be seen as a kind of return to a long-standing relationship between mathematics and the alphabet, going back to ancient Greece. But key to Oulipo's texts is the idea of using a formal constraint to generate new literature. To be sure, writers have always had to deal with constraints, whether because of the demands of patrons or those of a particular form (rhyme, metre, stress, scansion). The beauty of a sonnet or a sestina has always been due in part to the ability of a poet to fit his or her message to the strict formal requirements.

The question posed by Oulipo is: how can formal constraints be used to generate literature in our modern world? In a sense, Oulipo can be seen as reacting to a certain "anything goes" aesthetic of some "beat" writers – one thinks of Jack Kerouac (1922–69), for example – as well as to a sense of frustration with traditional forms of narration and poetic creation. This is certainly not the first time that twentieth-century writers have felt that the existing moulds for literary creation are inadequate. Oulipo will take over from the surrealists an interest in happenstance as a way of generating novel alphabetical combinations. But even more remarkable are the arbitrary constraints the Oulipo members often impose on their writing.

The desire to find new means for generating literature responds to a feeling, articulated in different ways in the 1960s, that "everything has already been done" in literature. The writer John Barth (b. 1930), in a book published in 1967, characterized a number of literary gambits of the period as a "literature of exhaustion." As the name of the Oulipo movement suggests, the goal has been to open up new potentialities for literature, and Oulipo members have sought to do this not by trying to tell new stories (again, "everything has been done") but rather by using the very medium of literature – the alphabetic letters – to generate new works. In a sense, Oulipo can be seen as similar to some of the alphabetical constraints Carolingian writers imposed on themselves, such as Hucbald de Saint Amand's ninth-century poem in praise of baldness in which every word for 146 verses begins with a "c."

One of the founders of Oulipo in 1960 was Raymond Queneau (1903–76) who came from the surrealist movement. Queneau made a number of experiments with constraints, the best known of which is his *Exercises de style* (1947) in which he describes the same banal scene ninety-nine times, each time using a different style. Each version carries a constraint: in "Surprises" each sentence has to be exclamatory; in "Negativity" all the sentences are written in the negative; "Double in part" says everything in two ways ("Toward the middle of the day and at noon …"). Queneau also creates an alphabetical labyrinth of sorts for poetry with his *Cent mille milliards de poèmes* or *Hundred Thousand Billion*

Poems (1961) in which he produces ten sonnets with exactly the same rhyme scheme and then cuts between the lines of each page so that one can mix and match the lines. The result is 100,000,000,000,000 possible poems.

In 1973 Oulipo published an anthology of their work ("travaux") in which they detailed many of the constraints designed to be catalysts for a new type of literature (*La Littérature potentielle*). The book demonstrates how the Oulipo members engage in lipograms (i.e., texts that deliberately omit a particular letter) and heterograms (ones that repeat no letter).

As an example of the ways in which the absence of a single letter can generate new literary configurations, the Oulipo group takes the first sentence of Marcel Proust's *Remembrance of Things Past* – one of the most celebrated lines in all of French literature ("Longtemps je me suis couché de bonne heure") – and rewrites it:

> without an "a": Longtemps je me suis couché de bonne heure
> without an "i": Longtemps nous nous couchâmes de bonne heure
> without a "c": Longtemps je me mis au lit de bonne heure
> without an "s": Enfant, on me mettait au lit tôt
> without an "r": Longtemps, je me suis couché à la tombé de la nuit (avec les poules)
> without an "e": Durant un grand laps, on m'alita tôt, trop tôt pour moi.

The nuances of this exercise are lost somewhat in translation; suffice it to say that one has to keep modifying lexical items, verb tenses, and "voice" (active/passive) in order to produce the same general idea. Some of the results are quite amusing. Upon observation several features come to the fore. First is that the original sentence is in fact a lipogram because it contains no "a"! Was Proust even aware of having engaged in an Oulipo-type of lettristic game in his first sentence? Probably not. What is more, the omission of certain letters makes for a more radical rewriting than does the omission of others: not all alphabetic letters have the same weight in lipogrammic writing. To not permit an "s" or an "e" prevents the inclusion of the famous first word "longtemps" ("for a long time"): the lack of an "s" turns *longtemps* into "as a child" (enfant) and the lack of an "e" into "for a long lapse [of time]."[2]

The greatest challenge for a heterogram would be one that uses all the letters of the alphabet without repeating any (called a "heteropangram"). This proves impossible in both French and English (except for the alphabet itself) though one can come close. The classic English school orthography exercise, "The quick brown fox jumps over lazy dog" comes close, but uses 32 letters (it repeats "o" [four times!], "u," and "r").

As did the authors of the *carmina figurata* in the Carolingian period, Oulipo also delights in palindromes, that is, texts that read the same forwards and backwards. But whereas in the Middle Ages the letters of the palindrome, however clever, were invested with a divine semiotics and served to remind the reader of his or her moral responsibilities, in the twentieth century the palindrome is designed to jumpstart literary creation in an entirely secular world. The emphasis is on the ludic quality of literature and on the alphabetical letter for the letter's sake. There is a need to resurrect the letter and revitalize it, and the palindrome is merely one of a number of means. The Oulipo members propose palindromes with an even number of letters ("Salut! Tu l'as?" [Hello! You have it?]) and with an odd number ("Et Luc colporte trop l'occulte" [And Luke peddles the occult too much]). They even compose bilingual palindromes ("Ted, I beg, am I not ever a venom?" which read backwards is the French "Mon Eva rêve ton image, bidet! [My Eve dreams of your image, bidet!]). Not quite worthy of Shakespeare, perhaps, but impressive as a linguistic feat.

In its concern for the letter as letter, the Oulipo movement is entirely in step with the "linguistic turn" of the twentieth century that sees linguistics as the model for the construction of larger meanings. Meaning does not reside in some transcendent signifier – God – but rather it slips away along a chain of minimal differences. The addition or subtraction of a single letter provokes nuances in meaning, as the Proustian example illustrates. And the imposition of a particular constraint, whether in the form of a forbidden letter or the strictures of a palindrome, instigates new meanings.

Surely the most demanding and dazzling palindrome of the Oulipo movement is that of Georges Perec, which is several pages long (reproduced in *Littérature potentielle* 101–6). Not surprisingly, it reads rather strangely, but that very strangeness is part and parcel of the "defamiliarization" of much twentieth-century literature. The Russian formalist Victor Shklovsky (1893–1984) argued that the role of literature is to pull us from our complacency and defamiliarize our world. Perec's palindrome certainly does that. At the same time, the sheer virtuosity of creating a palindrome of many hundreds of words such that it reads exactly the same from the front as from the back is a way of reclaiming one's position as a great "maker" of literature. Perec's palindrome amounts to a kind of proof of literary virility for which only the greatest figures have "the right stuff."

The most audacious Oulipo creations are undoubtedly the novels of Georges Perec for which reason he is probably the greatest representative of the movement as a whole. The apogee of Oulipo literature is Perec's 1969 novel *La Disparition* (*The Disappearance*). *La Disparition* (rendered into English as *A Void*) is a lipogrammic text from which the letter "e," which is the most common letter in French, as it is in English, is entirely absent. The novel is a tour de force of Oulipean strategy since it is so hard to avoid completely using an "e" for hundreds of pages. In French, the "e" appears in many of the pronouns (including "je" [I] and "elle" [she]); it characterizes almost all verbal forms of the most common class of verbs (known as "-er verbs"); it is the masculine definite article "le" (the); and it is included in most feminine adjectives. As a result, one must perform linguistic contortions in order to find circumlocutions that evade the "e." The novel has been translated into English (three times), Dutch, German, Romanian, Spanish, and Swedish. But it is a misnomer to suggest that it has been "translated." The novel must be adapted and effectively rewritten by each translator since many key terms in the original may not be able to be translated because an "e" appears in the corresponding word in the new language; for example, the very title of the novel in English could not be "The Disappearance," which would already contain three "e"s! Hence the clever circumlocution "A Void," which refers to both the space left by the missing item and the need to *avoid* the letter "e."

The plot mimics that of a classic detective novel and concerns the search for a missing person, Anton Voyl, who can never be named since the unstressed "atonic vowel" (*voyelle atone* in French) is precisely the "e." Perec plays on the notion of a "bourdon" which refers to the blank space typesetters set between letters.

The following passage will give some illustration of the tenor of the novel. It comes from *A Void*, the English translation/adaptation of *La Disparition*.

> Oh what was that word (is his thought) that ran through my brain all night, that idiotic word that, hard as I'd try to pin it down, was always just an inch or two out of my grasp – fowl or foul or Vow or Voyal? – a word which, by association, brought into play an incongruous mass and magma of nouns, idioms, slogans and sayings, a confusing, amorphous

outpouring which I sought in vain to control or turn off but which wound around my mind a whirlwind of a cord, a whiplash of a cord, a cord that would split again and again, would knit again and again, of words without communication or any possibility of combination, words without pronunciation, signification or transcription but out of which, notwithstanding, was brought forth a flux, a continuous, compact and lucid flow: an intuition, a vacillating frisson of illumination as if caught in a flash of lightning or in a mist abruptly rising to unshroud an obvious sign – but a sign, alas, that would last an instant only to vanish for good. (116)

Not bad for a lipogrammic paragraph that does not once use the letter "e"! Moreover, the whole novel reads in similar fashion.

Perec was proud of the fact that his novel had the lipogram not only as a function of the writing but as its thematic core as well. The "e" is missing, and the plot and the episodes repeatedly point to the missing letter. Indeed, the unspeakable "e" that has disappeared refers in part to the horrors of the twentieth century; the mutilated words ("Vowl," for example) and the gap left by the disappearance take on much greater proportions. There is strong reason to believe that Perec consciously alludes to the Holocaust through this alphabetic disappearance, and that the elimination of the letter "e" and the characters who would pronounce the letter is designed to recall the disappearance of the Jews under the Nazis.[3] A Jew himself, Perec was orphaned by the war, and his mother was deported to Auschwitz where she perished. The inability to use the letter "e" means that such words as "père" (father), "mère" (mother), "famille" (family), and "parents" are banished from the novel. Significantly, the form used in France after Second World War to document Jews who disappeared into the Nazi concentrations camps was called an *acte de disparition*, and the 1947 official government document testifying to the deportation and death of Perec's mother is, in fact, extant.[4] The ubiquitous letter "e" – or rather its absence – presents a vision of our world as denatured and mutilated by genocide. The old view that the letter carries a trace of the external world is redeployed in Perec's novel such that it is now the absence of a particular letter that reflects the greater world, the missing "e" alluding to the Nazis' attempted effacement of a whole people.

Interestingly, Perec followed up *La Disparition* with another novel *Les Revenentes* (1972), which is monovocalic, hence the *only* vowel that occurs in the whole novel is the "e."

It is worth noting that Perec is not the first writer to have knowingly produced a lipogrammic work. It is often pointed out that Ernest Vincent Wright (1873–1939) in 1939 wrote a much shorter novel *Gadsby*, which also did not employ any "e"s. In fact, lipogrammic writing reportedly goes back to sixth century BCE Greece and the lost works of Lasus of Hermione and his student Pindar (522–443 BCE). Classicists are familiar with Nestor of Laranda's third-century CE rewriting of Homer's *Iliad* and Tryphiodorus's rewriting of *The Odyssey* (third century CE? – the title is given variously). In each case the lipogrammic works are divided into twenty-four books, each of which successively suppresses one of the letters of the Greek alphabet: alpha, beta, etc. This systematic approach was picked up by the Fabius Planciades Fulgentius (late fifth–early 6th CE) in his *De aetibus mundi et hominis* (*On the Ages of the World and of Man*), though only fourteen of the original twenty-three chapters are extant. In the sixteenth century Petrus de Riga took a similar approach to the Bible, summarizing it in twenty-three chapters, each of which successively suppressed a different letter. Even the great Renaissance Spanish playwright Lope de Vega (1562–1635) who wrote over 1500 plays also produced five novellas, each of which avoided one of the vowels. A number of German writers intentionally suppressed the letter "r" (as did also a fair number of Italians), of whom the eighteenth-century German poet Gottlob Burmann (1737–1805) is perhaps the most amusing: he is reported to have hated the letter "r" to such an extent that in 130 poems he never used it and refused to pronounce his own last name. These lipograms were word games or compositional challenges that were similar in many ways to those of the Oulipo movement, with the key difference that they did not derive from a sense that literature had been exhausted and needed some kind of rejuvenation through manipulation of the alphabet.[5]

This abiding relationship between letter and external world is nuanced in the twentieth century by the view that there is not a divide between letter and world since alphabetic letters are as much a part of our real world as are other objects. Artists such as the surrealist René Magritte (1898–1967) and Paul Klee (1879–1940) make use of letters in and on their canvases, placing them on the same level as daily objects. Magritte argues in his essay "Les Mots et les images" (Words and Images) in *La Révolution surréaliste* (*The Surrealist Revolution*) that in paintings, words and images partake of the same substance. Similarly, the Uruguayan painter Joaquín Torres-García (1874–1949) was wont to install not only icons for objects into niches in his paintings, but also letters, thus giving them the same level of both "objectivity" and sig-nification. In his autobiography, Torres García states that he "puso ... en sus nichos respectivos una Casa (como esas que dibujan los niños) un Barco, una Ancora [*sic*], la letra B, un Hombre, un Pez" (*Historia de mi vida* 210: put ... in their respective niches a House [like those that children draw], a Boat, an Anchor, the letter B, a Man, a Fish). In the paintings by the Argentine Xul Solar (1887–1963) – often referred to as the Latin-American Paul Klee – letters appear like so many trees and bushes among which people wander. Towards the end of the twenti-eth century, the young artist Jean-Michel Basquiart (1960–88) included written lists as well as misspelled and crossed out letters in his can-vases, sometimes repeating the lists from one painting to another. And to cite one last case, Cy Twombly (1928–2011) managed to make the let-ters of Achilles's name, scrawled in a "violent" red, convey anger in his series "Fifty Days at Iliam" (now in the Philadelphia Museum of Art). In these many instances, the letters not only partake of a concept of the world, they become the world.

Still, the given alphabet proves insufficient to express the artist's rela-tionship to the world in the late twentieth century. Artists and writers create private mythologies and new letterforms. The Star Wars series has given rise to a complete Klingon-language grammar with its own alphabet. Joaquin Torres-García invents his own alphabet, which, rather like the script we have seen by Rambaud in the sixteenth cen-tury, carries echoes (and even some letterforms) of previous Western alphabets. "D, H, I, J, O, X, Y, Z" are carried over from the Roman alphabet; a few letters ("A, B") evoke Greek letters; and a few appear to be inspired by ancient Phoenician characters because they appear to be similar in shape to Roman letters but different in their orientation (the "K" is turned sideways, the "E" and the "L" are turned upside down and altered somewhat). As with Thomas More's utopian letters, both the Klingon and Torres-García's alphabets maintain a one-to-one corre-spondence with our everyday letters. In the case of the Uruguayan art-ist, this means that he has a version of both the "L" and an "LL," since his model is the Spanish alphabet. Interestingly, no avant-garde artist has, to my knowledge, tampered with the actual order of the letters in the alphabet, even in the cases of the most provocative transgressions; the alphabet order is always maintained, i.e., "A, B, C, D ..."

The suggestion is that the artist's unique personal vision must be matched by a personal alphabet: seeing the world in a new way means to write it in a new way, and vice-versa. Can the nature of the world no longer be expressed by the twenty-odd letters with which we are all familiar? Is this a descent into solipsism on the part of the artist or, on the contrary, an attempt to communicate better with the larger public? Could it be that the usual letters – in their various fonts – have lost their power to speak for the individual and to express a unique vision, and so an artist must find new graphic representations?

In a sense, advertising most loudly proclaims a new role for the alphabetic letter since it announces most directly the triumph of the industrial revolution and ushers in the age of consumerism. The letter is put in the service of sales and profits, and as such it bespeaks the new world of mass-production and the consumer society. The twentieth century is a world in which systems of education that are free and obligatory are instituted on a national level in most Western countries, resulting in a higher level of mass literacy than in any preceding period. As a result, public areas become spaces for lettered texts – usually, but not always, advertisements – and the urban setting is transformed into an alphabetic wilderness. People are surrounded by letters as soon as they step out into the street, and cities are turned into a collage of alphabetic messages of all sorts.

The letter thus participates as both a producer and a product of modernity, and the ubiquity of large public letters is a hallmark of modern urban spaces. Businesses that a couple of centuries earlier would have been identified by an image on their shop signs now have their names or their logo splashed across the storefronts. The sides of industrial buildings, trucks and carts, human sandwich advertisements – all are covered with alphabetic writing. The push to make the alphabet express and be expressive of modernity is fuelled by great creativity. Turn-of-the-century Viennese artists and typographers experimented with new typefaces and orientations, and with the advent of modernism in its various forms (German Bauhaus, Russian constructivism, Dutch De Stijl, etc.) typographers canted letters and made use of different sizes and spacings. Art deco artists like Cassandre (most famous for his train and ship travel advertisements in France) designed type that left out some strokes of the letters or combined solid and outlined portions in a single letter (Meggs and Purvis 294). Propaganda posters of both the fascists and communists put their hortatory texts at dramatic 45-degree angles.

If there is a single design feature that has seemed to "speak" the modern world, it is the sans-serif script. Whether we are speaking of the De Stijl school, Bauhaus, French Art Deco, the American modern

movement, or Swiss post-war designers, the elimination of the traditional serifs has been viewed as powerfully connoting the modern – as
a metaphorical sweeping away of many centuries of tradition. It would
of course be incorrect to say that this has been true in every instance –
witness, for example, the IBM logo – though even when serifs have
been retained, as with IBM, they tend to be forceful, slab serifs, not the
elegant serifs of the Didot-Baskerville-Boldoni sort. It should also be
noted that twentieth-century letter forms have often been cast as simply part of a larger revolution in style, and many of the great designers
of typefaces have also addressed questions of living spaces, furniture
design, and urban planning.

After the Second World War, the International Style in architecture
was paralleled to a certain extent by an International Typographic
Style. In both, clean lines, order, and clarity were championed. In many
cases – perhaps most – sans-serif letters were laid out according to
grids, often with left justification and ragged right margins (Meggs and
Purvis 373). One could undoubtedly argue that after the upheaval of
the Second World War, there was little interest in the exploding, violent typography of Marinetti's Futurist images. Stability was prized in
the alphabetic approaches to communication as the International Style
became the dominant mode of the post-war triumph of American-led
capitalism.

The International Style also became deeply intertwined with the
alphabetic approach to corporate identity and advertising (Meggs and
Purvis 412 ff.). The inauguration of the CBS corporate logo, and to a
lesser extent the type layout for the Olivetti corporation – both of them
done in sans-serif letters – were watershed events. They heralded what
has become common in corporate and institutional culture: the articulation of a particular typeface and alphabetic display that appears to
speak the values of the institution and will be recognized as such. The
company name, and increasingly simply the company logo, needs to
be distinctive – to stand out in the sea of textuality in which we swim
daily. For example, the great designer, Paul Rand, produced for ABC
television a logo, again with sans-serif letters, that could do battle with
CBS; the ABC trademark is one, to quote Meggs and Purvis, "in which
each letter form is reduced to its most elemental configuration" (420).

Finally late in the twentieth century, the International Style gives
way to what can loosely be called "postmodernism," in which clarity,
order, and stability are deliberately undermined or altered, whether by
jumbling different typefaces together or arraying them in haphazard

manners or bunching letters (for the last, consider the case of the UNION wall safes trademark in which the "overlapping and cropping [of] the logo ... brings [out] the vitality and impact of pure form" [Meggs and Purvis 463]). However, it is worth remembering that transgressions of a system in fact reinforce the system already in place since their transgressive status depends on the underlying system for meaning.

The logo is merely one late twentieth-century development in a long series of attempts to revitalize the alphabetic letter and make it "speak" the capitalist and corporate vision of modernity (and even what has come to be called "post-modernity"). How can new letter forms and combinations express the cacophony of the modern city? How can letters participate in the expression of twentieth-century cultural concatenations? The clever company logo is merely the final commodification of the experimentations with letters that characterize the century as a whole.

Never have there been so many fonts at the disposal of artists, writers, and the general public as towards the end of the twentieth century. And perhaps never have writers, publishers, graphic artists, and public officials devoted so much time and thought to the precise letter forms for books, billboards, announcements, cards, documents, etc. The "Note on the Type" at the end of a novel has become so common that a short story of that title in *The Paris Review* was able to parody its emotive discourse (Russell, "A Note"). With the advent of sophisticated personal computers, the general public has an astonishing array of fonts at its disposal through a convenient drop-down menu.

Yet, despite the wide range of font types to choose from, the modern world in fact has for the most part settled on only a few fonts that it repeats almost endlessly. The three fonts that people writing on computers most commonly choose to use are Times New Roman, Calibri, and Arial. Despite having a choice among hundreds of letter forms, the vast majority of the public at the end of the twentieth and early decades of the twenty-first centuries gravitates to the same letter shapes again and again, eschewing all other scripts. This conformity is astonishing, and one understands well why some artists or writers would attempt to break out of it. Do we not have anything original to say? Are we so afraid of appearing even a slight bit different?

Without the public being entirely aware of it, a sameness of alphabetic letters has come to cover the world – at least when the text is set in the Roman alphabet. People use Times New Roman on a daily basis without having any sense of the way in which it harkens back to the majestic letters that were carved on innumerable buildings in ancient Rome. Developed in 1931 for the London *Times*, it is based on earlier fonts, Plantin in particular, but the majuscule letter forms ultimately go back to the Roman monumental capitals.

Still, the most common font in our current world is one that individuals rarely use when sitting at their computers but which has blanketed the West since the Second World War. I am speaking of the font known as Helvetica. Helvetica was developed in 1957 by Mac Miedinger at the Haas Type Foundry in Switzerland. Originally called Neue Haas Grotesk, the name was changed to Helvetica to give it a more international appeal. Indeed, the choice of the Latinate version of the name for Switzerland can be seen as a decision in favour of "neutrality" that echoes Switzerland's well-known neutral stance in political affairs; in both cases the putative neutrality is, in fact, politically charged.

A sans-serif font – that is, it lacks the little "flags" or "serifs" at the edges of letters in older typefaces – Helvetica was derived from the nineteenth-century sans-serif "grotesque" fonts and in particular one called Akzidenz-Grotesk, developed in 1896. The worldwide acceptance and exploitation of the Helvetica font could not have been anticipated. In the intervening decades Helvetica has covered public spaces to an extraordinary extent, although most people are unaware of the font's ubiquity. It is used as the font for innumerable company names and logos: a small sampling includes American Apparel, American Airlines, BMW, ECM, J.C. Penny, Jeep, Lufthansa, Motorola, Panasonic, and Target. It is used for metropolitan transit systems (New York, Chicago, Washington), and also for many sports teams and franchises. It appears on store windows, flyers, and billboards. Indeed, it has become so ubiquitous that a documentary – a very interesting one, in fact – called simply *Helvetica* (2007) has been made about the font. As the documentary makes clear, the font has its admirers and detractors.

Indeed, the range of affective responses to the font, particularly on the part of typeface designers, is rather extraordinary. It may seem surprising that something as innocuous as a typeface can elicit such strong reactions. Even more startling, however, is the tendency to load the typeface with metaphorical values that speak to our contemporary world. More than one interviewee in the *Helvetica* film sees the typeface as quintessentially representative of the late twentieth century: the sparse, streamlined sans-serif forms become equated with the sleek, fast-paced, and impersonal urban lifestyle. Since no Cratylus-type argument is being propounded that would see a part of the physical world as carrying over into the letter forms, the thesis is based entirely on analogy and aesthetics. Serif letter forms such as Didot's become associated with a more staid, traditional society, whereas sans-serif forms are made analogous with modernity. Why should this be the case? Is it simply because sans-serif fonts were not used much until well into the nineteenth century (even though William Caslon first introduced them in 1816), so that the chronological parallel of serif fonts with earlier times makes Helvetica and other similar fonts connote the modern? But how much of the mass public knows anything about the history of serif and sans-serif fonts? Or might the serifs at the bases of letters in serif fonts themselves connote stability and tradition – and thus an older, more staid society? Are Roman capitals monumental simply because they are used on monuments, or are they perfect for monuments because the serifs make them seem more solid – hence, more monumental – despite the fact that serifs were probably originally a necessary device to accommodate the tip of the chisel used for carving? Do sans-serif fonts seem more likely to slip and slide because they lack the solid feet of the serifs?

If the serif/sans-serif aspect of a font subliminally affects the viewer, then the view that Helvetica somehow perfectly captures our contemporary world would suggest in a new fashion that the alphabetic letter encapsulates a vision of our world. The nature of our cosmos or at least how we experience it would be implied by the smooth contours of the Helvetica letter forms. Moreover the almost universal adoption of Helvetica (it has also been adapted for the Cyrillic and Greek alphabets and even for Chinese characters) would suggest that the font somehow speaks globalization and the universal triumph of Western capitalism as the dominant culture worldwide. Helvetica's forms would appear to trumpet the late-capitalist view of reality.

Are we loading a typographic font with too much meaning? Besides, did it have to be this way? After all, does this argument not constitute an essentialist argument of the Cratylus type? If Roman capitals had been characterized by a lack of serifs, would then a font like Didot, with its graceful serifs, perhaps be seen as quintessentially modern rather than a bit old fashioned?

Might it be that people see in the font what they want to see? Typographers' opinions on Helvetica are far from universal, after all. Some celebrate the font, arguing that it is somehow democratic and accessible to all – a font of universal acceptance and the perfect font for a world in which many barriers have come down. Yet others view Helvetica

as cold and impersonal, associating it with a world in which the individual no longer has any importance and huge international and mul-
tinational forces, whether private corporations or government entities,
control our lives. How can the font have such diametrically opposed
values? Are letter forms simply a slate onto which one can project
whatever one wishes? Is there nothing that inheres in the font itself in
order to determine, at least to a small extent, its meaning?

The wide range of responses to Helvetica calls into question the values of typography itself. What is the point of developing fonts if one
has absolutely no control over the effects they have on viewers? Perhaps the whole history of letter forms was misguided, and the repeated
reformations of letter styles a complete waste of time? Was it wrong
to see Carolingian scripts as an improvement over Merovingian writing and emblematic of a more ordered world and worldview? Was it
equally wrong to credit Baskerville and Didot with devising letters that
had grace and balance without being intrusive? Do we simply attribute
qualities to alphabetic letters or do we respond, as we think, to traits in
the letters themselves?

Despite these questions, many institutions devote much attention
and thought to the letter types they use for their logos and their letter-
heads. The choice of a font is seen as crucial to "branding," and institutions often spend large amounts of money on consultants and graphic
designers to choose or even design fonts that they then copyright. Not
only private business enterprises consider that the implications of certain letter forms are crucial to their images, but non-profit agencies,
universities, printing houses, and even cities sometimes have unique
typefaces designed, and they develop complex rules and requirements
for how the fonts are to be used in official communications. Harvard
University has its own unique typeface, as does my own university,
and in both cases the letter forms supposedly connote erudition and
serious intellectual endeavours. Some cities have developed unique letter forms that seem to speak their metropolis; one of the most ingenious
is the official font for Lisbon, the skeletal LX Type whose letters are
taken from the crisscrossing cables that hang above Lisbon's beloved,
aging streetcars. As the official pronouncement from the city makes
clear, the cable crossings, now made letters, "speak" something essential about Lisbon:

Os eléctricos de Lisboa fazem parte da paisagem lisboeta e tornaram-se
um ícone da cidade. Para além de pintarem as ruas de amarelo riscam o

céu azul da capital com os seus cabos. Da complexa malha feita por estes, surgiu a ideia de criar uma tipografia, cujo traço é formado pelo cruzamento aleatório dos mesmos. Assim, a LX Type passa a ser a fonte oficial de Lisboa. (See: http://acidadenapontadosdedos.com/2014/01/27/lx-type-a-nova-tipografia-de-lisboa/)

(The trams of Lisbon are part of the Lisbon cityscape and have become an icon of the city. Besides painting the streets with yellow [the colour of the streetcars] they score the blue sky of the capital with their cables. From the configuration of the complex network of cables arose the idea of creating a typography whose lines are formed by their random crossings. Thus, LX Type becomes the official font of Lisbon.)

In our time, however, there are also those who have suggested that it is time to move beyond the twenty-odd letters of the Western world – as though the alphabet had outlived its usefulness.

Interestingly, rather than moving in the direction of a universal language or alphabet, as the seventeenth century wished to do, the tendency in recent years has been to go in the direction of private scripts and personal alphabets. In other words, some of the recent changes wrung on alphabetic letters have swung towards solipsism rather than universal communication. We have already considered the personal alphabet of the Uruguyan Torres-García. Others are attempting to move beyond letters to what is called "asemic writing." Asemic writing is writing for which the letters or characters do not have a particular sign value (from the Greek a + seme = without + sign). In other words, one cannot attach a specific signifier, sound, or semantic value to individual graphic marks within a known system, and yet the overall impression is one of writing. In a sense, we have seen this many times in people's signatures since often we cannot distinguish any individual letters but instead merely read the writing globally as "signature"; indeed, signatures can hover between asemic writing and monograms.

Not that asemic writing is without meaning. It is simply without specific semantic value. These non-letters are still inscribed within a writing culture such that the values of certain types of writing can be activated even if a specific message cannot. Asemic writing can imitate handwriting, different types of typography and calligraphy, characters such as one finds for Asian languages, medieval manuscript scripts, or any other manner of graphic writing. It thus evokes and plays with the overall meanings one associates with different sorts of documents, private missives, ancient texts, etc. Moreover, an asemic text either means more or less than conventional writing: less in the sense of a clear semantic message from a sender to a receiver, but more in that the "meaning" can vary with the viewer. Indeed, asemic writing opens itself up to multiple meanings because it is *viewed* more than *read* and stands somewhere between an organized system of communication and a work of visual art.

Recent writers, artists, calligraphers, and typographers have engaged in the production of asemic texts. Perhaps the most famous of all asemic works is Luigi Serafini's 1981 *Codex Seraphinianus*, a hand-written, illustrated manuscript published in a facsimile edition. There have been attempts to crack the "code" and decipher meanings for the calligraphy in the tome, but it appears increasingly likely that the writing is asemic and meanings for individual words and letters cannot be pinned down (but then, asemic writing is not interested in "pinning down" meanings). In some ways the codex resembles the fifteenth-century Voynich codex, although the latter may not be asemic writing but rather an abbreviated, late-medieval "semic" script. The key difference is that the Voynich codex's writing probably has specific semantic content whereas the *Seraphinianus* does not. That the two books should nevertheless seem so similar, at least superficially, informs us about how much of alphabetical texts' meaning derives from the overall "look" of writing and not from the individual letters per se.

To take but one example of asemic writing, let us consider the "interventions" of the Canadian artist Sylvia Ptak. Ptak "intervenes," as she puts it, in early-printed and preprint manuscript books by covering part of the written text with a thin textile veil from which she removes some threads and then paints the loops of remaining threads in order to create what appear at first glance to be medieval-looking letters (fig. 43). The curves and swirls imitate the curves and undulations of incunabula or gothic scripts, complete with what seem from a distance to be illuminated initials. But on closer inspection, the letter forms melt away into threads of loops and curves that are not quite letters. What is this near-alphabetical script supposed to signify for us as viewers? Is this a postmodern reminder that sure meanings always slip from our grasp, since as soon as we actually try to identify Ptak's letter forms they become meaningless shapes? Or are the interventions reminders of the alterity of an earlier age found in books from before 1500, which are generally written in languages and scripts that the modern reader cannot read? After all, except for specialist readers, the parts of the pages that Ptak has not covered with asemic writing are no more accessible than the parts she has created. Perhaps the point of the textiles is to remind us of the aesthetic qualities of old books (or all books) by turning the page into a meditation on the beauty of writing? Another possibility is that we are being drawn back to the very origins of written texts and to the association of texts and textiles that inheres in the word *textus*. After all, the origin of the first written works of Western culture has an impenetrable, mysterious quality for us, whether we are speaking of Homer's two great epics or the composition of the Hebrew Bible. Penelope, we should remember, provided the counterpart to her husband Odysseus's adventures as she kept weaving and deferring the resolution of her story until Odysseus came home to write the end of his tale in the blood of the suitors with his bow.

The asemic loops of Sylvia Ptak's interventions return us, in a sense, to the very origins of alphabetic writing, shrouded as they are in mystery. The basic outlines of the development of writing are well known. As early as the seventh millennium BCE, peoples in Anatolia inscribed meaningful signs, though specialists would be wary of calling the signs "writing." But around 3300 BCE in the Sumerian city of Uruk the first writing – still partly pictographic – is attested along with a numeric system, and shortly thereafter, around 3100 BCE, the first Egyptian writing appears. The earliest texts from Uruk refer to titles and professions, while the Egyptians seem to have quickly put writing in the service of royal power, recording the dates and doings of the dynasties. Some time after the year 2000 BCE, the *Epic of Gilgamesh* was composed in cuneiform writing (portions of which are preserved in the clay tablets in the Ashmolean Museum, Oxford, dating from 2000 to 1600 BCE). Most alphabetic letters that have survived into the modern era, regardless of the language, derive as is well known from Phoenician letters, themselves developed out of what is called a proto-Siniatic writing. The key change made by the Phoenicians was to modify pictogrammic forms into purely linguistic signifiers, standing for sounds and not objects.

So much for the historical facts, such as they are. But what that transition from pictogrammic signs to alphabetic letters, which took place some time between about 1700 and 1200 BCE, felt like we cannot know. Did the early lines and curves strike Phoenician eyes the way Sylvia Ptak's forms, which seem to hover either before alphabetic writing or

after it, provoke ours? Did a sense of mystery characterize those letters or proto-letters? Did they seem to radiate power? In the twentieth century, the great French anthropologist Lévi-Strauss wrote, as we
have seen, of a writing lesson (*Leçon d'écriture*) among the Nambikwara
in Brazil in which the chieftain understood that power resided in the
anthropologist's scribblings, even if he did not understand the details
of the alphabetic system, and he began to imitate the Frenchman's writing by drawing wavy lines (347–60). In a sense his writing was asemic:
he understood the cultural powers that surrounded writing even
though he knew nothing of the alphabet (see also Martin). In the early
sixteenth century, Hernán Cortés (1485–1547) of course describes a similar phenomenon during his conquest of Mexico. The Meso-Americans,
he recounts, were dumbfounded that the marks on paper could deliver
messages across great distances; they, too, realized that the system of
letters the Spanish used had enormous power even if they did not yet
know how the system worked.

Asemic writing reminds us that we will never be able to lift the veil
fully from the mysteries that surround the transition from non-lettristic
marks to lettristic ones. As mentioned in chapter 2, we would love to
know what is meant by the reference in Homer's *Iliad* to the signs carried by a messenger, but we will never know what the nature of those
signs was.

As a reflection of and on our approaches to alphabetic letters, asemic
writing is certainly thought-provoking. It hardly constitutes the death
of alphabetic writing, however, as some of its proponents have claimed.
Alphabetic writing does not appear to be headed for its demise. On
the contrary, as linguists write down languages that have only existed
orally hitherto, they invariably use some version of the Latin alphabet
to do so. The development of the internet, of blogs, of email, and of
ebooks means we use and are exposed to alphabetic letters more than
ever before. More and more people worldwide are literate, and as English becomes the universal second language, it brings with it the Latin
alphabet into cultures that have hitherto used other systems. Naturally,
the alphabetic letters and spellings of English cannot help but have an
effect on other cultures. The linguistic domination carries with it elements of cultural domination as well.

At the same time, the worldwide embracing of English as the *lingua
franca* of our planet also has implications for the alphabet of English
users. The advent of text messaging and the different uses of English
by speakers whose native language is very different mean that over

time the spellings, the grammar, the vocabulary, and perhaps even the worldview implied by our alphabetic letters will change. The alphabetic letters with which we are so familiar will still carry with them a sense of how the world or the cosmos is viewed, but that sense may differ from what it was in the past.

This is a true globalization of the alphabet. The English alphabet has taken over the world in a certain respect but at the same time the world has taken over the English alphabet. The world is seen as speaking alphabetic letters but from a new perspective. In 2015 Google announced that it intended to reincarnate itself and bring its various endeavours, many of which are quite unrelated to its original function as an internet search engine, under the umbrella of a new, multi-faceted company called Alphabet. There are those who were surprised by the name chosen, but they need not have been. What the deep thinkers at Google have understood is that the alphabet has consistently been a lens which our culture has used to understand the world. In the new name Google has demonstrated an awareness of how our ABCs provide a conceptual order that aids us in making sense of reality while providing at the same time an elastic, flexible framework that can house many disparate elements, as when we file very different topics in alphabetic order.

But if the alphabet can be a tool, it can also be a plaything. Readers will be familiar with the sets of alphabetic refrigerator magnets that guests rearrange into ludic messages during dinners and parties. The installation artist Camille Utterback earned fame with the 1999 "Text Rain" she created with Romy Archituv. This is how she describes her project:

> Text Rain is an interactive installation in which participants use the familiar instrument of their bodies, to do what seems magical – to lift and play with falling letters that do not really exist. In the Text Rain installation participants stand or move in front of a large projection screen. On the screen they see a mirrored video projection of themselves in black and white, combined with a color animation of falling letters. Like rain or snow, the letters appear to land on participants' heads and arms. The letters respond to the participants' motions and can be caught, lifted, and then let fall again. The falling text will 'land' on anything darker than a certain threshold, and "fall" whenever that obstacle is removed. If a participant accumulates enough letters along their outstretched arms, or along the silhouette of any dark object, they can sometimes catch an entire word, or

even a phrase. The falling letters are not random, but form lines of a poem about bodies and language. "Reading" the phrases in the *Text Rain* installation becomes a physical as well as a cerebral endeavor.[6]

In an entirely virtual manner the letters "that do not really exist" (though one must ask what it means for a letter to "exist" apart from its representation) interact with the human body, even though the two are in different ontological and physical spaces.

Another playful, but also highly significant, example can serve to finish out this chapter. Available online is a "geogreeting" that differs a bit from other such e-cards common to the internet. This site (http://www.geogreeting.com) allows one to select letters that are in fact formed by the tops of buildings whose shapes look like alphabetic letters when seen from the sky. These "letters" are scattered all over the world. As one composes a message one does so from a truly cosmic perspective; the program zeroes in on a rooftop that forms the desired alphabetical shape. The resulting message is both highly specific, from one person to another, while also "global." In fact, the ability to see so many buildings as letters from above would have been almost unthinkable before the twentieth century, and the ability to draw from satellite photographs that cover the world would not have been possible before the twenty-first century. At the same time, such a program hints at the hegemony of alphabetic signs. One could not produce such a program for character languages.

This global architectural alphabet is very different from the experiments in earlier centuries in which architects intentionally designed buildings in the shapes of letters. Here architectural intention has not played a role. Indeed, many of the buildings are industrial and may not be the least bit attractive. Rather, what we have is an example of the cosmic eye, powered by technology, that "sees" the tops of buildings as letters, quite apart from the intentions of the architects. In yet a new way, our world is viewed as an alphabetical text – as a planet that speaks letters to a sentient viewer high in the sky and surveying the whole planet.

Moreover, users the world over can enter new instances into the program as they discover new examples of buildings that form letters when seen from the air. At the present time, Europe and North America are represented much more than other continents – a new example of cultural hegemony – but China and Latin America are catching up. Left somewhat behind is Africa, which is underrepresented.

The distribution of these rooftop "letters" thus mirrors, not by chance, the political power of the various regions of the world in our present time. As has been the case from the invention of letters until our day, these alphabetic letters say something about our world and the way we view it. The satellites we have built all over the world speak our alphabet back to us, and the planet becomes one giant alphabetic text.

10

Into the New Millennium

Thou whoreson zed, thou unnecessary letter.

Shakespeare (King Lear)

The arbitrariness of language and of letters is a hallmark of twentieth-century thinking and has been summed up most powerfully in Ferdinand de Saussure's teachings early in the twentieth century on the linguistic signifier. As Saussure and his followers (of which we are all descendants) have shown, the relationship between the linguistic sign, whether oral or written, and what it signifies is purely a matter of social convention. Not that this view is entirely new in the twentieth century. In the late eighteenth century, Charles de Brosses considered the view that language was conventional and arbitrary already to be the dominant one.

We have seen, nevertheless, over the course of the preceding chapters that there has also been a recurrent tendency in Western culture to see letters as "motivated," that is, as maintaining or reflecting some sort of organic or analogical relationship to the things of our world. Indeed, it is due to this view, sometimes only in a diluted, residual form, that the alphabet has repeatedly provided a lens through which Western culture has viewed and assessed both itself and the world. In its strong form, this conception sees the alphabetic letter as actually *containing* some portion of the real world. This is the view espoused by Cratylus in Plato's dialogue of the same name, and it was inherent in many aspects of the ancient Greek and Roman conception of alphabetic letters: letters were the *stoicheia* or *elementa* and hence the very building blocks of the cosmos. While Socrates largely rejects Cratylus's position, even he, in Plato's dialogue, considers that there is carry-over, albeit imperfect and incomplete, from the real world into some letters, as for example, the trilled Greek letter "ρ" ("rho") which, for Socrates, does not just convey motion but actually *is* motion (represented also by the movement of the tongue in trilling), for which reason the "rho" is used, he says, in words referring to movement.

Although a consistently "strong" view of motivation has been largely set aside, beginning with Plato's Socrates, it has made periodic returns in later centuries, as we have noted during the course of this book. Certainly the analogy between the alphabet and the world has had great frequency, especially in what we can think of as a "weak" version of the motivated letter. In this view, letters do not necessarily contain actual bits of the world, but they are seen as representing the world in terms of their oral form (their names or pronunciation) or their written shapes. On the one hand, such a view is justified historically, given that the first Phoenician letters were in fact pictograms that lost, quite early, their visually mimetic aspects. However, even long after the loss of any sort of visual representation, the weak view of motivation has remained. To an extent, we are all subject to this view. Our various responses to changes in orthography – for example, our very different attitudes towards "c" and "k" and even "q" when they represent the same sounds – attest to a difficulty in viewing the letter as an entirely arbitrary signifier. "Amerika" strikes us as vaguely militaristic in a way that "America" does not, largely because the "k" is far more frequent in German than in English, and Germany has been seen as responsible for two world wars in the twentieth century. Surely that is a lot to load onto a single letter! Furthermore, a few letters of the alphabet are seen as a bit strange or exotic – "x" above all, but also "z" – largely due to their infrequency. If all letters are completely arbitrary as signifiers, we should not think of some as being more "natural" in a particular language than others. "A" and "e" are so ubiquitous in many western European languages, including English, that it seems an extraordinary feat to write a lipogrammic novel with no "e"s whatsoever, as George Perec did in *La Disparition* (*A Void*). For all we know, there may be many novels without a single "z" or "j," since both are infrequent, but no one has bothered to check to make sure. In any event, a lipogrammic novel that lacked a "z" would hardly strike us as remarkable.

In various ways, then, we reinstate a mild or "weak" view of letters as motivated on many occasions. Christian culture, in viewing its Saviour as the complete alphabet ("I am the Alpha and the Omega"), invokes the alphabetic order as a template that can be laid over the whole of the cosmos. In our time, most Christians probably do not reflect consciously on the fact that their religion views the alphabet as a compendium that expresses and is expressed by the actual order of the letters (A, B, C …). By contrast, in the Middle Ages people were far more aware of this analogy, as we have seen. In illuminations the "t" was often turned into a cross on which Christ's crucifixion was depicted, especially for the opening of the Canon of the Mass that begins "Te Igitur, clementissime Pater." Both the Drogo Sacramentary (850–5 CE) and the Sacramentary of Metz (ca. 870 CE) make use of this iconography; in the former various scenes of prefigured sacrifices inhabit an enormous "T" and in the latter Christ himself is emblazoned on the large letter (fig. 44).[1]

In its weak form, the "motivated" approach still subtends the Christian view of things, even in the modern world. The alphabetic order of the Messiah can be taken as shorthand for the notion that he rules and orders the whole cosmos. Certain letters of the alphabet also stand out, largely for their form. To this day, the "x" and the "t" can be seen as images of the Cross. One can ward off evil by making an "x" (or a "t") with one's fingers. A "p" or an "o" would not have the same effect. The degree to which people currently believe that making the shape of the letter has actual power may not be great, but the gesture has remained nevertheless. Since the two letters reproduce *grosso modo* the shape of the Cross, the gesture inevitably alludes to the possibility of salvation and redemption through divinely instituted letters.

The weak form of motivated letters also reasserts itself in many ABC books for children. Along with the ones that catalogue the names of animals in alphabetical order are ABC books that provide a list of moral values or good conduct. Similarly, there are many "city alphabet" books for children in which an "ABC of Toronto" or the "Chicago Alphabet" provides cityscape examples that form the letters; such books are designed to foster civic pride and aid in the socialization of a young person.

Because alphabetic letters have both a graphic form and an oral pronunciation, either aspect can become the source for "motivation." Indeed, for a few letters their placement in the order of the alphabet can also become part of their "meaning," as with the alpha and omega in Greek or the "A to Z" expression to suggest completion of a whole range. The shape of an "o" as well as the articulation ("oh") suggests meanings in numerous languages. Moreover, the successive ideologies of different historical periods can establish new analogies between the letter and the world. As we saw in the chapter on the Renaissance, Geoffroy Tory abandoned the medieval Christianization of alphabetic letters but then remapped humanistic views onto their forms, seeing in the letters a human body and the Graeco-Roman tradition.

A few letters have been endowed with consistent meanings throughout much, even most, of the Western tradition. The most persistent of these is probably the "Y," derived from the ancient Greek upsilon. Although in earlier chapters we have briefly seen some views of the letter, a more detailed consideration of the letter might be of value here as a final example. Indeed, the letter "Y" seems to encapsulate in little the thesis of this whole book; it can be seen as emblematic of the way in which Western culture returns again and again to the alphabet as a means of conceptualizing the world.

Very early on in Western culture, the form of the forked capital letter was metaphorized as a moral "fork in the road" such as every person encounters in life. The creation of the "Y" was attributed by classical, medieval, and Renaissance writers to the mathematician Pythagoras (sixth century BCE), and its origin ostensibly grew out of a tale told precisely of a fork in the road that Heracles (Hercules) encountered. In a sense, then, the legend, rather than simply metaphorizing the letter in terms of geography, made of the letter a representation of the geography of our world. Pythagoras supposedly created the letter in remembrance of the road. This tale seems to provide the background for an episode in Hesiod's *Works and Days* (ca. 700 BCE) and is made explicit in Book II of Xenophon's (430–354 BCE) *Memorabilia* (1965) in which Socrates retells Prodicus of Ceos's anecdote about Heracles having to choose between two paths, the good and the bad, personified by two women.

Cicero (first century CE) alludes in his *De Officiis* (I.118) to Socrates's narrative in Xenophon's *Memorabilia*. The key elements are by now well known: the path to the left is broad and has a sensual and comely woman who beckons to Hercules while the path to the right is narrow and has a beautiful, but more austere, woman. Hercules understands that the two paths represent, respectively, *voluptas* (pleasure) and *virtus* (virtue), and he chooses the correct path – that of virtue. Half a millennium later, Isidore of Seville makes the relationship between the alphabetic letter "Y" and the moral choices in life explicit. "Y litteram Pythagoras Samius ad exemplum vitae humanae primus formavit" (I.iii.7: Pythagoras of Samos first formed the letter Y as an example of human life). A bifurcation of the trunk takes place in adolescence ("ab adolescentia incipit"), the right branch being arduous but leading to a blessed life ("[ad] beatam vitam"), while the left is easier but it leads to disgrace and death.

This view of the road as a "Y" that presents one with two paths in life – or of the "Y" as representing that road – has had extraordinary currency throughout Western culture. This powerful metaphor subtends, for example, the whole of Dante's *Divine Comedy* in which the narrator has veered from the "correct path" in life. It is found as well throughout the medieval romances in which knights are presented with two paths and must choose the proper one. In the thirteenth-century French *Quest of the Holy Grail*, one knight (Melian) at a fork in the road chooses the path that knights traditionally take and learns later that this denoted a moral failure because it represented the path of "terrestrial chivalry" not "celestial chivalry," which was represented by the other branch of the "Y" (see de Looze, "Story" 130–1). Even the modern poem by Robert Frost, "The Road Not Taken," subtly reworks the metaphor of the forking road as referring to one's choices in life:

Two roads diverged in a wood, and I
Took the one less traveled by,
And that has made all the difference.

It is this last line of the well-loved poem that establishes the moral valence of the "Y" marked out on the earth.

While some of these instances do not specifically mention the letter "Y," the instances that explicate the "Y" as representative of the moral choices on the road of life are so many that this view can be said never to be very distant. We cannot, of course, get all the way back to Pythagoras to verify that he first associated the fork in the road with the Greek upsilon, but the later tradition attributes this view to him, and by the Middle Ages it is a commonplace. Moreover, numerous medieval and Renaissance writers also attribute to Virgil a poem that explicates the "Y" in precisely these terms. The pseudo-Virgilian poem begins as follows:

Littera Pytagorae discrimine secta bicomi
Humanae vitae speciem praeferre videtur ...

(Tory, *Champ Fleury*, fol. 62r)

(Pythagoras's letter divided into two horns
Appears to signify the manner of human life ...)

This poem may be as old as the sixth century CE. Certainly it is to be found in manuscripts of the tenth and eleventh centuries. In the poem, the pseudo-Virgil goes on to explain that the right side of the "Y" is narrow and more difficult to follow but leads eventually to repose and virtue whereas the left branch of pleasure is wider and easier but ends in misery.

By the Middle Ages this explication of "Y" is widely known, and it continues to be repeated in successive centuries. In his 1529 book on the alphabetic letter, *Champ Fleury*, Tory explicates what are for him the meanings of each letter of the alphabet. When he arrives at the "Y" he cites the same pseudo-Virgilian poem to which he adds an exhortation to youth, telling them not to ignore

> la conoissance des bonnes lettres qui sont le vrai bouclier pour surmonter adversite & tous vices, & pour paruenir a la souueraine felicite de ceste vie humaine, qui est parfaicte vertus (fol. 62v.)

> (the knowledge of good letters which are the true shield in order to conquer adversity and all vices, and to arrive at the crowning happiness of this human life, which is perfect virtue.)

Tory then illustrates the "Y" twice, to which he attaches an explanation of the "sens moral de la lettre Pythagorique" (moral sense of the Pythagorian letter). The capital "Y" he presents has, as we would expect, a left branch that is thicker than the right one. From the left branch hang a number of objects, beginning with a sword and whip and ending with gallows and a fire to demonstrate that pleasure and worldly pursuits lead to "miserables maulx & griefz torments" (fol. 63r) (miserable evils and terrible torments). By contrast, the thinner branch on the right is harder to follow but finishes with a laurel wreath, palms, a scepter, and a crown.

Tory's second illustration (fig. 45) is perhaps more striking for the way in which it associates the letter "Y" with a Dantean fork in the road. Taking this image from Fra Lucas Pacioli's own treatise on the alphabetic letter, the *Divina proportione* (1509), Tory engraves a capital "Y" with detailed itineraries for both the left and right branches. The easy ascent of the wide left branch leads to food and wine, but then a fall into (eternal) flames; the right branch is much coarser and harder to climb, but leads to a throne over which a palm branch extends. Most interesting are the three beasts which one must get around on the right branch, which are labelled in ascending order: "libido," "superbia," "invidia."

Although the correspondence to the three beasts at the beginning of Dante's *Inferno* is not exact, "libido" would seem to refer to the sins of incontinence in the *Inferno*, and while "superbia" or "pride" is not usually seen as a sin of violence (the second of Dante's categories of sin) the second animal does appear to be a lion, which is of course the second animal that stands in Dante's way in *Inferno* and which represents the sins of violence.

The moralized view of the "Y" continues well beyond the Renaissance period. We saw in an earlier chapter how children in the seventeenth century were taught to attribute moral values to each letter of the alphabet. The 1633 manual *Methodes pour apprendre à lire, à écrire, à chanter le plein-chant et compter...* (*Methods for Learning to Read, Write, and Sing the Plainsong and Count ...*) displays on its title page the complete alphabet on two large stone-like tablets. In between the two halves of the alphabet is a large capital "Y," and once again the left side is wide and smooth while the right side is narrow and coarse and crowned with a laurel wreath (fig. 46). There is no explication for the image, though the trunk leading up to the bifurcation is marked "CHOISYS" (CHOOSE). It is assumed that the viewer knows and understands the moral significance of the "Y" as representing the geography of our world and the choice of a life path.

The degree to which a moralizing view of the alphabet has permeated Western culture is evidenced by the fact that in many periods the "meaning" of a letter such as the "Y" needs no explanation whatsoever. It is seen as self-evident, as though the ideological dimension of the letter is simply part and parcel of what the letter most profoundly *is*. One finds this again in the great *Apocalypse Tapestry* in Angers, France, woven between about 1377 and 1382. This enormous tapestry comprising ninety different scenes from the biblical Apocalypse (Book of Revelation), and of which seventy-one have survived, presents vivid images drawn from what is undoubtedly the most "visual" of all the books of the Bible. Panel 64 depicts the "Whore of Babylon" sitting on a mound, gazing at her beauty in a mirror and surrounded by fifteen "Y"s in floating mandorlas (fig. 47). There is no need to provide any explanation for the presence of the "Y"s. Fourteenth-century viewers would have known all too well the significance of the letter and the message that the whore had taken the wrong branch in life.

There are recent examples as well. Consider, for example, the graphic novel *Y: The Last Man* (sixty issues between 2002 and 2008) in which the

Y poses the question "Why?" for the protagonist Yorick (the "Y" man) who is the only man left living on earth. The title page of the first issue presents the protagonist along with his evolutionary ancestor and side-kick, a monkey, against a large "Y" on which are overlaid maps of the chromosomes X and Y, the latter one of course defining the masculine sex.[2] Marjorie Celona also notes the quintessentially modern value of the Y as a chromosome, to which her novel *Y* will add also the "Y" of the YMCA. Her book opens with a passage that could almost be from Victor Hugo:

> Y. That perfect letter. The wishbone, fork in the road, empty wineglass. The question we ask over and over. Why? Me with my arms outstretched, feet in first position. The chromosome half of us don't have. Second to last in the alphabet: almost there. Coupled with an L, let's make an adverb. A modest X, leg's closed. Y or N? Yes, of course. Upside-down peace sign. Little bird tracks in the sand. (no page number)

From the fork in the road to the male chromosome, the letter becomes a catalyst for a meditation on meaning in the world.[3]

In a similar manner the splendid *Virgin of the Dry Tree* painted by the Flemish painter Petrus Christus around 1462 (fig. 48) can count on the viewer understanding the significance of a letter's presence with no need of explanation. Petrus's beautiful image portrays the Virgin Mary with Child appearing against a dessicated tree. The image com-memorates a vision Philippe the Good allegedly had before a battle with the French in which he was ultimately victorious. Like the Whore of Babylon, the Virgin is also surrounded by fifteen letters, but this time the letter is a lower-case "A." The reference, as viewers of the period would have known, is to the beginning of "Ave Maria," the "Ave" being the typological counterpart (and reversal) of the Old Testament "Eva" or Eve.

In the case of both the Angers Tapestry and the Petrus Christus painting, the world surrounding the personages is filled with a moral letter. But then, from Augustine on, Christian culture views the world as so many letters that make up a text that the good Christian reads for his or her salvation. Every object and every event in one's world is an opportunity to read "charitably" in Augustinian terms or, to use a more lettered expression, to take the right branch of the "Y."

As we might expect given the overall thesis of this book, in more recent centuries the meanings attached to the letter "Y," even when it is viewed as a metaphor of the world, might move in the direction of secularization. We have already briefly considered the personalized mythology of Victor Hugo for whom the "Y" loomed large. However, it is worth glancing at a larger portion of the passage by the great nineteenth-century master:

> Avez-vous remarqué combien l'Y est une lettre pittoresque qui a des significations sans nombre? L'arbre est un Y, l'embranchement de deux routes est un Y, le confluent de deux rivières est un Y, une tête d'âne est un Y, un verre sur son pied est un Y, un lys sur sa tige est un Y, un suppliant qui lève les bras au ciel est un Y.
>
> Au reste cette observation peut s'étendre à tout ce qui constitue élémentairement l'écriture humaine ... Toutes les lettres ont d'abord été des signes et tous les signes ont d'abord été des images.
>
> La société humaine, le monde, l'homme tout entier est dans l'alphabet. La maçonnerie, l'astronomie, la philosophie, toutes les sciences ont là leur point de départ, imperceptible mais réel; et cela doit être. (*Alpes et Pyrenées* 50)

(Have you noticed how the Y is a picturesque letter that has innumerable significations? A tree is a Y, the forking of two roads is a Y, the running together of two rivers is a Y, a donkey's head is a Y, a glass on its stem is a Y, a lily on its stalk is a Y, a supplicating person who raises his arms to the sky is a Y.

For the rest this observation can be extended to everything that constitutes in an elementary way human writing ... All letters were signs first, and all signs were images first.

Human society, the world, man in his entirety is in the alphabet. Masonry, astronomy, philosophy, and all the sciences have their point of departure there, imperceptible but real. And that is as it must be.[4]

In this passage Victor Hugo returns of course to the "Y" as a fork in the road. But he also sees the letter as much more than that. The "Y" is a ubiquitous presence that characterizes countless aspects of our world and has, as he says, an infinity of meanings. While not referencing Christianity in any direct way, Hugo nevertheless restates the longstanding analogy between the alphabet and the cosmos. He finds, as he says, "human society, the world, [and] man in his entirety ... in the alphabet" even as he finds a letter such as the "Y" mapped countless times onto the world.

The letter "Y" is a prime example of how the letter-world analogy holds true throughout many periods even as the ideological particulars evolve over the course of two millennia. Other letters could lend themselves to similar diachronic analysis, though there is little point in demonstrating this phenomenon twenty-six times or more. The degree to which the alphabet is viewed as a structure that both represents the world and also makes up our reality appears to be considerable, regardless of the historical period.

To be sure, the persistence of these associations has implications for our current society and for the future. Fears that alphabetic writing is somehow in danger of being "lost," either because of modern technologies of communication (smart phones, text messaging, etc.) or because our culture is remarkably "visual" (by which people seem to mean it is driven by icons and graphics) appear to be overstated. Text-messaging is textually based above all, and the shortcuts in terms of orthography in no way endanger alphabetic culture; certainly text-messaging is less radical in its orthographical revisions than were some medieval manuscript abbreviations or the proposals of sixteenth-century reformers. On a different front, proponents of "asemic" writing are fond of claiming that alphabetical writing is doomed or dead, but they offer no evidence of this beyond their own claims and their esoteric productions. Alphabetical writing is all around us, and for many people in the third millennium of the Common Era, not a day goes by without reading some lettered text, whether in a public space, a book, a set of directions, or on the internet.

Our culture may be enamoured of the visual, but for the communication of precise and specific information, visual images are of only limited use. To the degree that they are icons that are conventionally accepted they become consensual signifiers – as, say, for the pictograms for hand dryers in public washrooms. Over time they may even, with simplification, become completely arbitrary signifiers (already not all hand dryers correspond to the current pictogram). Some pictograms are not clear to all observers. The pictograms for some Olympic sports are anything but self evident, even though such common ones as those for running or cycling may seem transparent. Moreover, they are often modified from one Olympiad to another (see Meggs and Purvis 428–34).

We know of cultures for which only pictogrammic writing existed: such was the Meso-American society Hernán Cortés came upon when in 1519 he began his conquest of what we now call Mexico. The pre-Columbian texts that have survived are pictogrammic with only the rare image that is a rebus referring to pronunciation. The result is a kind of writing that no one but a highly trained priest or scholar could decipher; only a person with the requisite training and erudition could understand and explain the meaning of the text since what was encoded was not the specific words to be pronounced. Although a pictogrammic text can contain great amounts of information to be decoded, one cannot, nevertheless, write a sonnet or a sestina in a pictogrammic manner. It is impossible to encode the exact words to be used.[5]

It seems unlikely that Western culture will abandon alphabetic writing in the near or even relatively distant future. We are far too attached to the ease of communication that it affords us within any given language, even if it requires learning a new set of grammatical and phonetic structures, though not often a different alphabet, whenever we move to a different language, which is not the case for pictogrammic writing. Our computers may communicate with each other in the language of 1s and 0s, but we need those long binary strings to be retranslated into our strangely ungainly but remarkably succinct system of about twenty-six letters in order for us to send and receive messages.

If the ancient Greeks marvelled at the power of their alphabet and considered that, despite their knowledge of the historical origin of their letters, the power of their small repertoire of graphic signs was such that it seemed only to have been able to come from a divine source, several millennia later we are still often in awe of what our letters are capable of, whether it is a matter of a great Shakespearean poem or, as in the case of William Carlos Williams (1883–1963), a note left in the kitchen that becomes the great poem, "This is just to say ..."

In 2013 I was in Berlin for a week. Berlin is a city with an enormous variety of public graphic art, whether mimetic images many stories tall on the sides of abandoned buildings or personalized graffiti. What caught my eye, however, was a spray-painted message on the wall of a construction site in the centre of the city on the small island where Berlin's great museums are found. It read simply in capital letters, "I don't want to spread my name. I just want [to] write letters," with a large 2013 written just beneath (fig. 49).

This message seemed to me to be of particular significance. First of all, one had to consider that this anonymous statement was of sufficient importance to some person for him or her to procure a can of black spray paint, search out a suitable spot – one sufficiently large and in a place where many people would pass by – and then go there, probably in the dead of night when there was not likely to be anyone else present, in order to leave this message. Significant as well was that the statement was written in English, though probably not by a native English speaker despite the fact that the writer seemed to know English quite well. Writing in English would, of course, be a way of reaching the largest possible international audience in an area of Berlin through which people of many nations pass daily. The grammatical oversight in the second sentence was telling. The missing "to" was probably due more to haste than to ignorance since the first sentence also had "want to + infinitive," so the author must have been familiar with that English construction but did not sense it intuitively the way a native speaker would (in German, for example, the modal verb *wollen* would be followed directly by an infinitive). One can see, however, that a second person has faintly added the missing "to" as an editorial emendation, the way readers in medieval manuscripts would make marginal corrections a thousand years ago. The missing apostrophe in the first sentence and the missing word in the second were probably the result of working fast: the writer could not know whether or not the *Polizei* might appear out of nowhere at any moment.

As for the content of the graffiti, it says a lot with only a few words. It is not only anonymous, but in fact it calls specific attention to its anonymity. The author refuses to give – or, as s/he tellingly puts it, "to spread" – his or her name, pointedly declining to participate in a name/fame discourse (I suspect that the writer was familiar with that common rhyme). The author did not want to be known as a person, but rather as pure alphabetic text. Indeed, s/he signs off with simply a non-alphabetical squiggle under the graffiti. S/he wished to leave his or her mark in the world as simply a series of so many alphabetic marks. The alphabet was both the medium and the message, to paraphrase Marshall McLuhan. Personal identity was shunned in favour of the satisfaction of becoming pure text. The great twentieth-century French critic Roland Barthes might say that the author chose to be dead in order for life to be bestowed completely on the letters. The writing of the letters was to leave a message about the writing of letters, and the tautology is strangely poetic and haunting.

What is more, the very visual style of these letters makes for a kind of "anti-graffiti graffiti." We are accustomed to ballooning graffiti letters, usually that identify a particular person by means of a "tag" (indeed, the casual observer may find the tag almost unreadable). Here we have the opposite. The author has taken pains to provide us with letters of extraordinary clarity and regularity, such as we find in printed books (the same does not apply to the numbers), while refusing to give an identity.

What is more, the author does not speak of writing *words* but of writing *letters*. In other words, the statement references the almost infinite combinations that the alphabetic letters are capable of creating. Before they gel into words, letters are pure possibility, pure potentiality. Perhaps this is why the author chose a site that was ephemeral. In the midst of Berlin's great museums, which are designed to house the past for as much of eternity as we can conceive (the week I was in Berlin, the Pergamonmuseum had a large exhibit that included texts from Uruk written 6000 years ago, including cuneiform tablets of *Gilgamesh*), this graffiti was penned on the side of a temporary wall surrounding a construction site for an as-yet-unrealized future. Here today, gone tomorrow. If books (which is to say writing) are the key of remembrance, as Chaucer put it in *The Legend of Good Women*, the letters themselves are like so many leaves in the wind, like the folios on which Sybil tends to write her prophecies, according to Virgil's *Aenead*. The gift of writing is, as Plato tells us in the *Phaedrus*, a *pharmakon* – that is, both a poison for memory and a remedy for forgetting. The graffiti writer knows that the individual message on the side of this wall will be forgotten, but the desire to write letters will endure. New messages will be written and forgotten and more still that will follow them.

The Berlin graffiti writer does not, then, hope that his or her name will stay on peoples' lips, as Ovid does at the end of the *Metamorphoses*, but that people will recognize the desire that is inscribed in all alphabetical letters – the desire to communicate across time and distances. Curiously, but also fittingly, the ellipsis of the "to" in the second sentence hurries us forward to the real point of the message: the excitement and power of letters and the desire to use them. Countless scribes, calligraphers, typesetters, graphic artists, and of course writers of the present time and of past centuries will recognize themselves in that second sentence. The graffiti celebrates the magic and power of alphabetic letters.

Our graffiti writer is not the first person to be drunk with the power of letters, nor the last. The inebriation of alphabetic combinations is found perhaps most obviously in Ovid (43 BCE–17/18 CE), in Petronius (27–66 CE), in Jean de Meun (1250–1305), in Rabelais, and in James Joyce (1882–1941), but it inheres in the works of countless other writers as well as in the more private correspondences of millions of people over the course of several millennia. We cannot imagine Western culture apart from the writing of Western culture by means of a succession of alphabets. Prior to that all is mystery – "the night of time," as the French say.

Which is to say not only that light was shed on our culture by the alphabet but that the alphabet was that very light and thus is also the culture itself.

Notes

Preface

1 In modern Japan, four writing systems are actually in operation in the modern world: kanji (traditional characters originally from Chinese), hiragana (for elements not treated by kanji), katagana (mainly for the transliteration of foreign words), and the Latin alphabet. But the fact that the Latin alphabet is used here and there does not mean that a Japanese person grows up internalizing it in the way that Westerners do.

1 Introduction

1 The *OED* notes that the alphabet refers, in the first instance, to Greek letters but then goes on to define "alphabet" as "any set of characters representing the simple sounds used in a language or speech generally" (I. 252). The *OED* definition is pretty standard. Cf. Meggs and Purvis who define an alphabet as "a set of visual symbols or characters used to represent the elementary sounds of a spoken language" (22).

2 It is important to distinguish between writing (which may or may not be alphabetic) and alphabetic writing, even though there is often overlap in peoples' comments and discussions. For example, the quotation at the beginning of the preface to Gelb's book references writing in the widest sense whereas in the passage by Honorat Rambaud at the beginning of the chapter on humanist letters Rambaud is almost surely thinking of alphabetic writing.

3 Despite its rather similar title, Logan's *The Alphabet Effect* develops no thesis about the effect of the alphabet on Western culture. A generalized and highly simplified history of the West, the book only occasionally

mentions the alphabet, usually to make a sweeping generalization with no supporting details, as for example on the ancient Greeks: "The abstractness of the phonetic alphabet promoted a divorce of brain and hand, a disdain of empiricism, excessive adherence to logical rigor among Greek thinkers, each of which inhibited the development of modern science" (167).

4 It is worth noting that Chinese, as it exists today, is not purely an ideographic writing system since it often marries ideogrammic signs with phonetic signs. See DeFrancis, especially 89–130.

5 1. Litterae autem sunt indices rerum, signa verborum, quibus tanta vis est ut nobis dicta absentium sine voce loquantur. Verba enim per oculos non per aures introducunt. 2. Vsus litterarum repertus propter memoriam rerum. Nam ne oblivione fugiant, litteris alligantur (1.3.1–2). Unless otherwise noted, all translations in this book are my own.

6 "hic enim est usus litterarum, ut custodiant voces et velut depositum reddant legentibus, itaque id exprimere debent quod dicturi sumus" (1.7.31).

7 Claude Lévi-Strauss's famous "writing lesson" (Léçon d'écriture) in Tristes tropiques, 347–60, illustrates well the power dynamics, even the purely social power, inherent in writing. While Lévi-Strauss's interpretation of the events has been challenged by Jacques Derrida, it remains that the chief of the Nambikwara in Lévi-Strauss's account realized almost immediately that power accrued to writing even if he did not understand the exact function of the Westerners' letters. Hernán Cortés also recounts in his Cartas de relación that during the conquest of Mexico in the early sixteenth century the indigenous peoples attributed magical powers to the Westerners' written texts that allowed speech to be sent over long distances and then perfectly recovered. See also, Martin, Histoire et pouvoirs de l'écrit.

8 It is interesting to see how space and time become mapped onto one another. Anthony Pagden has noted the moral nature of geography in the European imagination, such that everything beyond the known was cloaked in "darkness," a view that conceived of the New World as "unnatural" (Pagden, European 7). The view of America as characterized by an earlier cultural stage (they did not have alphabetic letters, but "only" pictogrammic writing) meant that the continent had to be more recent. Pagden notes that even Humboldt believed that America was a younger continent (European 9).

9 See Barasch 64. In an interesting essay Michael Camille has discussed the ways in which "Gregory's statement is, like all texts, shifting not stable" in terms of its meaning in the Middle Ages (91).

10 I discuss this in more detail in chapter 4. David Hiley 424 gives a reproduction of the page and provides discussion on p. 425.

11 In *Alpes et Pyrénées* 51, Hugo goes through the whole alphabet, giving images for which each letter stands, in his view. He concludes in architectural fashion: "l'A, l'E, l'F, l'H, l'I, le K, l'L, l'M, l'N, le T, le Y, l'Y, l'X et le Z ne fussent autre chose que les membrures diverses de la charpente du temple."

12 The *salone sistino* is discussed by Boeckeler. It is also the object of a brief video documentary on CBS's *60 Minutes*: http://www.cbsnews.com/videos/a-tour-of-the-salone-sistino/.

13 See, for a recent overview and many examples, Heller and Anderson, *The Typographic Universe*.

14 Most of the letter-building images have been made available online by the Academia di Belli Arte di Bologna (http://www.storiaememoriadibologna.it/antonio-basoli-lalfabeto-pittorico-840-opera).

15 On Gobert, see Massin.

16 See http://jewmus.dk/fileadmin/files/webpage/documents/Arkitektur/mitzvah_english.pdf and Libeskind, "Mitzvah" for notes on the use of the architect's use of the word "Mitzvah" for the building's structure. To see Libeskind's drawing of the Hebrew word becoming the floor plan, see http://jewmus.dk/en/architecture/.

17 http://www.thecjm.org/about/building and Libeskind, "Contemporary."

18 Defining literacy is notably problematic. My brief categorization here is drawn from the 1958 UNESCO definition of "illiterate" as referring to anyone "who cannot with understanding both read and write a short simple statement on his everyday life" (cited in William Harris 3). Clearly, there is a great deal of grey in this statement, beginning with what constitutes "understanding" and with what would qualify as a "short simple statement."

2 Ancient Greek Letters

1 For the information on the development of early alphabets, I am indebted to Boulanger and Renisio, *Naissance de l'écriture* 171–93 and the more recent *Cuneiform* by Finkel and Taylor. The Egyptian inscription actually reads "alksindrs" and is part of the Paris Louvre's Guimet collection (AE/MG 23090). It is reproduced in *Naissance de l'écriture* 176.

2 The classic study of the transition from orality to literacy is that of Walter Ong (*Orality*).

3 The scholar is Barry Powell (221–37). As William Harris notes (45, n. 3) this "romantic notion" has a long tradition, stretching back into antiquity. However, just because the earliest surviving documents are literary texts does not mean they were the first things written; less important writing would have been on materials that were perishable. "The fact that the innovation occurred in a period of drastically increased contact with the Phoenicians favours the view that commercial uses were the earliest" (45, n. 3).

4 David Diringer asserts that the Latin "elementum" is due to the collation of three Etruscan letter names "ell," "em," and "en" (1: 420).

5 See Snyder 31–51 for extensive discussion and examples.

6 The Talmudic scholars of the Kabbala were also interested in the numeric value of the letters of the Hebrew alphabet – to the point of obsession. I do not treat them in detail because their interest was less in the actual letters of the alphabet than in turning them into mathematical calculations and manipulating the numeric values in an effort to get to what they believed to be the occulted messages of the Hebrew Bible. The approaches of these scholars did consider that the Hebrew Bible spoke the cosmos, but that the "real" text was not that of the actual letters one encountered but an occulted set of signifiers to which the letters referred. On mystical approaches to the alphabet in Early Christian culture, see Franz Dornseiff.

7 The twentieth-century French critic Roland Barthes (1915–80) has also asserted in a much-cited statement that for the Greeks trees were alphabets ("Les arbres sont des alphabets, disaient les grecs," 47). I am hard pressed to find a classical source for this claim, for which reason I suspect that Barthes is ludically linking the French word for "tree" (*arbre*) with the word for "arbitrary" (*arbitraire*), which, according to Saussurian linguistics, is the hallmark of all linguistic signification. "Arbitraire" could then be construed as the pun "to draw out the tree ("arbre" + "traire") if one takes the ancient meaning of French "traire" (not the modern one). We should remember that in Saussure the key example of the arbitrary nature of the signifier is precisely the word and image of an "arbre."

8 See Lucretius, *De rerum natura* I: 196–8; 907–14, and II: 688–94; 1013–22; Sedley 39; Drucker, *Alphabetic* 56. The satirical ideas of Lucilius are contained in Cicero. *Nat. D.*2.3 (fig. 93). For the specific point regarding Lucilius's satirical view, see Papangheghelis 128, footnote 61.

9 See Jennifer Wise 15–17.

10 "ut nobis dicta absentium sine voce loquantur." *Etymologiarum sive originum* Bk 1: 3.

11 The seminal text is Jacques Derrida's famous essay, "La Pharmacie de Platon," in which the French philosopher deconstructs Plato's dialogue

through an analysis of Plato's designation of writing as a "pharmakon" (meaning both "remedy" and "poison" in Greek).

12 See Montaigne, *Les Essais* (1: 26 151).

13 Frances Yates gives many examples of references in antiquity to memory as writing on wax tablets in her seminal *The Art of Memory*. See especially chapters 1 and 2.

14 I take the concept of a "motivated" sign from Ferdinand de Saussure's *Cours de linguistique générale* (181–4), though with a different emphasis. For Saussure, the motivated sign bifurcates from the arbitrary sign, though these are not absolutes for Saussure. Since Saussure considers the motivated sign to be associative ("farmer" gestures toward "farm," for example; the friend "vachier" recalls "vache," making it somewhat motivated, whereas "bergier" is not associated at all with the sheep [moutons] one tends, hence the sign is completely arbitrary). I tend to use the term "motivated" less for letters or words that gesture towards other items in a semantic field and more to designate signs seen as gesturing towards the real world.

15 The brief discussion of Aeschylus's treatment of letters in *Prometheus Bound* recapitulates material developed by my classicist colleague Aara Suksi over the course of several conference presentations.

3 Latin Letters and the Enduring Influence of Roman Scripts

1 I have given a loose dating for this phenomenon because the distinguishing of i/j and u/v was not uniform across the western European languages. It took place at different times in different languages, and even often had variation among printers, though many printers began to make this distinction in the late sixteenth century. Nina Catach (*L'Orthographe*) provides a table of printers in France and the low countries in which she notes the date they first began using "j," "j," and "v," or only "v" (315–17). It must be remembered that sometimes printers would distinguish "i" from "j," but not "u" from "v," or vice versa.

2 Linguists generally agree that the basic distinctions between the languages of Italy, France, and Spain were already in place in the vulgar Latin spoken in each of these respective regions prior to the breakup of the Roman Empire in the fifth and sixth centuries CE.

3 "Or ne say ie qui est ce Meigret, sinon que l'on le m'ha dit estre vn de ces triuiaux, & vulgaires translateurs, qui ne savent rien faire, sinon de iour à autre nous rompre les oreilles de leurs sottes versions, diray ie ou plustot peruersions?" (Guillaume des Autels 1551, 8)

4 I draw this example from Bernard Cerquiglini (*Roman* 60). See also de Looze, "Orthography."

5 "siempre la lengua [romana] fue compañera del imperio: 7 de tal manera lo siguió, que juntamente començaron, crecieron 7 florecieron, 7 despúes junta fue la caida de entrambos" (ed. Antonio Quilis, 97).

6 "les Romains ... ont eu domination sus la plus grande partie du monde, [et] ont plus prospere, & plus obtenu de victoires par leur langue que par leur lance" (fol. 4v).

7 The winning essay by Antoine de Rivarol famously declared that "ce qui n'est pas clair n'est pas français" (what is not clear is not French). He lauded French for its clarity and for the fact that French, unlike German, generally followed the syntactical order of subject-verb-object which, Rivarol argued, was the "natural" order of thinking.

4 Christian Letters: The Middle Ages

1 What constitutes "literacy" is problematic, as we have already seen (ch. 1, n. 16) and studies of literacy in the Middle Ages have focused on Britain more than on other countries (but see also Petrucci on medieval Italy). M.T. Clanchy has noted a tendency to simplify matters and associate too easily the cleric ("clericus") with the literate ("litteratus") and the laity ("laicus") with "illitteratus" (177–81). M.P. Parkes distinguishes three types of literacy in the Middle Ages: that of the professional reader ("the scholar or professional man of letters"), that of "the cultivated reader, which is the literacy of recreation," and that of the "pragmatic reader," which is the necessary level needed for business transactions (274; for this last group William Harris prefers the term "craftman's literacy," 7–8). As Parkes indicates, the literacy of the cultivated reader was on the rise throughout the Middle Ages. In Parkes's opinion, there has been a tendency on the part of scholars to underestimate the level of literacy in the medieval period (296). For example, in the late Middle Ages, literacy was growing, Parkes asserts, among the middle class. He does, however, also mention the "cautionary example" of the twelfth-century book collector, Count Baldwin II of Guines, who could not read and had his tomes read aloud to him (276). It may be that recent scholars now tend to overestimate levels of literacy. After all, William Harris estimates that at the height of ancient Greek civilization only 10–15 per cent of society could read (328; see also 24). Should we assume that the level of literacy was higher in the Middle Ages than in classical Greece? Finally, as Brian Stock makes clear, "literacy" in medieval society had many implications for the lives of illiterate people, despite their inability to read

since the knowledge that a written document endowed certain rights and privileges would affect peoples' actions whether or not a particular person could read. Finally, a single number for the thousand-year period and huge geographical expanse of the Middle Ages would be almost meaningless.

2 See *On Christian Doctrine*, Book 2.

3 *Sermon*, Mai 126.6. Cited and translated in Augustine, ed. Bourke, *Essential* 123. See also Curtius 319–26 in which he traces the appearances of this conceit during the High Middle Ages in both "pulpit eloquence" and then in "mystic-philosophical speculation" (321).

4 "Dicturus sum canticum, quod novi: antequam incipiam, in totum expectatio mea tenditur, cum autem coepero, quantum ex illa in praeteritum decerpsero, tenditur et memoria mea, atque distenditur vita huius actionis meae in memoriam propter quod dixi, et in expectationem propter quod dicturus sum: praesens tamen adest attentio mea, per quam traicitur quod erat futurum, ut fiat praeteritum ... quum tota illa actio finita transierit in memoriam. et quod in toto cantico, hoc in singulis particulis eius, fit atque in singulis syllabis eius, hoc in actione longiore, cuius forte particula est illud canticum, hoc in tota vita hominis, cuius partes sunt omnes actiones hominis, hoc in toto saeculo filiorum hominum, cuius partes sunt omnes vitae hominum" (ed. W. Watts, 276–8).

5 "et tu scis, domine, tu scis, quemadmodum pellibus indueris homines, cum peccato mortales fierent. unde sicut pellem extendisti firmamentum libri tui, concordes utique sermones tuos, quos per mortalium ministerium superposuisti nobis ... laudent nomen tuum, laudent te supercaelestes populi angelorum tuorum, qui non opus habent suspicere firmamentum hoc et legendo cognoscere verbum tuum. vident enim faciem tuam semper,et ibi legunt sine syllabis temporum, quid velit aeterna voluntas tua" (ed. W. Watts, 402–6).

6 A good example of this analogy is to be found in the cathedral at Albi (fourteenth century) in which the large depiction of the Last Judgment covering the wall at the front of the congregation depicts the saved as standing with the books of their lives open on their chests.

7 Matthew 5:27 is a key incident that expresses Jesus's view of sin as residing in intentions above all. In the passage, Jesus famously reinterprets the Exodus commandment, "Thou shall not commit adultery" to apply to intentions as well as acts: "I say to you that everyone who looks at a woman lustfully has already committed adultery with her in his heart."

8 The Christian view of the old law as locked into an overly literal reading of the covenants is an exaggeration and misreading of Hebrew culture. The passage in Romans 2:25 to which I have alluded in fact echoes Moses's metaphorical expression in Exodus 6 that he has "uncircumcised lips."

9 Gregory the Great, *In librum I regum*, 4:123 (*PL* 79:268; *CCL* 144:359): "Nam
   scritum est: *Littera occidit, spiritus vivificate*. Hoc quidem facit omnis divina
   littera. Nam littera corpus est; huius vero corporis vita, spiritus."

10 Don Pascual de Gayangos, who has edited the *Ejemplos por ABC*, has done
   so under the alternate title *El Libro de los enxemplos por abc*, presumably
   because, as Gayangos contends, the collection recalls Book I of Juan
   Manuel's fourteenth-century *El Conde Lucanor*. The more recent edition by
   John Esten Keller (1961) also calls the work the *Libro de los ejemplos por ABC*.

11 I am indebted to my colleague Paul Potter for this example. As one of
   my graduate students pointed out, we often view the ABCs deployed
   horizontally in a different fashion from a vertical ABC list. The verticality
   often creates a hierarchy in which A is superior to or more important than
   B, which is superior to C, and so on.

12 I am a bit hard-pressed to understand the train of thought in a comment
   by Elizabeth Eisenstein: "[P]rinted reference works encouraged a
   repeated recourse to alphabetical order. Ever since the sixteenth
   century, memorizing a fixed sequence of discrete letters represented by
   meaningless symbols and sounds has been the gateway to book learning
   for all children in the West" (*Printing Revolution* 71). There are several
   strands here. Eisenstein's comments about reference works is on the mark;
   ditto that the entrance into alphabetical order continues to be a "gateway"
   experience for children. Where matters get muddy is in the sentence
   about the sixteenth century. Well into the early modern era, the learning
   of one's ABCs was an entry into a deeply moral order, as I discuss later
   in this chapter, and as a result the alphabetic order was hardly seen as
   "meaningless sounds and symbols." The example Eisenstein cites from
   Daly following the quoted passage above illustrates precisely this fact: the
   thirteenth-century Genoese compiler sees the alphabetical order as coming
   from God (see Daly 91).

13 "Prima conexio est 'doctrina domus plenitudo tabularum ista,' quo
   uidelicet doctrina ecclesiae, quae domus Dei est, in librorum repperiatur
   plenitudine diuinorum. Secunda conexio est 'et haec vita.' Quae enim alia
   potest esse uita sine scientia scripturarum, per quas etiam ipse Christus
   agnoscitur qui est uita credentium?" (ed. Labourt 33).

14 For a description of the Beatus of Fernando and Sancha (also known as
   the Facundus Beatus after the scribe's name), see O'Neill, Howard, Lucke,
   et al. 289. There are twenty-six illuminated Beatus manuscripts from
   Spain, all of which derive from the Beatus of Liébana, an eighth-century
   illustrated commentary on the Book of the Apocalypse by a monk at
   Liébana, Spain. The manuscripts show remarkable similarity in terms of

iconographical programs and are among the most celebrated works of Mozarabic art.

15 The Latin Vulgate reading is, "Ego sum α, et ω, principium, et finis, dicit Dominus Deus: qui est, et qui erat, et qui venturus est, omnipotens." Isidore of Seville mentions this passage and discusses it in his *Etymologies* I.iii.9.

16 There are many instances of this iconography in the Beatus manuscripts. For example, very similar is the alpha with Christ underneath in the Girona Beatus (975 CE) (Girona, Girona Cathedral 7, fol. 19r) as well as the prayer book of Fernando and Sancha (1055) (Biblioteca universitaria de Santiago de Compostela, ms. 609 Ms, Res. 1, fol. 1r, reproduced in O'Neill, Howard, Lucke, et al. 129).

17 The early Christian church was in fact reticent about portraying Christ and saints pictorially, afraid that the faithful would not perceive the images as simply representations but rather would see them as imbued with the living presence of the person figured. This concern surfaced most dramatically in the Iconoclast Controversy of the eighth century CE, which pitted the Eastern Orthodox Church against the Western Catholic Church. The Western position, accepting representational images, was articulated at the Council of Nicaea in 787 CE.

18 For more information, go to http://www.metmuseum.org/collection/the-collection-online/search/466190.

19 I am grateful to Leann Wheless Martin for bringing this manuscript to my attention.

20 Wolfenbüttel, Herzog August Bibliothek, Cod. Guelf. 84.5 Augusteus 2°, fol. 41.

21 In this paragraph and the next I am indebted to Laura Kendrick's *Animating the Letter* (1999), chapter 3.

22 François Rabelais will parody the mastication of the divine text in his *Fifth Book* (*Cinquieme Livre*) when Panurge drinks the sole word from the calligrammic bottle, *dive bouteille*. The world is "TRINCH" which is explained as meaning "Beuvez!" (Drink!). The mastication of divine words, which would lead to greater understanding, becomes in Rabelais a riotous drinking of an alcoholic alphabetic text. See Rabelais, *Cinq livres* 1509–15.

23 See also the "T" of the "Te Igitur" in the Metz Sacramentary (fig. 44) in which the "t" becomes the cross on which Jesus was crucified (see my conclusion for discussion). Other Carolingian sacramentaries offer a similar treatment, as for example the Gellone Sacramentary (790 CE or later), which, according to Jean Massin, is the oldest extant instance of this treatment (see Massin 39 for the claim and a reproduction of the image. Massin also situates the Metz Sacramentary slightly earlier, placing it

between 755 and 787 CE [268]). Cf. also the Figeac Sacramentary (Paris, BnF Ms. Lat. 2293, fol. 19v; reproduced in Alexander, Plate 23).

24 For discussion, see Brian Stock, *Implications*.

25 See also the sketchbook of Giovannino de' Grassi, Bergamo, Biblioteca Civica, Ms. VII. 14, fol. 29v. This corporeal approach to the alphabet – often quite playful – continues right up through the nineteenth century (Massin gives copious examples). By the twentieth century such alphabetic contortions have been relegated largely to the realm of children's literature. By contrast, the "serious" letters of the modern book are designed to be unobtrusive so that we simply "read through" them.

26 Drogo Sacramentary (BnF Lat. 9428, fol. 58).

27 For figs. 19 and 21 I am indebted to the discussions in Alexander, *The Decorated Letter*.

28 For a reproduction of this folio, see Backhouse 74.

29 I follow here the discussion given in the Bibliothèque Nationale (Paris) CD-ROM, *L'aventure des Écritures*.

30 The tradition goes back to the sixth century BCE. See Curtius 282–7.

31 Discussed by both Curtius 283–4, and Zumthor 26, 41.

32 The shield, for instance, begins with: "Nam scutum fedei depellit tela nefanda " (For the shield of faith repels evil arrows).

33 See John Williams, vol. 1, for a discussion of these Beatus manuscripts. The Fanlo Beatus in the Pierpont Morgan Library is in fact a seventeenth-century facsimile of a Spanish Beatus from ca. 1050 (for discussion, see Williams, vol. 1).

34 Patricia Crain has a good discussion of the "God's Cross" or "Christ's Cross," as it was called, in seventeenth-century America (19–26). Crain shows no awareness, however, that the association of cross and alphabet was also typical of France in earlier centuries and probably ultimately derived from there.

35 It is interesting to note that the illuminator may not have been fully literate. Some letters are omitted from the alphabet and some are written backward. For figures 24–7 I am indebted to the discussions and descriptions of the BnF CD-ROM *L'Aventure des écritures*, most of which have now been put on line in a slightly altered form and for which individual authorship is not given. I give here the current BnF websites for each of the figures:

Figure 24: http://classes.bnf.fr/ecritures/grand/e111.htm
Figure 25: http://classes.bnf.fr/ecritures/grand/e110.htm
Figure 26: http://classes.bnf.fr/ecritures/grand/e107.htm
Figure 27: http://classes.bnf.fr/ecritures/grand/e168.htm

36 This image, with a description, is available on the BnF website as part of the *L'Aventure des écritures* project at: http://classes.bnf.fr/ecritures/grand/e107.htm.

37 Patricia Crain has noted the same phenomenon in seventeenth-century hornbooks in North America. She points out that the alphabet serves here to associate letters with Christian ideology more than to teach children how to read (23). To enter the alphabetic order is also to enter the Christian order.

38 The Folger Library (Chicago) has examples of Trevelyon's moralizing alphabets of which images can be seen on the library's website, as for example:

http://luna.folger.edu/luna/servlet/s/t195p7
http://luna.folger.edu/luna/servlet/s/2d89l9

5 The Letters of Humanism

1 Elizabeth Eisenstein's two volumes (1979) launched a whole industry of study regarding how the introduction of the printing press affected early modern Europe. There has been criticism of Eisenstein's conception of a "print culture"; see in particular Joseph Dane's vociferous complaints (10–20) (Dane's more gratuitous attacks are tempered by the problems in his own argumentation, as James McLaverty has mentioned [313, 315]). One must ask whether the advent of the printing press represented a true "revolution" in thinking. Was it instead a "slow revolution" or perhaps simply part of a larger "evolution," as some historians of the book have argued? Indeed, in the early modern era not everyone was impressed by the new technology of the printing press; Giovanbattista Palatino (1515–75) (1533) asserts that "[la] stampa ch'altro non è, che vno scriver senza penna" (Aiii verso: "printing is nothing but writing without a pen"). Eisenstein has countered that the printing revolution represented a genuine shift in attitudes, and it affected maps and other "non-book materials," and thus refers to a larger field than historians of the book generally consider (*Printing Revolution* 317, 319).

2 We have an unfortunate tendency to characterize the movement from manuscript to printed book in terms of a sharp epistemological break, but in fact the two modes of writing co-existed for a good half-century, and for the first fifty years printed books (called incunabula) imitated manuscripts. One of the interesting features of the printing press is that it changed forever the centres and nature of writing. In the late Middle Ages the copying of manuscripts in the monastery scriptorium was considered a sort of divine service, capable of reducing one's years in purgatory.

The printing press may have sounded the death knell of the medieval scriptorium, depriving many monks of their daily work, though by the end of the Middle Ages there were also many secular workshops (and with the rise of universities the *pecia* system allowed students to copy the works they needed for their courses, quire by quire). The older view of J. Destrez, which saw the *pecia* system as lasting until the entry of printed texts, has been nuanced by Graham Pollard who shows that while in some universities it died out in the fourteenth century there are also instances of *pecia* copies made after printed copies are also in circulation. Johannes Trithemius (1462–1516) famously reflected on the two modes of writing in his *De laude scriptorium manualium* (*In Praise of Scribes*), itself published as a book in 1494. Aware of the threats the printing press posed, Trithemius nevertheless also saw that it posed new possibilities for evangelizing.

3 See Fra Luca Pacioli's *De Divina Proportione* (Venice, 1509) and Giovanni Battista Palatino's *Libro nuovo d'imparare a scrivere tutte sorte lettera antica et moderna …* (Rome, 1540).

4 Petrucci goes on to comment, "Questa scrittura, vechia e nuovissima insieme, rispondeva in modo mirabile al gusto estetico ... [e] alle propensioni ideali della nuova *élite* umanistica che si veniva organizzando intorno alle corti signorili italiane, e che, allonganandosi sempre piu dalla scuola, dale università … veniva forgiando una nuova ideologia intellettualistica in netto contrasto con i valori tradizionali e tutta fondata sul mito del ritorno all'antico" (*Libri* 29–30). See also Petrucci, *La Scrittura*.

5 I am indebted to my research assistant, Lina El Shamij, for this observation. The application of the new printing technologies was much slower to take hold in the alphabetic languages of the Middle East, for example.

6 "fue escrita en esperanza cierta del Nuevo Mundo, aunque aún no se habia navegado para descubrirlo." Menéndez Pidal 50.

7 "[S]iempre la lengua [romana] fue compañera del imperio: 7 de tal manera lo siguió, que juntamente començaron, crecieron 7 florecieron, 7 después junta fue la caida de entrambos. (Nebrija 97: "the [Roman] language always accompanied the empire; and it followed it in such fashion that together they began and grew and flourished, and later together they both collapsed.")

8 "[L]es Romains qui ont eu domination sus la plusgrande partie du mõde, ont plus prospere, & plus obtenu de victoires par leur langue que par leur lance. Pleust a Dieu que peussions ainsi faire" (The Romans, who had dominion over the greater part of the world, prospered more and obtained more victories on account of their language than of their arms. May it please God that we might do the same"). Tory, *Champ Fleury* fol. 4v.

9 See Laurence de Looze, "Orthography."

10 I am simplifying here. Europeans often vacillated between seeing the island natives as innocent and peaceful or savage and cannibalistic (see Todorov). The initial "discovery" of the island communities did not impress Europeans overly much, but when the Spanish came upon the imperial empire of the Aztecs, the reaction was different. The Spanish Empire was nothing if not impressed by other empire cultures.

11 Geoffroy Tory states that Roman letters were also designed around the perfection of geometric forms: "Les anciēs voulāt mōstrer la singuliere perfection de leurs lettres, les ont formees & figures par deue p[ro]portion des trois plusbōnes & parfaictes figures de Geometrie. Qui sont, la figure Rōde, la Quatree, & la Trigulaire" (fol. 10r).

12 It should be noted, however, that although Juan de Torquemada comments "que estos Indios no sabian escrivir," he nevertheless notes that they maintained their laws in memory very well, which would have been the goal of writing them down. Similarly, José de Acosta clearly did not believe that the Meso-Americans were somehow ignorant because they did not have alphabetical writing. Book 6 of his *Historia natural* takes issue with those who believed that the indigenous peoples of Mexico were characterized by a "falta de entendimiento."

13 One of the most sympathetic European observers of indigenous New World culture, Fray Bernardino de Sahagún (1494–1590), also comments that "Esta gente no tenía letras, ni caracteres algunos, ni sabían leer ni escribir, comunicábanse por imágenes y pinturas" (These people had neither letters nor any characters, nor did they know how to read or write, [rather] they communicated with each other by means of images and pictures. Quoted in Thouvenot 393).

14 *Relación de las cosas de Yucatán*, cited in Léon-Portilla 325.

15 Las Casas 2:638 (cited in Mignolo, 312–13): "carezcan de ejercicio y studio de las letras."

16 "de tierra nueva de ayer conquistada sale nueva y verdadera manera de bien escribir para todas las naciones" (Medina 2:40).

6 Baroque Variations and the Search for a Universal Language

1 "Or comme la terre est estrangement grande: la paresse, la couardise & indiscretion des hommes telle, qu'ils ne veulent en descouvrir davantage que leurs vieux peres leur en ont tracé par escrit: il se faut asseurer, qu'il en reste beaucoup plus à cognoistre, voire en quelque cartier des 4. principaux du monde, vous desireriez aller, que noz modernes n'en ont fait voir" (La Popelinière 77).

2 Patricia Crain has taken a post-structural approach to Hawthorne's novel in her 2000 book. It is interesting that Reverend Dimmesdale, whose own letter "A" is hidden under his clothes, hallucinates a divine "A" as coming out of the sky at him: the moral order of the Puritan world is seen as a divine alphabetical order in that moment. The twentieth-century American novelist John Updike has responded to Hawthorne with his own 1988 novel entitled simply *S*.

3 See Harkness 177–81 and Salmon.

4 Dee here picks up in part a notion that the Talmudic scholars of the Kabbala fervently held, namely a belief in the alphanumeric character of the originary or Primitive Hebrew language. For Kabbalistic scholars the Hebrew letters of the Old Testament represented occulted mathematical calculations that revealed a second, hidden text. As for whether the original, uncorrupted Hebrew of creation had been completely lost or not, there were divergent opinions. Kircher held that one tribe had survived the Babelian scattering. The early seventeenth-century linguist Claude Duret also believed that Primitive Hebrew may not have been completely lost (see Duret, *Thresor* 44 ff. and Cornelius 12–16).

7 Logical Letters: The Alphabet in the Age of Reason

1 See also in France, Jacques La Rue, *Exemplaires de plusieurs sortes de lettres* (1575) as well as his *Alphabet, de dissemblables sortes de lettres italiques, En vers Alexandrins* (ca. 1575), and Pierre Hamon's *Alphabet, Plusieurs sortes de lettres* (1567).

2 "du genre à l'espèce et de l'espèce à l'individu" (5).

3 Drucker makes these comments while preparing her discussion of the modern, nineteenth- and twentieth-century printing practices used for most literary texts. As it happens, however, the actual context of this passage seeks to apply the "unmarked" practices retrospectively back to Gutenberg's printed bibles in the fifteenth century. In this application, Drucker is mistaken. Gutenberg was imitating manuscript styles, with two columns to a page, Gothic lettering, and the full apparatus of display scripts, etc. Moreover, in the sixteenth through eighteenth centuries, as we have seen, letters were still often "marked" or "motivated" in printed texts. The real turning point for modern printing comes with Baskerville, Bodoni, and Didot.

8 The Alphabets of the Industrialized World

1 The poem appears on the final page (unpaginated) of Jean-Charles Gateau's book *Abécédaire Critique*.

2 For example, *Le Confédéré*, 25 December 1895 (Switzerland); *La Vendé
   républicaine* 1895 (France); *O Mirandez*, 10 Julio 1894, p. 2 (under the title
   "Phantazia Alphabetica") (Portugal); etc.
3 One of the key figures was Walter Crane who, influenced by the flat colour
   areas of Japanese art, set the prevailing tone with his *Railroad Alphabet*
   (1865). See Meggs and Purvis 168–9.
4 Victor Hugo's initials, including the mutilated "VH," are discussed by Jean-
   Charles Gateau 82–3.

9 From Modern Experiments to Post-Modern Experiences

1 Meggs and Purvis have numerous examples in part IV of their book.
   For one early example, see the pages reproduced from *Die Scheuche* (*The
   Scarecrow*) by Kurt Schwitters, Théo van Doesburg, and Kate Steinitz in
   which "type and image are wedded literally and figuratively as the B
   overpowers the X with verbage" (266).
2 Similarly, Georges Perec rewrites famous French poems as lipogrammic
   texts. For example, he rewrites Rimbaud's "Vowels" (already discussed in
   the previous chapter) as a lipogrammic text lacking an "e," so that even the
   title has to be changed: "Vocalisations." See *La Littérature potentielle* 99).
3 The three-pronged Hebrew letter that most approximates the shape of a
   capital "E" is ש (*Shin*), which is seen as standing for *Shaddai*, one of the
   Hebrew names for God.
4 The "Act de Disparition" is reproduced and this aspect of the novel is
   discussed in Bellos.
5 For a review of the history of lipogrammic writing, see Green and Cushman
   809 and Perec's own much more complete essay on the history of the
   lipogram (*La Littérature potentielle* 77–93; English translation: Motte, *Oulipo*
   97–108). Perec's account makes clear that there has been a long tradition of
   lipogrammic writing, some of it of very good quality.
6 http://camilleutterback.com/projects/text-rain/. Utterback's site has a
   video of people manipulating the alphabet.

10 Into the New Millennium

1 For a reproduction of the Drogo Sacramentary "T" and discussion, see
   Gaehde 16, 90–2. For a detailed description of the Metz "T," Gaehde 101.
   Both manuscripts are now in the Bibliothèque Nationale, Paris.
2 I am indebted to my graduate student Alexandre Desbiens-Brassard for
   bring this example to my attention.

3 Marjorie Celona's is not the only novel named "Y." The 1972 Spanish novel
   by Tomás Salvador is named Y…. Clearly there is something striking about
   a title that has only alphabetic letters. The 2009 French novel by Laurent
   Binet – characterized by some critics as the first post-modern historical
   novel – has the striking title, *HHhH*. The four "h"s – three capitals and
   one lower case – refer to the German slogan regarding Reinhard Heydrich
   whom Hitler put in as dictator in Prague during the Second World War:
   "Himmlers Hirn heist Heydrich" (Himmler's brain is called Heydrich).
4 Hugo's meditation on the meanings of letters goes on for another page,
   during which he goes through the whole alphabet. A is a roof, J is a military
   catapult, T is a hammer, etc.
5 For discussion, see Boone, *Stories* 28–39.

Works Cited

Manuscripts and Early Printed Books [through the 16th century, excluding modern facsimile editions]

Arrighi, Lodovico degli. *La operina da imparare de scrivere littera cancellaresca.* 1522. Online.

Berlin, Staatsarchiv, Charter of Emperor Henry IV written by Sigehardus. 1067.

De Furtivis literarum notis vulgo de Ziferis libri IIII, Joan Baptista Porta ... autore. Paris, 1563. Bnf, Rés.-V-1896.

Des Autels, Guillaume. *Replique de Guillaume des Autels aux furieuses défenses de Louis Meigret.* Lyon, 1551.

Dubois, Jacob. *Iacobi Syluii Ambiani in linguam gallicam Isagoge, unà cum eiusdem Grammatica Latino-gallica ...* Paris: Robert Estienne, 1531.

Dürer, Albrect. Engraving of schoolmaster. Paris, 1510. BnF Estampes, Ca 4b Res fol.

Giovannino de' Grassi. Bergamo, Biblioteca Civica. MS VII. 14.

Girona [Spain], Catedral Num. Inv. 7 (11) (Girona Beatus).

Hamon, Pierre. *Alphabet, Plusieurs sortes de lettres.* Paris: Robert Estienne, 1567.

La Rue, Jacques. *Alphabet, de dissemblables sortes de lettres italiques, en vers Alexandrins.* Paris: Charles Micard, ca. 1575.

– *Exemplaires de plusieurs sortes de lettres.* Paris: Charles Micard, 1575.

London, British Library, Cotton MS Nero D. IV (Lindisfarne Gospels).

London, British Library, Harley MS 2799 (Arnstein Bible).

Madrid, Biblioteca Nacional, Cod. 80 (Moralia in Job).

Madrid, Biblioteca Nacional, MS Vitrina 14–2 (Beatus of Fernando and Sancha, 1047 CE; also called "Facundus Beatus")

More, Thomas. *Utopia.* Louvain, Thierry Martens, 1516. (London, Sir Paul Getty, K.B.E – Wormsley Library).

New Haven, Beineke Rare Book and Manuscript Library MS 408 (Voynich Manuscript).

New York, Cloisters Collection. Beatus leaf (1991.232.1 – .14).

New York, Pierpont Morgan, M 1079 (Fanlo Beatus).

Pacioli, Lucas. *De Divina proportione*. 1509. Bibliothèque de Genève, MS Langues Étrangères 210. Online.

Palatino, Giovanni Battista. *Libro de M. Gianbattista Palatina citadino Romano nel qual s'insegna à scriver ogni sorte lettera* … Rome: Antonilo Blado Asolano, 1553. (Morgan Library 151011).

Paris, BnF MS français 888 (models for writing).

Paris, BnF MS Lat. 1141 (Metz Sacramentary).

Paris, BnF MS Lat. 1156B (Marguerite d'Orléans, Book of Hours).

Paris, BnF MS Lat. 1171 (Henri IV, Book of Hours).

Paris, BnF MS Lat. 1173 (Charles D'Angouleme, Book of Hours).

Paris, BnF MS Lat. 2293 (Figeac Sacramentary).

Paris, BnF MS Lat. 8878 (Saint Sever Beatus).

Paris, BnF MS Lat. 9428 (Drogo Sacramentary).

Paris, BnF MS Lat. 10525 (Beatus Vir).

Paris, BnF Rothschild IV. 4. 145 (moralizing alphabet).

Torniello, Francesco. *Opera del modo de fare le littere maiuscole antique*. Milan, 1517.

Trithemius, Johannes. *De laude scriptorium manualium*. Mainz, 1494.

Valladolid [Spain], Biblioteca de la Universidadad Ms. 433 (Valladolid Beatus).

Vienna, Kunsthistorisches Museum, Schatzkammer, Inv. XIII 18 (Coronation Gospels, late 8th century CE).

Vienna, Österreichische Nationalbibliothek, Cod. 652, fol. 3v, fol. 33v (Hrabanus Maurus).

Von Kayserberg, Geiler. *Ein Heysamelere und Predigi*. Engraving. J. Zainer (Ulm), 1490 (1st edition 1489). Paris, BnF Imprimés, C46159.

Wolfenbüttel [Germany], Herzog August Bibliothek Cod. Guelf. 84 Augusteus 2. (Pericope ms).

Books and Articles

Acosta, José de. *Historia natural y moral de las Indias*. Mexico City: Fondo de cultura económica, 1962.

Aeschylus. [*Prometheus Bound*] *Aeschylus*. 2 vols. Ed. and trans. Herbert Weir Smyth. London: Heinemann, 1922–6.

Alemán, Mateo. *Ortografía Castellana*. Mexico City, 1609.

Alexander, J.J.G. *The Decorated Letter*. London: Thames and Hudson, 1978.

Anderson, Donald M. *Calligraphy: The Art of Written Forms*. New York: Dover, 1969.

Apollinaire, Guillaume. *Calligrammes dans tous ses états: édition critique du recueil de Guillaume Apollinaire*. Ed. Claude Debon. Vanves: Calliopées, 2008 [1918].

Aristotle. *Metaphysics*. Trans. Hugh Tredennick. Cambridge, MA: Harvard UP, 1996.

Atkinson, Geoffroy. *The Extraordinary Voyage in French Literature before 1700*. New York: Columbia UP, 1920.

Augustine of Hippo, Saint. *On Christian Doctrine*. Trans. D.W. Robertson. New York: Bobbs-Merrill, 1958.

– *The Confessions of Saint Augustine*. Trans. John K. Ryan. New York: Doubleday, 1960.

– *The Essential Augustine*. Ed. Vernon J. Bourke. Indianopolis: Hackett, 1974.

Austin, J.L. *How to Do Things with Words*. Cambridge. MA: Harvard UP, 1962.

L'Aventure des écritures. Dir. Anne Zali and Anne Berthier. Paris: Bibliothèque de France. CD-Rom. No publication date.

Barasch, Moshe. *Theories of Art from Plato to Winckelmann*. New York: New York UP, 1985.

Barth, John. "The Literature of Exhaustion." *The Friday Book: Essays and Other Nonfiction*. New York: Putnam, 1984 [1967]. 67–79.

Barthes, Roland. *Roland Barthes par Roland Barthes*. Paris: Seuil, 1975.

Beck, Cave. *Universal Character, by which all the nations in the world may understand one anothers conceptions, reading out of one common writing in their own mother tongues…* London: Tho. Maxey, 1961 [1657]. Online.

Bellos, David. *Georges Perec: A Life in Words*. Boston: David Godine, 1993.

Biggs, John R. *Basic Typography*. London: Faber and Faber; New York: Watson-Guptill, 1968.

Bischoff, Bernhard. *Latin Paleography: Antiquity and the Middle Ages*. Trans. Dáibhí Ó. Cróinín and David Ganz. Cambridge: Cambridge UP, 1986.

Backhouse, Janet. *The Illuminated Page: Ten Centuries of Manuscript Painting in the British Library*. Toronto: U of Toronto P, 1997.

Boeckeler, Erika. "Building Meaning: The First Architectural Alphabet." *Push Me Pull You: Imaginative and Emotional Interaction in Late Medieval and Renaissance Art*. Ed. Sandra Blick and Laura D. Gelfand. Leiden: Brill, 2011. 149–96. Online.

Boone, Elizabeth Hill. *Stories in Red and Black: Pictorial Histories of the Aztecs and Mixtecs*. Austin: U of Texas P, 2000.

Boone, Elizabeth Hill, and Walter D. Mignolo, eds. *Writing without Words: Alternative Literacies in Mesoamerica and the Andes*. Durham: Duke UP, 1994.

Boulanger, Jean-Paul, and Geneviève Renisio. *Naissance de l'écriture: cunéiformes et hiéroglyphes*. Paris: Éditions de la Réunion des musées nationaux, 1982.

Bouvelles, Charles de. *Liber de differentia vulgarum linguarum, & Gallici sermonis varietate*. Trans. C. Demaizière. Paris: Klinsieck, 1973 [1533].

Brunot, Ferdinand. *Histoire de la langue française des origines à nos jours*. 13 vols. Paris: Armand Colin, 1966–7.

Camille, Michael. "The Gregorian Definition Revisited: Writing and the Medieval Image." *L'Image: fonctions et usages des images dans l'Occident medieval*. Actes du 6e International Workshop on Medieval Societies, Centre Ettore Majorana (Erice, Sicily, 17–23 octobre 1992). Ed. Jérôme Baschet and Jean-Claude Schmitt. Paris: Le Léopard d'or, 1996. 89–107.

Cassirer, Ernst, Paul Oskar Kristeller, and John Herman Randall, eds. *The Renaissance Philosophy of Man*. Chicago: U of Chicago P, 1948.

Catach, Nina. *L'Orthographe française à l'époque de la Renaissance*. Geneva: Droz, 1968.

Celona, Marjorie. *Y*. Toronto: Hamish Hamilton (Penguin, Canada), 2012.

Cerquiglini, Bernard. *Le Roman de l'orthographe: au paradis des mots, avant la faute 1150–1694*. Paris: Hatier, 1996.

Cicero, Marcus Tullius. *De Officiis*. Ed. and trans. Walter Miller. London: W. Heinemann, 1947.

Clanchy, M.T. *From Memory to Written Record: England 1066–1307*. London: Edward Arnold, 1979.

Comenius, J.A. *The Way of Light*. Trans. E.T. Campagnac. London: UP of Liverpool, 1938.

Conrads, Ulrich, and Hans G. Sperlich. *Fantastic Architecture*. Trans. Christiane Crasemenn and George R. Collins. London: Architectural P, 1963.

Cornelius, Paul. *Languages in Seventeenth and Early Eighteenth-Century Imaginary Voyages*. Geneva: Droz, 1965.

Cortés, Hernán. [*Cartas de relación*] *Historia de Nueva España escrita por su esclarecido conquistador Hernán Cortés*. Ed. Miguel Angel Porrua. Mexico: n.p., 1992.

Cossard, Jacques de. *Méthodes pour apprendre à lire, à écrire, à chanter le plain-chant et compter*. Paris, 1633.

Court de Gébelin. *Le Monde primitif*. Paris: Plancher, Eymery, and Delaunay, 1816.

Crain, Patricia. *The Story of A: The Alphabetization of America from* The New England Primer *to* The Scarlet Letter. Stanford: Stanford UP, 2000.

Cram, David. "George Dalgarno on *Ars signorum* and Wilkins' *Essay*." *Progress in Linguistic Historiography*. Ed. Ernst F.K. Koerner. Philadelphia: J. Benjamins, 1980. 113–21.

- "Language Universals and 17th-Century Universal Schemes." *John Wilkins and 17th-Century British Linguistics*. Ed. Joseph L. Subbiondo. Amsterdam Studies in the Theory and History of Linguistic Science 67. Philadelphia: J Benjamins, 1992. 191–203.

Curtius, Ernst Robert. *European Literature and the Latin Middle Ages*. Trans. Willard R. Trask. New York: Pantheon, 1953.

Dalgarno, George. *Ars signorum, vulgo character universaliset lingua philosophica*. London: Hayes, 1661. Online.

Daly, Lloyd W. *Contributions to a History of Alphabetization in Antiquity and the Middle Ages*. Collection Latomus 90. Brussels: Revue d'études latines, 1967.

Dane, Joseph A. *The Myth of Print Culture: Essays on Evidence, Textuality and Bibliographical Method*. Toronto: U of Toronto P, 2003.

David, Madeline V. *Le Débat sur les écritures et l'hiéroglyphe aux XVIIe et XVIIIe siècles*. Paris: École pratique de hautes études, 1965.

De Brosses, Charles. *Traité de la formation méchanique des langues*. Paris: Chez Saillant, 1765.

Dee, John. *A True and Faithful Relation of What Passed for Many Yeers between Dr. John Dee ... and Some Spirits*. London: D. Maxwell, 1659; London: Askin, 1974, facsimile edition.

de Looze, Laurence. "'Mon nom trouveras': A New Look at the Anagrams of Guillaume de Machaut – the Enigmas, Responses, and Solutions." *Romanic Review* 79 (1988): 537–57.

- "Orthography and National Identity in the Sixteenth Century." *Sixteenth-Century Journal* 43 (2012): 371–89.

- "A Story of Interpretations: The *Queste del Saint Graal* as Metaliterature." *Romanic Review* 76 (1985): 129–47.

DeFrancis, John. *The Chinese Language: Fact and Fantasy*. Honolulu: U of Hawaii P, 1984.

Derrida, Jacques. "La Pharmacie de Platon." *La Dissémination*. Paris: Seuil, 1972. 69–200.

Desnos, Louis-Charles. *Dissertation historique sur l'invention des lettres*. Paris: Chez Desnos, 1772.

Destrez, J. *La Pecia dans les manuscrits universitaires du xiiie et xive siècle*. Paris: Jacques Vautrain, 1935.

Díaz del Castillo, Bernal. *Historia verdadera de la conquista de la Nueva España*. Ed. Carmelo Saenz de Santa Maria. Madrid: Instituto Gonzalo Fernández de Oviedo, 1982.

Diderot, Denis, and Jean le Rond d'Alembert, eds. *Encyclopédie: ou Dictionnaire raisonné des sciences, des arts et des métiers....* 28 vols. Paris, 1751–72.

Dioscorides, Pedanius. *De materia medica libri quinque* [Περὶ ὕλης ἰατρικῆς]. Ed. Max Wellman. Berlin: Weidmannos, 1958.

Diringer, David. *The Alphabet: A Key to the History of Mankind.* 3rd ed. 2 vols. London: Hutchinson of London, 1968.

Dornseiff, Franz. *Das Alphabet in Mystik und Magie.* Berlin: B.G. Teubner, 1925.

Drucker, Johanna. *The Alphabetic Labyrinth: The Letters in History and Imagination.* London: Thames and Hudson, 1995.

– *The Visible Word: Experimental Typography and Modern Art, 1909–1923.* Chicago: U of Chicago P, 1994.

Du Bellay, Joachim. *La Defense et illustration de la langue françoise.* Geneva: Slatkine, 1972 [1547]. Facsimile edition.

Dubois, Claude-Gilbert. *Mythe et langage au XVIe siècle.* Paris: Eurédit, 2010.

Duret, Claude. *Thresor de l'histoire des langues de cest univers.* Geneva: Slatkine. 1972 [1613]. Facsimile edition.

Eco, Umberto. *The Search for the Perfect Language.* Trans. James Fentress. Oxford: Blackwell, 1995.

Einhard, and Notker the Stammerer. *Two Lives of Charlemagne.* Trans. Lewis Thorpe. New York: Penguin, 1969.

Eisenstein, Elizabeth L. *The Printing Press as an Agent of Change: Communications and Cultural Transformations in Early-Modern Europe.* 2 vols. Cambridge: Cambridge UP, 1979.

– *The Printing Revolution in Early Modern Europe.* Cambridge: Cambridge UP, 2005.

Ellis, Alexander John. *The Alphabet of Nature.* London, 1845.

La Farce de Maître Pierre Pathelin. Ed. Jean Dufournet. Paris: Flammarion, 1986.

Finkel, Irving, and Jonathan Taylor. *Cuneiform.* Los Angeles: The J. Paul Getty Museum, 2015.

Foigny, Gabriel de. *A New Discovery of Terra Incognita Australis, or, The southern world, by James Sadeur, a French-man, who being cast there by a shipwreck, lived 35 years in that country and gives a particular description of the manners, customs, religion, laws, studies and wars of those southern people, and of some animals peculiar to that place.* London: printed for John Dunton, 1693.

Gaehde, Joachim E. *Carolingian Painting.* New York: George Braziller, 1977.

Gambarota, Paola. *Irresistible Signs: The Genius of Language and Italian National Identity.* Toronto: U of Toronto P, 2011.

Garipzanov, Ildar H. *The Symbolic Language of Royal Authority in the Carolingian World (c. 751–877).* Leiden: Brill, 2008.

Gateau, Jean-Charles. *Abécédaire critique: Flaubert, Baudelaire, Rimbaud, dadas et surréalistes, Saint-John Perse, Butor, etc.* Geneva: Droz, 1987.

Gelb, I.J. *A Study of Writing.* 2nd ed. Chicago: U of Chicago P, 1963.

Genette, Gérard. *Mimologiques: Voyage en Cratylie*. Paris: Seuil, 1976.

Gobert, Thomas. *Traité d'architecture*. Paris, 1690. Online (Bayern StaatsBibliothek Cod. Icon. 188).

Goody, Jack. *The Domestication of the Savage Mind*. Cambridge: Cambridge UP, 1977.

Grafton, Anthony. *Defenders of the Text: The Traditions of Scholarship in the Age of Science 1450–1800*. Cambridge, MA: Harvard UP, 1991.

Gray, Nicolette. *A History of Lettering: Creative Experiment and Letter Identity*. Oxford: Phaidon, 1986.

– *Lettering as Drawing: The Moving Line*. 2 vols. Oxford: Oxford UP, 1970.

Green, Roland, Stephen Cushman, et al., eds. *The Princeton Encyclopedia of Poetry and Poetics*. 4th ed. Princeton: Princeton UP, 2012.

Gregory the Great. *Librum I regum*. PL 79:268; CCL 144:359.

Gropius, Walter. *The New Architecture and the Bauhaus*. Trans. P. Morton Shand. Cambridge, MA: MIT P, 1965 [1935].

Harkness, Deborah E. *John Dee's Conversations with Angels: Cabala, Alchemy, and the End of Nature*. Cambridge: Cambridge UP, 1999.

Harris, Roy. *La Sémiologie de l'écriture*. Paris: CNRS, 1993.

Harris, William V. *Ancient Literacy*. Cambridge, MA: Harvard UP, 1989.

Havelock, Eric. *The Muse Learns to Write: Reflections on Orality and Literacy from Antiquity to the Present*. New Haven: Yale UP, 1986.

Heller, Steven, and Gail Anderson. *The Typographic Universe*. London: Thames & Hudson, 2014.

Helvetica [film]. Dir. Gary Hustwit. New York: Plexifilm. 2007.

Herodotus. *The Landmark Herodotus: The Histories*. Trans. Andrea L. Purvis. Ed. Robert B. Strassler. New York: Pantheon Books, 2007.

Hesiod. *Theogony*. Trans. Apostolos N. Athanassakis. Baltimore: Johns Hopkins UP, 1983.

Hiley, David. *Western Plainchant: A Handbook*. Oxford: Clarendon P, 1993.

Homer. *The Iliad*. Trans. Robert Fitzerald. Garden City: Anchor P, 1974.

Houston, Stephen. "Literacy among the Pre-Columbian Maya: A Comparative Perspective." Boone and Mignolo, 27–49.

Hugo, Victor. *Alpes et Pyrénées*. Paris: J Hetzel, 188? Online.

– *Notre Dame de Paris*. Paris: Ollendorff, 1904.

– *Portefeuille dramatique. Œuvres complètes de Victor Hugo*. Ed. Lucrèce Borgia and Marie Tudor. Vols 17–18. Paris: Club Français du Livre, 1970 [1839–51].

Huon de Cambrai. "ABC par ekivoche." *Oeuvres*. Ed. Artur Långfors. Paris: Champion, 1911. 1–15.

Isidore of Seville. *Etymologiarum sive Originum Libri XX* [*Etymologies*]. Ed. W.M. Lindsay. 2 vols. Oxford: Oxford UP, 1911.

Jalley, Michèle. "Remarques sur le projet de langue universelle de Leibniz." *Langue et langages de Leibniz à l'Encyclopédie*. Ed. Michèle Duchet and Michèle Jalley. Paris: Union Générale d'Éditions, 1977. 69–81.

Jerome, Saint. *Lettres*. Ed. Jérôme Labourt. Vol. 2. Paris: Les Belles Lettres, 1949.

Kendrick, Laura. *Animating the Letter: The Figurative Embodiment of Writing from Late Antiquity to the Renaissance*. Columbus: Ohio State UP, 1999.

Knowlson, James. *Universal Language Schemes in England and France 1600–1800*. Toronto: U of Toronto P, 1975.

Kraitsir, Charles. *The Significance of the Alphabet*. Boston: Peabody, 1846.

LaCapra, Dominick. "Two Trials." *A New History of French Literature*. Ed. Denis Hollier. Cambridge, MA: Harvard UP, 1989. 726–31

Lafont, Robert. *Anthropologie de l'écriture*. Paris: Centre Georges Pompidou, 1984.

Leibniz, Gottfried Wilhelm. *Nouveaux essais sur l'entendement humain*. Paris: Flammarion, 1990.

Léon-Portilla, Miguel. "Have We Really Translated the Mesoamerican 'ancient word'?" *On the Translation of Native American Literatures*. Ed. Brian Swann. Washington DC: Smithsonian Institution P, 1992. 313–38.

Lévi-Strauss, Claude. *Tristes tropiques*. Paris: Plon, 1955.

Libeskind, Daniel. "Contemporary Jewish Museum." *Daniel Libeskind and the Contemporary Jewish Museum: New Jewish Architecture from Berlin to San Francisco*. Ed. Connie Wolf. San Francisco: Contemporary Jewish Museum, 2008. 107–9.

– "Mitzvah: The Concept for the Danish Jewish Museum." *The Danish Jewish Museum*. Ed. Henrik Sten Møller. Denmark: Danish Jewish Museum, 2004. 40–51.

La Littérature potentielle: créations, re-créations, recreations. [No editor named]. Paris: Gallimard, 1973.

Lodwick, Francis. *A Common Writing: Whereby Two, Although Not Understanding One the Others Language, yet by the Helpe thereof, May Communicate Their Minds One to Another*. London. Menston: Scolar P, 1969 [1647]. Facsimile edition.

Logan, Robert K. *The Alphabet Effect: The Impact of the Phonetic Alphabet on the Development of Western Civilization*. New York: St Martin's P, 1986.

Lucretius. *De Rerum natura*. Ed. Martin Ferguson Smith. Trans. W.H.D. Rouse. Cambridge, MA: Harvard UP, 1975.

Magritte, René. "Les Mots et les images." *La Révolution surréaliste* 12 (1929): 32–3.

Maimieux, Joseph de. *Pasigraphie, ou premiers elements du nouvel art-science*. Paris, 1797. Online.

Mallarmé, Stephane. *Un coup de deś jamais n'abolira le hazard*. Paris: Table Ronde, 2007 [1897].

Manuel, Don Juan. *El conde Lucanor*. Ed. Guillermo Serés. Barcelona: Círculo de Lectores, 2006.

Marinetti, F.T., Boccioni, et al. *I Manifesti del futurismo*. Florence: Lacerba, 1914. Online.

Martin, Henri-Jean. *Histoire et pouvoirs de l'écrit*. Paris: Perrin, 1988.

Massin, Jean. *La Lettre et l'image*. Paris: Gallimard, 1970.

McLaverty, James. Review of Joseph A. Dane, *The Myth of Print Culture*. *Review of English Studies* 224 (2005): 313–15.

McLuhan, Marshall. *The Gutenberg Galaxy: The Making of Typographic Man*. Toronto: U of Toronto P, 2011 [1962].

Medina, José Toribio. *La Imprenta en México (1539–1821)*. 2 vols. Mexico City: UNAM, 1989.

Meggs, Philip B., and Alston W. Purvis. *Meggs' History of Graphic Design*. 5th edition. Hoboken: John Wiley, 2012.

Meigret, Louis. *Louis Meigret: Le Tretté de la grammere françoeze 1550 with La Reponse 1550, Defenses 1550, and Reponse 1551* . Ed. R.C. Alston. Menston, England: Scholar P, 1969. Facsimile edition.

– *Traité touchant le commun usage de l'escriture francoise*. Ed. Keith Cameron. Exeter: U of Exeter P, 1979 [1545]. Facsimile edition.

Menéndez Pidal, Ramón. *La lengua de Cristóbal Colón*. Madrid: Espasa-Calpe, 1958.

Mercati, Michele. *Gli Obelischi di Roma*. Ed. Gianfranco Cantelli. Bologna: Cappelli, 1981 [1589].

Mersenne, Marin. *Harmonie universelle*. Paris: CNRS, 1963 [1636]. Facsimile edition.

Michon, Jacques. *Mallarmé et les mots anglais*. Montreal: Presses de l'université de Montréal, 1978.

Mignolo, Walter. *The Darker Side of the Renaissance: Literacy, Territoriality, and Colonialization*. Ann Arbor: U of Michigan P, 1995.

Montaigne, Michel de. *Les Essais*. 3 vols. Ed. Pierre Villey. Paris: PUF, 1965.

Morison, Stanley. *Politics and Script: Aspects of Authority and Freedom in the Development of Graeco-Latin Script from the Sixth Century B.C. to the Twentieth Century A.D.* Ed. Nicolas Barker. Oxford: Clarendon P, 1972.

Motte, Warren F., Jr, ed. and trans. *Oulipo: A Primer of Potential Literature*. Lincoln: U of Nebraska P, 1986.

Mukařovský, Jan. *The Word and Verbal Art: Selected Essays by Jan Mukařovský*. Ed. and trans. John Burbank and Peter Steiner. New Haven, Yale UP, 1977.

Nebrija, Antonio de. *Gramatica de la lengua castellana*. Ed. Antonio Quilis. Madrid: Editora Nacional, 1980 [1492].

O'Neill, John P., Kathleen Howard, Anne M. Lucke, et al. *The Art of Medieval Spain, 500–1200*. New York: Harry N. Abrams, 1993. Online.

Ong, Walter. *Orality and Literacy: The Technologizing of the Word*. New York: Methuen, 1982.

Pagden, Anthony. *European Encounters with the New World*. New Haven: Yale UP, 1993.

– *The Fall of Natural Man: The American Indian and the Origins of Comparative Ethnology*. Cambridge: Cambridge UP, 1982.

Papanghelis, Theodore D. *Propertius: A Hellenistic Poet on Love and Death*. Cambridge, Cambridge UP, 1987.

Parkes, M.B. *Scribes, Scripts and Readers: Studies in the Communication, Presentation, and Dissemination of Medieval Texts*. London: Hambledon , 1991.

Perec, Georges. *La Disparition*. Paris: Gallimard, 1969.

– "History of the Lipogram." In Motte, 97–108.

– *Les Revenentes*. Paris: Gallimard, 1972.

– *A Void* [English adaptation of *La Disparition*]. Trans. Gilbert Adair. London: Harvill, 1994.

Petrucci, Armando. *Libri, scrittura e pubblico nel Rinascimento: Guida storica e critica*. Bari: Editori Laterza, 1979.

– *La Scrittura: ideologia e rappresentazione*. Turin: Einaudi, 1986.

– *Writers and Readers in Medieval Italy: Studies in the History of Written Culture*. Trans. Charles M. Radding. New Haven: Yale UP, 1995.

Plato. [*Cratylus*] *Platonis opera*. Vol 2. Ed. John Burnet. Oxford: Clarendon P, 1905.

– *The Statesman*. Ed. and trans. H.N. Fowler. Cambridge: Harvard UP, 1952.

Plutarch. "The E at Delphi." *Moralia*. Vol. 5. Trans. Frank Cole Babbit. Cambridge: Harvard UP, 1949–69. 194–253.

Pollard, Graham. "The *pecia* System in the Medieval Universities." *Medieval Scribes, Manuscripts and Libraries: Essays presented to N.R. Ker*. Ed. M.B. Parkes and Andrew G. Watson. London: Scolar P, 1978. 145–61.

Pons, Emile. "Les jargons de Panurge dans Rabelais." *Revue de littérature comparée* 11 (1931): 185–218.

Popelinière, Lancelot Voisin, sieur de la. *Les trois mondes de La Popelinière* . Ed. Anne-Marie Beaulieu. Geneva: Droz, 1997 [1582].

Powell, Barry. *Homer and the Origins of the Greek Alphabet*. Cambridge, Cambridge UP, 1991.

Psalmanazar, George. *An Historical and Geographical Description of Formosa*. London: Robert Holden, 1926 [1704]. Facsimile edition.

Ptak, Sylvia "Intervention: Sallust. *Works, 1495.*" *Commentary: An Exhibition of Work by Sylvia Ptak*. Thomas Fisher Rare Book Library (Toronto): 24 May to 4 September, 2004. Printed Catalogue.

Queneau, Raymond. *Cent mille milliards de poèmes*. Paris: Gallimard, 1961.

– *Exercises de style*. Paris: Gallimard, 1947.

Quintilian. *The Institutio Oratoria of Quintilian*. Ed. and trans. H.E. Butler. Cambridge, MA: Harvard UP, 1920–2.

Rabelais, François. *Les cinq livres*. Ed. Jean Céard, Gérard Defaux, and Michel Simonin. Paris: Livre de Poche, 1994.

– *Pantagruel*. Ed. V.L. Saulnier. 2nd ed. Geneva: Droz, 1965 [1532].

– *Le quart livre de Pantagruel*. Ed. Jean Plattard. Paris: Champion, 1910 [1548].

Rambaud, Honorat. *La Declaration des Abus que l'on commet en escrivant et le moyen de les euiter et representer nayuement les paroles; ce que iamais homme n'a faict*. Lyon: Jean de Tournes, 1578.

Rasula, Jed, and Steve McCaffery. *Imagining Language: An Anthology*. Cambridge: MIT P, 1998.

Rico, Francisco. "*Laudes litterarum*: Humanismo y dignidad del hombre en la España del Renacimiento." *Homenaje a Julio Caro Baroja*. Ed. Antonio Carreira, Jesús Antonio Cid, Manuel Gutiérrez Esteve, and Rogelio Rubío. Madrid: Centro de investigaciones sociológicas, 1978. 895–914.

Rivarol, Antoine de. *Discours sur l'universalité de la langue française*. Paris: P. Belford, 1966 [1784].

Ronsard, Pierre de. *Oeuvres*. Ed. Charles Marty-Laveaux. 6 vol. Paris: Lemerre, 1887–93.

Russell, Ray. "A Note on the Type." *Paris Review* 82 (1981): 193–6.

Sacks, David. *Language Visible: Unraveling the Mystery of the Alphabet from A to Z*. New York: Broadway Books, 2003.

Salmon, Vivian. "Language-Planning in Seventeenth-Century England: Its Contexts and Aims." *In Memory of J.R. Firth*. Ed. C.E. Bazell et al. London: Longmans, 1966. 370–97.

Sanchez de Vercia, Clemente. *Los Ejemplos por ABC* [*El Libro de los enxemplos*]. *Escritores en prosa anteriores al siglo XV recogidos é ilustrados por don Pascual de Gayangos*. Ed. Pascual de Gayangos. Biblioteca de autores españoles 51, Madrid: Ediciones Atlas, 1952. 443–560.

– *Libro de los ejemplos por ABC*. Ed. John Esten Keller. Madrid: Consejo superior de investigaciones científicas, 1961.

Sarafini, Luigi. *Codex Seraphinianus*. Parma: Franco Maria Ricci, 1981.

Saussure, Ferdinand de. *Cours de linguistique générale*. Paris: Payot, 1972.

Sedley, D.M. *Lucretius and the Transformation of Greek Wisdom*, Cambridge, Cambridge UP, 1998.

Singh, Simon. *The Code Book: The Science of Secrecy from Ancient Egypt to Quantum Cryptography*. New York: Anchor Books, 1999.

Snyder, Jane McIntosh. *Puns and Poetry in Lucretius'* De Rerum natura. Amsterdam: B.R. Grüner, 1980.

Stahl, P.J. *Devinez l'alphabet*. [Scheler, Théophile. Etching of Waterwheel]. 1978. Online.

Steingruber, Johann David. *Architectural Alphabet 1773*. Trans. E.M. Hatt. London: Merrion P, 1972.

Stock, Brian. *The Implications of Literacy: Written Language and Models of Interpretation in the Eleventh and Twelfth Centuries*. Princeton: Princeton UP, 1983.

Thouvenot, Marc. "Fray Bernardino de Sahagún et le *Codex de Florence*: un exemple de non-découverte de l'écriture aztèque." *Amerindia: revue d'ethnololinguistique amérindienne* 19/20 (1995): 389–401.

Todorov, Tzvetan. *La Conquête de l'Amérique: la question de l'autre*. Paris: Seuil, 1982.

Top, Alexander. *The Olive Leaf or Universall Alphabet*. Menston: Scolar P, 1971 [1603].

Torquemada, Juan de. *Monarquia Indiana*. Intro. Miguel León Portilla. 3 vols. Mexico City: Porrua, 1969 [1615]. Facsimile of 1723 edition.

Torres García. *Historia de mi vida*. Montevideo, 1938. Facsimile edition.

Tory, Geoffroy. *Champ Fleury*. New York: Johnson Reprint, 1970 [1529]. Facsimile edition.

Trudeau, Danielle. *Les Inventeurs du bon usage (1529–1647)*. Paris: Minuit, 1992.

Utterback, Camille, and Romi Archituv. *Text Rain*. Interactive video installation. http://camilleutterback.com/projects/text-rain/. Online.

Vairasse [d'Allais], Denis. *Grammaire méthodique contenant en abrégé les principes de cet art et les règles les plus nécessaires de la langue française dans un ordre clair et naturel*. Paris: published by the author, 1681.

– *The History of the Sevarambians: A People of the South-Continent. In five parts. Containing An Account of the Government, Laws, Religion, Manners, and Language of that Nation. Translated from the memoirs of Captain Siden, Who lived fifteen Years amongst them*. London: printed for John Noon, at the White-Hart near Mercer's-Chapel, Cheapside, 1738 [1677]. Online.

Valdés, Diego de. *Rhetorica christiana*. Perugia, 1579.

Valla, Lorenzo. *De linguae latinae elegantia*. Ed. S. López Moreda. Cáceres: Universidad de Extremadura, 1999 [1441].

Virgil. *Aeneid*. Paris: Firmin Didot, 1798.

– *Publii Virgilii Maronis Bucolica, Georgica, et Aeneis.* Birmingham: Typis Johannis Baskerville, 1757.

Watts, Pauline Moffit. "Prophecy and Discovery: On the Spiritual Origins of Christopher Columbus' 'Enterprise of the Indies.'" *American Historical Review* 90 (1985): 73–102.

Webster, John. *Academiarum examen, or, The examination of academies: wherein is discussed and examined the matter, method and customes of academick and scholastick learning, and the insufficiency thereof discovered and laid open: as also some expedients proposed for the reforming of schools, and the perfecting and promoting of all kind of science...* London: Printed for Giles Calvert, 1654. Online.

Wilkins, John. *Essay towards a Real Character and a Philosophical Language.* London: Sa. Gellibrand and John Martyn, 1688.

– *Mercury, or The Secret and Swift Messenger: Shewing how a Man May with Privacy and Speed Communicate his Thoughts to a Friend at any Distance.* London: I. Norton, 1641.

Williams, John. *A Corpus of the Illustrations of the Commentary on the Apocalypse.* 5 vols. London: Harvey Miller, 1994–8.

Wise, Jennifer. *Dionysus Writes: The Invention of Theatre in Ancient Greece.* Ithaca: Cornell UP, 1998.

Wright, Ernest Vincent. *Gadsby.* Los Angeles: Wetzel, 1939.

Xenophon. *Memorabilia and Oeconomicus.* Ed. and trans. E.C. Marchant. London: W. Heinemann, 1965.

Yates, Frances. *The Art of Memory.* London: Routledge and Kegan Paul, 1966.

Zumthor, Paul. *Langue, texte, énigme.* Paris: Seuil, 1975.

Illustration Credits
(all images used with permission)

Index